RE-VISIONING THEOLOGY

A Mythic Approach to Religion

NORVENE VEST

Paulist Press

New York / Mahwah, NJ

Portions of Chapter 2 under "An Erotic Mythic Narrative" were originally published in *Journal of Feminist Theology* as "Is Rêverie to be Trusted? The Imaginal and the Work of Marija Gimbutas," in January 2005 (Vol. 13.2), and are republished with permission.

Portions of Chapter 3 under "Psychoanalysis" were originally published in *Spring: A Journal of Archetype & Culture* as "Hermeneutical Philosophy in Dialogue with Freud," in Spring 2007, and are republished with permission.

Selections from this book were originally published in summary form in *Presence: An International Journal of Spiritual Direction* as "Faith that Works in a Disbelieving World," in September 2008, and are republished with permission.

The chapter epigraphs are authored by the Rev. Douglas C. Vest, originally appeared in his books of poetry *Homes for the Heart*, *Entering the Mystery*, and *Churchianity Lite: An Insider's Loving Look*, and are republished with permission.

Cover design by Sharyn Banks
Book design by Lynn Else

Library of Congress Cataloging-in-Publication Data

Vest, Norvene.
   Re-visioning theology : a mythic approach to religion / Norvene Vest.
     p. cm.
   Includes bibliographical references and index.
   ISBN 978-0-8091-4688-8 (alk. paper)
   1. Philosophical theology. 2. Theology. 3. Christianity—Philosophy. 4. Mythology. 5. Myth. I. Title.
   BT40.V47 2011
   230.01—dc22

2010025386

Published by Paulist Press
997 Macarthur Boulevard
Mahwah, New Jersey 07430

www.paulistpress.com

Printed and bound in the United States of America

Contents

Contents

In gratitude to:

The School of Mythological Studies at
Pacifica Graduate Institute, especially Patrick Mahaffey,
Elizabeth Terzian, and Dennis Slattery

My husband, Douglas, who not only gave permission
for his poems to be used for the epigraphs, but also shared
deep reflective conversations with me that produced
the parallels between his poetry and my theology

Introduction:
Problem and Possibility:
Literalism and a Mythic Response

Life's unfolding traces helixes
...filled with twists and turns
into three dimensions.
What seems at first like tracing circles
getting nowhere slowly,
brings depth and forward movement.

...I choose
deliberately
to walk imagined separation
between "the church"
and "world"
with one foot lovingly emplaced in each
and walking
in both doubt and faith,
not ambivalently strung out,
to abandon either.

Such interlacing, I've concluded,
begets objectiveness
about a fuller universe—
finding truth in each,
though sometimes feeling bridge-like,
and walked on from each side
long posed as mutually opposing.

"More Than A Metaphor," in *Entering the Mystery*
by Douglas C. Vest

LITERALISM

Theology today is at an impasse, despite the efforts of scholars and laity to lift theology out of its slough. At least at the level
of popular Western culture, a divide exists now between what are
commonly called science and faith. To some extent, the notion of
such a divide is contrived, because both the best of science and the
best of religion are beyond the popular caricature. Nonetheless,
popular perception is important and powerful, limiting dynamic
movement within a culture and shaping even the terms of possible alternatives.

Speaking primarily of Christianity in industrialized nations,
it can be said that at one end of the continuum are those who
cling to a set of literal dogmas, and at the other end are those who
cling equally to an insistence that nothing is true unless it can be
demonstrated empirically, that is, by repeated experiments that
produce the identical results time after time. Literal religious
dogma can be seen in such statements as "Of course God created
the world in seven literal days!" Clinging to the letter of biblical
language may actually be a means of avoiding contact with God's
lively Holy Spirit continuing to inspire people of faith.[1] Literal *scientism* can be found in recent books arguing against the notion of
an outmoded vision of God, instead defining rational secularism
or empirical science as the place of final and definitive Truth.
For example, a recent issue of the esteemed news journal, *The
Economist*, headlined a special report on faith and politics that
spoke of "a populist revolt against the overreach of elitist secularism." However, the full text of the article referred to religion as
"the opium of the people," "a barrier to change," and "supersti-
tion," suggesting that only barbarians and terrorists maintain a
serious belief in a Divine Being, a belief that is always dangerous
to democracy.[2] Such an extreme skepticism about religion is also
a form of literalism, both in its inability to sense the mystery at
the heart of religion, and in its viewpoint that secularity and
rationality are the only demonstrable, and thus the only valid
realities. This way of thinking is not science at its creative best; it
is merely technological fixation, clinging to the certainties of tech-
nique, and can be called scientism.

Introduction: Problem and Possibility

It is not just the uneducated who perceive an impasse between religion and science; the impasse permeates Western culture and limits creative conversation among people of differing viewpoints, as if either religion or science must ultimately be victorious, eliminating the other.[3] In general it seems clear that a scientistic and analytical approach lacks language with which even to speak of the sacred. Moreover, religious efforts to speak in the language of the rational mind tend to produce deadlock. The classic romantic solution to this problem was to leave science to its own explanatory devices, staking out a separate and distinct arena of understanding and empathy for the soul and the sacred.[4] But this proved unsatisfactory because it merely reinforced the split between the reasoning mind and the rest of life.

Seldom do the strengths of science speak to the strengths of faith in public discourse in the West today. Why is this apparent impasse between a literal view of religion and a literal view of science so hard to dislodge? And what tools might help restore a genuinely creative conversation leading toward increasing vitality in both science and religion?

In my view, the problem is less that there are two extremes on the continuum than that the continuum itself reveals a kind of addiction to simple, unambiguous "reality." It represents a heightened desire for control, especially in times when life seems to be more complex, when old certainties seem less stable. Literalism's inadequacy can be seen in its single-minded focus on the evident and manifest and its quest for clear, stable answers. The demand for singleness of meaning, in symbols, in science, in religion, renders life less flexible, hardens hearts, and closes out the mystery of expanding circles of reality surrounding the manifest—circles that create a rich and fulfilling texture in life. In both science and religion, literalism can be seen as a disease that squeezes the juice out of life by stabilizing everything, by removing tensions in favor of certainties. Ongoing ambiguity can be difficult to bear, and frequently in history, a move toward literalism accompanies periods of radical change. When religious or scientific dogma in the form of literalism seems fixated on either-or, simplistic answers, it signals a culture resisting the creative destabilization necessary for renewal. For example, when the mixed-

3

race Barack Obama was running for president of the United States, a sermon given by his black pastor stirred controversy. Media commentators were quick to literalize the controversy as an old black-white conflict, whereas Obama's response was to address the rich complexity of feelings among black, white, and mixed-raced Americans, an address that was immediately challenged because it bypassed the simplistic worldview that keeps racial discussion superficial and racism alive. Religious and cultural vitality is blocked by unthinking acceptance of literalism and refusal of the complexity characteristic of the deeper dimensions of life.

These issues haunt me and they stimulate this book. Pondering these questions, I propose the hypothesis that a contemporary and expansive view of mythology might be able to intervene effectively in the pervasiveness of a limiting literalism in contemporary Christian religious talk. Like religion, mythology also has often been relegated to the realm of barbarians and terrorists, but a contemporary look from a depth psychological viewpoint reveals strengths in mythology that are of considerable value in addressing this theological and cultural impasse.

STRENGTHS OF MYTHOLOGY

Because the term *myth* is not well understood today, it is often taken to mean a lie or untruth. More accurately, while myth is hard to penetrate because of its inherent ambiguity, it is closely associated with the soul's desire for something beyond the surface of things. Myth "is one of a small but interesting group of words that mean both one thing and its opposite (like *cleave*—meaning both 'adhere (to)' and 'split (apart)')."[5] Thus the use of the word *myth* to mean a falsehood ironically reveals that mythology is about the revealing of truth deeper and more real than facts can describe.

My definition of myth is a people's understanding of the sacred and the way ultimate truths impinge on human experience, especially as unfolded in a depth psychological framework. Different from individual mythic stories, the depth mythological substructure of a culture is seldom visible to those living in it. A people's most deeply felt understandings of the sacred are often background

4

rather than foreground: they are the dimension of soul, forming the implicit container for daily experience. The mythic stories that are most visible are often only the topmost layer of powerful motivating factors, suggesting rich but obscure layers of fundamental convictions below. Psychologist C. G. Jung described this phenomenon with his terminology of archetypes, powerful thematic networks hidden away in a culture's collective unconscious, ready to bond with particular incidents as they occur in ordinary individual or cultural life.[6] The mythic or archetypal substructure of a culture is not usually one of lucid clarity but rather exists as the "explanation through enigma" that shapes society.[7]

Myths are about what might be called boundary questions: what does it mean to be alive and then to die; why are we born into life; what is wholeness or fullness of life and how do we gain it? In dealing with these questions, myth speaks of our relationship with the unknown even as it gives us a sense of purpose. The symbols and metaphors of myth carry meaning, even when their deeper narratives are not regularly told. Because of its depth psychological dimension, mythology refers to the relatively hidden story lines embedded in a culture that surface in repetitive themes or common sense ideas. For example, the mythology of individual freedom is so deeply and unthinkingly embedded in the U.S. culture today that even the phrase "the common good" tends to raise cries of "socialism!"

Because myth is always engaged with mysteries, with what remains ultimately unknown, it does not speak definitively; a mythic perspective hints and points and winks. A mythic approach carries sacred meaning for a group of people in the form of stories, symbols, images, and metaphors because these tools are rooted in the visible and sensory realm of ordinary human experience, even as they suggest something beyond themselves as deeper mysteries that can never be comprehended. Mythic awareness links the material realm intimately with the spiritual realm, although the two realms are complementary and neither can be collapsed into the other. Symbols and stories, like soul itself, function in a round-about way, slipping away from a tight grasp, revealing truth in glimpses at the edge of awareness. Metaphor can transport thought toward new understanding by pointing to

5

a resemblance not previously observed, thus setting forth "a tension between identity and difference."[8] The tension or destabilizing effect created by metaphor offers a way to participate in the creation of new meaning. And there is no end to meaning—the living metaphor, symbol, or myth continually points beyond itself, and cannot be expressed as having only one, already known, meaning. Myth can indeed be recognized by its capacity to bear many vibrant meanings. However, any specific cultural myth can in time become hardened and resistant, rather than remaining pliant and flexible in accordance with genuine mythic orientation toward the always unknowable realm of soul and divinity.

In contrast to the notion of a single fixed or certain meaning, mythic awareness at its best views literal or historical understanding as simply a first outer circle of meaning, alongside which lie additional concentric symbolic layers, each of which reveals further meaning. The first centuries of Christianity applied just such a multidimensional method to scripture, calling it (somewhat confusingly) the allegorical method of scriptural exegesis, in which the reader is opened to four different meanings in every text. The *literal* or *historical* meaning is followed by three kinds of "spiritual" meanings. The *allegorical* finds Christ in the text, in "the conviction that Christ is so inherent in the structure of the universe...that everything speaks of him."[9] The *tropological* finds moral or behavioral implications, and the *anagogical* explores eternal or ultimate meaning. While the specifics of this method are not central here, my re-visioning of theology seeks to reclaim a Christian appreciation of polyvalent meanings ordinarily characteristic of vital mythic thought.

A mythic approach seems to be an ideal way to address the excesses of literalism, whether in religion or science—those tendencies toward simple either-or, hence "certain" answers that have strengthened the power of literalism in our time. Mythic thinking can identify old cultural and theological myths that have hardened into literalism, and can likewise offer alternative mythic themes appropriate for a time of cultural and theological shift. The work of theology at any time is to translate the good news into cultural idioms that evoke stronger connections to the living God. This book proposes that a mythological perspective enables breakthrough beyond the literalism impasse and offers a means of dissolving the powerful popular forces of Western culture that hold theology hostage today.

EPIC MYTH AND PERSONAL/
CULTURAL DISORIENTATION

Commentators from Thomas Cahill to Phyllis Tickle have used the term *hinge of history* to describe periods of human history that in retrospect appear to involve major shifts in attitudes and events.[10] In the language of this book, such periods might be considered times when major reinterpretations of mythic archetypal materials are linked to momentous changes in behavior and culture. When a mythic interpretation becomes rigid, literal, and one-dimensional, emerging forces that are constrained by old dogmas tend to press at the edges of personal and cultural consciousness until eventually new receptivity allows fresh exploration of the ambiguity inherent in any mythic substratum.

The lived shift during a major re-interpretation of mythic archetypal materials is strenuous, because typically it involves periods of serious disequilibrium. This disorientation occurs at the individual and the cultural level, and is similarly necessary at the theological level. The form of myth called *epic* is intended for just such times, and is a way of re-visioning sacred narrative that arises when a new cultural worldview is emerging but not yet in place. Epic is a form of myth that lends itself particularly well to concerns of Christian theology, because epic's goal is to honor the sacred values of the past even as it reframes or reimagines those values so as to create new possibilities for the future. When culture and religion stand on the threshold between past and future, a liminal and potent place, epic is capable of holding the old sacred myth, both in its ideals and in its betrayals, in conversation with all that is represented by the unknown future, in a way that transforms and reshapes myth and meaning.

The epic form of myth is particularly helpful when "an entire way of life [is] caught at a moment of radical change,"[11] just as Western culture is now experiencing a period of movement away from the old certainties, while new frameworks of understanding have not yet been stabilized. Epic is a form of poetry involving an entire people; it is the realm of the attempt to create and/or restore a new mythos. It follows and builds on the tragic clearing of the ground and the comedic creation of a community and speaks to an entire way of life in transition. Thus epic encompasses a double vision—both backward toward a past remembered through the lens of loss and longing and forward toward a persuasive mythic vision of the future.[12] Epic enables the past to be seen with clarity and compassion, and the future in an authentic re-visioning.

Classical Epic Patterns

The classic epic myths are the *Odyssey* of Homer and the *Aeneid* of Virgil, both stories to help a people move through a time of great change. For example, Augustus Caesar commissioned Virgil to write something that would help legitimize his new imperial regime (replacing the Roman senate of the people) as having a divine mission to rule and spread the blessings of civilization, while at the same time reasserting the personal qualities of the old model Roman as essential to the success of the new regime.[13] Virgil's Aeneas is forced to flee Troy, carrying his father and his household gods on his back. He embarks on a long period of wandering, including a trip to the underworld, and a brief romantic involvement in a decadent culture on the mainland, finally arriving to claim the land of Rome, full of promise for the future. Here we see how Virgil integrates the sacred ideals of the past with all that is represented by the promised but unknown future. Virgil acknowledges the betrayals of the past, its limits in holding back the unfolding future as witnessed in the destruction of Troy, the time of darkness and confusion, the existence of corrupt neighbors. And just this acknowledgement enables him to re-vision a sacred narrative for the unfolding future that transforms both past and future, an epic reshaping of the mythic substratum of the culture.

Epic movement tends to be regarded as the work of a single hero like Aeneas. Indeed, Joseph Campbell elaborates this view of epic in his so-called monomyth, *The Hero with a Thousand Faces*, where he describes the nuclear unit of the epic hero as follows:

> A hero ventures forth from the world of common day into a region of supernatural wonder: fabulous forces are there encountered and a decisive victory is won: the hero comes back from this mysterious adventure with the power to bestow boons on his fellow man.[14]

A close parallel thus seems to exist between the path of the hero and the essential work of epic poetry. However, such an expectation for epic is itself shaped by a mythic fixation—a perspective that sees the hero as a unique individual visionary who makes a decisive break with the community, later returning to share the largess that he himself has won.[15]

In contrast to this way of thinking, I believe that the current task of epic re-visioning is not the work of a solitary hero, but is rather a summons to a whole people, to be lived out in the ongoing story of personal and institutional life. The shape of epic in this time may take a new form, a form that may not initially even seem like epic because of its new garb. A return to the foundations for epic poetry laid down in Aristotle's *Poetics* may illuminate alternative models.[16]

The pattern Aristotle explains is that epic myth is not so much intended to describe what has happened, but rather to show what may happen, what is possible according to the laws of probability or necessity. Epic's imaginative exploration is a movement outward toward the world of the heart's inner knowing, creating a potent space of new possibilities. Yet the epic story will necessarily enfold dissonance and discordant elements, just as life does. Aristotle has in mind the Greek play *Oedipus* in his description, a play not technically an epic but nonetheless containing the elements Aristotle considers central to epic. First, there is a *complication*: a sequence of events unfolds that leads toward a conflict. Second, an *unraveling* happens: an event occurs that interrupts the apparently steady flow and brings one up short. This event involves shock, but in some way also *recognition*—the interruption actually shows how the present moment has come to be. The present is seen truly, in its strengths and its limits, and initially this causes suffering. This narrative will seem so real—so true to life experience yet seemingly hidden until now—that it evokes both pity and fear. So, third, the turning point offers an opportunity for *reversal* through an event that is both perfectly probable and yet unforeseeable until it happens. A shift occurs within consciousness that evokes new awareness calling forth new action. And fourth and finally, the movement of unraveling is *also a turn toward the future*, because the past has been seen and remembered in a new way.

Aristotle's familiar model of an epic story begins with a king who abandons his son, Oedipus, because an oracle has foretold the son will kill the father. Raised in the country by shepherds who do not know his origins, Oedipus eventually returns to the country of his birth as a bright young warrior. Unknowingly, Oedipus approaches a crossroads blocked by an arrogant man in a chariot (his father). They engage in an angry fight, during which Oedipus kills the man, not even aware his opponent was king of that country. After Oedipus arrives at the capital, events unfold in such a way that Oedipus marries the queen, his mother, and becomes ruler of the country himself. However, despite his stewardship of the country, a drought ensues and the whole country suffers. (All this is the complication, the sequence of events leading to the unraveling.)

Oedipus calls his seers, declaring that whoever is responsible for this ill fate that has befallen the country will die. Finally, one old man is brought forth, the old king's steward who had been ordered to abandon the child. The old steward tells Oedipus to his face that he has murdered his father and married his mother, and when he sees the truth of this fact, Oedipus is horrified. (This is the unraveling, bearing shock and recognition.)

Oedipus blinds himself, a symbol of his previous blindness to the truth, and in a dramatic shift, he becomes a wandering "seer," a figure both pitied and feared, for now he is a symbol of the power of the gods as well as the capacity of humans to delude themselves. (The reversal here shows a new consciousness that makes possible a different kind of future, not only for Oedipus himself, but also for the neighboring peoples.)

Epic, Psychic Wholeness, and Spiritual Formation

Aristotle's model suggests that the work of epic myth involves a kind of disorientation corresponding both to ancient Christian spiritual formation patterns and to the kind of experience that C. G. Jung refers to as a "confrontation with the unconscious."[17] In all three of these patterns, a person's or culture's old organizing myth seems to collapse and a new way of being emerges only slowly and painfully. The psychic process of such a shift involves "watching as one certainty after another is dismantled and turns to dust [while realizing that] another kind of certainty grows stronger in us every day as we begin to make a new spiritual vessel out of the shards of the old one, [...trusting] the questions themselves."[18]

Jung demonstrates this depth psychological process not only in his personal engagement with the unconscious, but also in his professional work, providing a psychic model for others with his theories about the way the psyche moves toward greater wholeness and health—not linearly, but in a spiraling fashion that seems now up, now down. Being brought up short by something one resists, encountering a problem or an anomaly is often the opportune moment for personal transformation. The turmoil and conflict involved may seem to destabilize the ego temporarily, but this can be understood as an authentic engagement between the ego and the unconscious or the archetypal complex that will change both entities in the movement toward greater psychic wholeness.

This pattern, with its pivotal place for disorientation in the passage to greater maturity, has long been recognized by Christian theology as occurring in spiritual formation. For example, the *dark night* terminology found in the writings of sixteenth-century Carmelite monk John of the Cross offers a way to think theologically about psychic confrontation with the unconscious or epic shifts.[19] John's theology is an attempt to describe spiritual growth in light of the experience of impasse, an experience that feels like disintegration. He suggests that "it is *in* the very experience of darkness and joylessness, in the suffering and withdrawal of accustomed pleasure (in the felt sense of God's presence), that this transformation is taking place."[20] The process described by

11

St. John is not just personal but also one of societal impasse, where "God makes demands for conversion, healing, justice, love, compassion, solidarity, and communion."[21]

These individual psychic and spiritual patterns are similar to those occurring in social and cultural events of disorientation as an element of change toward growth. Scientist Thomas Kuhn emphasizes that new thought paradigms require "changing the meaning of established and familiar concepts," and demanding "more than additive adjustment of theory."[22] Kuhn adds that this shift in paradigms is not just an interior, personal change, but also involves a communal shift.

When such communal shifts in paradigms are happening, it is important to have a place of conversation where many can come together to explore the boundaries of the shift and gain some sense of positive potential. Yet such conversations are often difficult because the very people who might most assist in exploration, those more or less on the margins who see events with less attachment to maintaining the status quo, may be excluded from the conversation.[23] In speaking of the dynamics of a communal paradigm shift, Elisabeth Schüssler Fiorenza suggests, for example, that a helpful practice would be to read the Bible not as solitary readers, but rather in "a forum, that is, a public space where the *ekklesia* (literally church), the radical democratic assembly, can debate and adjudicate the public meanings of the scriptures."[24] Much of the early momentum of the liberation theology movements came from just such a communal reading practice centered in the Gospel. Poetic and prophetic voices emerging from a people help individuals negotiate mythic shifts. The most successful epic work involves communal cocreation.

In some respects, epic re-visioning is best led by people and ideas not in the centers of power, and today epic tends to be articulated in powerful and satisfyingly dramatic novels from the margins. One such story is Khaled Hosseini's *The Kite Runner*, in which an Afghani boy, who as a child abandoned his friend to the cruelty of a bully, later discovers that his childhood friend was actually his own brother. As an adult man, he finds himself face to face with that same bully, whom he must now fight if he is to retain his hard-won new integrity.[25] Another such epic novel is

Toni Morrison's *Beloved*, in which a runaway slave woman kills her child rather than allow the child to be taken back into slavery, later to find that the ghost of the child is gradually drawing the mother into a kind of mental possession.[26] Both of these epic novels ask the reader to gaze at something horrific long enough to find the gift of life that can be received only by acknowledging the reality of the horror. Being offered from the perspective of people "on the margin," these novels offer the gift of telling otherwise than the usual master story, so that an authentic healing of memory and myth can begin for all those willing to listen.[27]

Epic myth is a mode of mythic understanding specifically designed to invite disorientation and reorientation. Theological maturity—both individually and communally—can be seen in recognizing a disorienting impasse as an opportunity to view cultural signs not as bringing death, but instead as bringing "a fundamental evolutionary change and transcendence, [with] crisis as the birthplace and learning process for a new consciousness and harmony."[28]

A MYTHIC RE-VISIONING

Although Western Christianity has been reluctant to identify itself with the term *mythology*, the symbols and images of Christianity have dominated Western thinking about the sacred and its relation to human experience for the last two thousand years. Like any good myth, the elements of Christian mythic understanding take various forms in different ages, depending on the presuppositions and inclinations of that age. But the influence also occurs in the opposite direction: Christianity's myths and symbols have been significantly shaped by secular mythologies in Western society since its birth.

Certainly since Constantine legislated that Christianity be the official religion of the Roman Empire in the fourth century CE, a close alliance has existed between the symbols and myths of Christianity and those of Western culture. Major cultural paradigm shifts have previously occurred in Christianity's history, such as the Enlightenment or the Industrial Revolution, which were accompanied by shifts in Christian theology to strengthen its relevance. Corresponding to the Enlightenment's emphasis on the reasoning subject, Martin Luther proclaimed the need for the scriptures in the vernacular, and the right of every Christian to read and interpret the Bible. Corresponding to the Industrial Revolution, Max Weber showed how the Protestant work ethic supported the rise of capitalism. Yet today Christian theology seems to be hardening within previous patterns, rather than responding with flexibility to the challenges of the movement to postmodernism and beyond.

The Old Image of the Rational Heroic Ego

Although in many respects Western culture is no longer monolithic, I see much evidence that at a mythic, or depth psychological level, the basic mythic orientation of Western culture is fixated on the image of the *rational heroic ego*.[29] Archetypal psychologist James Hillman explores that pervasive image in his *Re-Visioning Psychology* from the point of view of soul.[30] Hillman explains that the hero archetype, so dominant in contemporary thought, "appears not so much in a list of contents as it does in maintaining the heroic attitude toward all events, an attitude now so habitual that we have come to call it the 'ego.'"[31]

Hillman's work is a radical challenge to the rational heroic ego. He observes what he calls the "steady withdrawal of soul into the narrow confines of the human skin…shrinking soul to its single and narrowest space, the ego," and points out that an ego's specific function is to represent the literal view.[32] The present cultural attitude tends to be "hero-based and ego-centered," fond of making problems and solving them by will power, as a defensive literalistic screen against ambiguity and the many things humans cannot control in the world.[33] In contrast to the heroic fixation, Hillman proposes *soul* as referring to reflection that enables the deepening of events into experiences, acknowledgement of death, and the "imaginative possibility in our natures…which recognizes all realities as primarily symbolic or metaphorical."[34]

The powerful image of the rational heroic ego emerges from many sources in Western culture, including the early Greek epics, and the Enlightenment movement, to name only two. Again, this image emphasizes the model of a bold hero who strikes out from the masses, vanquishes the dark danger that opposes reason, and saves the benighted poor people. Various elements of the mythic image are emphasized more strongly in one story or another, but familiar examples include Robin Hood, Luke Skywalker of *Star Wars* fame, and Spiderman. The image is so dominant in the West that, not infrequently, Jesus of Nazareth is viewed within the lens of this myth, despite theology's recent efforts to redefine Jesus' life and mission.

In certain respects, the rational heroic ego is the image that was adopted by the U.S. government in the early twenty-first century—in the name of (the hero) Christ, a solitary mission of the United States in the world to (or perhaps against) the benighted masses of the two-thirds world, disregarding other voices to the contrary. The notion of a rational heroic ego operates as a centripetal force, inevitably drawing into its field even new trends. A mythic analysis makes clear that Western theology's central religious beliefs are repetitively sidetracked or misaligned in their interaction with the culture's deep presuppositions that have become inflexible and literal, resisting change.

A New Image of an Imaginal Erotic/Creative Soul

I suggest that the mythic fixation on the rational heroic ego be challenged at a mythic/depth psychological level by the addition of, or new emphasis on, an alternative image. The mythic response I propose involves three major re-visioning components, each corresponding to one of the three presuppositions involved in the myth of the rational heroic ego. The proposed new perspectives are imagination, a feminist vision, and the "open" philosophy of Paul Ricoeur. Together, these three perspectives circumscribe a new mythic emphasis on an *imaginal, erotic (or creative) soul*.

IMAGINATION

The first re-visioning lens, imagination, holds an ambiguous place in Western culture and Christianity, and thus offers an effective position from the margin with which to challenge the status quo. In the West, imagination has often been perceived as either dangerous or foolish personal fantasy, possibly at odds with creedal religion. Sufi mythology suggests an alternative role for imagination. The Sufi cosmos consists of three realms, including not only the sensory and the conceptual but also the imaginal, which mediates between the other two.[35] The human functions in the imaginal world as mediator between the two realms, on one hand transmitting God's light and truth to the world; on the other, reflecting back to God the sparkling wonder of the world.[36] The place where the human learns what and how to effect this mediation is the imaginal world, reached through prayer and meditation; imagination is the faculty that makes that mediation possible.

This perspective contrasts with rationality not by excluding reason from conversations about what it is to be human, but because it recognizes that reason has unjustly extended its domain to cover the whole of human experience. Empirical reason works very well in some fields; but it is a very poor tool for speaking of values of any kind. Reason can never demonstrate that my husband loves me, or that a rose is beautiful. While reason can advance theological conversation in some ways, theology also requires other tools. Paul Ricoeur points out that truth can be revealed, for example, through a "logic" of probability, discovery, or through metaphor or attestation.[37] Imagination and the imaginal world open experience and conversation to the rich variety of avenues toward truth. For Sufis, one learns what it is to be fully human only when the practice of imagination is linked to sensation and thought.

A FEMINIST VISION

My proposed mythic image is the imaginal, erotic soul. The erotic component is intended to convey not primarily genital sexuality but rather a much richer feminist vision of spirituality as involving a joyously creative relationship with the material world. The erotic is the creative, life-affirming impulse that sees the world not as one of scarcity but as one of abundance.[38] The erotic perspective contrasts with the heroic mythical worldview expressed in a fixed notion of a male, kingly, triumphant warrior God. The erotic/creative view is not limited to women or is it valued by all women, but as used here, it represents a composite view of profound structural changes advocated by feminists as ways to expand theology's capacity to understand and love the divine. A feminist vision offers a view of human life not primarily shaped by such "commonsense ideas" as the inevitability of war, the necessity of dualistic oppositions such as body and spirit, or a so-called "natural" hierarchy in relationships. Instead, a mythic feminist template includes respect for the physical world, equality rather than dominance, the importance of community, nonviolence and complementarity rather than dualism.

THE "OPEN" PHILOSOPHY OF PAUL RICOEUR

The third and final re-visioning element is the philosophy of Paul Ricoeur, here as an expression of the reality of soul, referring to that part of human experience that is ambiguous, humble, and wondering, in the face of ultimate mystery. Paul Ricoeur, a philosopher whose life roughly spans the twentieth century, believes that science and faith, critique and conviction, are necessary partners, and he articulates a way to unite them that includes a dynamic and lively sense of the sacred. Ricoeur takes seriously the critical attacks on the pseudoinnocent self (cogito), while insisting that a suspicious interpretive scheme is just the first step of probing beneath the obvious. There is more to the self than these reductions; the human self is also an aspiration to grow beyond its limitations toward the divine. Transcendent longings are the province of soul.

One of Ricoeur's important insights, expressed in all his work, is that in an encounter dense with meaning, there will be conflicts of interpretation.[39] This insight speaks to the situations so common today with conflicts across cultural divides, where there seems to be no sense of common ground. Ricoeur offers a way of reaching across such chasms, maintaining personal authenticity, while genuinely hearing the other.

Ricoeur's philosophy unfolds into something called *phenomenological hermeneutics*, with phenomenology being the work of giving attention to the stuff—the phenomena—of life, and hermeneutics being the art of interpretation. He endeavors not to get caught in a dualistic opposition between a hermeneutic of suspicion and a hermeneutic of symbols (an interpretive stance that celebrates multiple meanings). Ricoeur wants to integrate both in a broad concept of interpretation that encompasses an initial move of suspicion, looking for an explanation *beneath* the evident meaning, in dialectical engagement with a second move of symbolism *between* meanings, meanwhile being alert to possible worlds *beyond* evident meanings in a dense third position not previously visible to either party.[40] Another way to say this is that one can enter conflict creatively by adding critique to personal conviction, participating deeply in another's experience as a way of critiquing personal attachments to certainties that in dialogue may be revealed as partial truths that can be expanded toward greater wholeness. When distancing oneself from one's own position for a time, an opening occurs to a reality beyond either side, a reality that appears only when each is listening in-depth not only to one another, but also to the possible worlds beyond the present moment.[41]

This opening to possible worlds is an opening to the unknown, the not-yet always hovering nearby. Possible worlds are best revealed by a mythological approach, one that accounts for the semantic innovation inherent in metaphoric language, as well as a return to the roots of a society's or theology's identity. Soul, not ego, is the place where such listening in depth engages possible worlds beyond.

Reflections

Summarizing the proposed re-visioning toward an imaginal, erotic soul, the lens of imagination offers a way to inform and direct spiritual passion toward wholeness beyond mere reason, serving a mediating and integrating role for sensation and thought, bringing the divine reality into the world and vice versa. The lens of a feminist vision challenges a mythic posture that not only sees God as exclusively male, but also carries a series of corollaries creating a closed story of inevitable power struggles hostile to an erotic appreciation of the world. The lens of Paul

Introduction: Problem and Possibility

Ricoeur's philosophy provides a philosophical foundation for soul, from which many interpretative positions can become mutually creative within an open story of uncertainty and change. In the aggregate, these three perspectives destabilize the tacit grasp of the rational, heroic ego myth on the underlying mythic substructure of the West, offering the renewed vitality of the imaginal, erotic soul myth for Western Christian theology and experience. Each of these perspectives offers a way of seeing that has generally been marginalized in the current Western cultural and theological worldview, yet none is inherently hostile to the foundational Christian experience. Each of these perspectives also abounds with ambiguity, uncertainty, and corresponding creativity. They all resist an impulse toward stability and control, which is to say, they retain an ongoing opening to the unexpected presence so characteristic of the living God. My hypothesis is that these shifts in perspective can loosen the "hardened arteries" of literalism and bring about a mythic re-visioning in mainstream Western Christianity's self-understanding and presence in the world. My hope is that this re-visioning might also benefit other religious or spiritual perspectives and various cultural arenas, but the focus here is on Western Christianity.

I write here not mainly about or to the individual Christian dealing with his or her soul, but rather primarily for and to the collective and epic soul of our times. Just as Hillman hopes to be a psychologist for the culture, so I hope to be a reflective "spiritual director" for Western culture and Christianity's theology. I write as a practicing Episcopal laywoman deeply formed by Benedictine spirituality who has authored seven books on Christian spirituality. As a feminist, I prefer to use the term *Godde* rather than God, because although the sound is the same, the additional letters are a reminder that the divine being is far beyond any categories that can be assigned to it. I approach theology itself with a similar initial disorientation, turning to mythology as a way to speak about the sacred beyond familiar New Testament language—a way to speak about the tacit background that supports and frames the explicit foreground of contemporary Western Christian lives. While I am aware that there are many streams in Western Christianity, my previous experience well suits me to speak to a central stream of these traditions. This book employs insights gained from my graduate degrees in theology, depth psychology, and mythology, drawing on the strengths of all three. I also bring to bear another previous graduate degree in political theory, where my concerns were centered in public philosophy, that is, with the way meaning is mutually created among individuals, the sociopolitical community, and concepts of the divine. I seek to respect differences, and I am especially sensitive to feminist concerns, even as I am primarily a generalist or synthesizer, seeking to evoke broad themes in a collective mythic-religious consciousness in the context of Western Christianity.

One of the primary characteristics of the mythic re-visioning process, or of any truly formative process, is that it cannot be understood until it has been suffered for a while. In moving from one major mythic understanding to another, a person or culture is not simply collecting information but becoming involved in a process of formation and transformation. Formation is a costly notion because it means that understanding only comes when we have been changed by the process itself. There is a necessary dying to the old ways of being before the shape of the new life begins to emerge. If this dying to the old ways is refused, if it is impossible for person or culture to accept or reconcile the past, old wounds and scars are repeated endlessly. Movement forward into the creative future does not happen until both the beauty and the violence of the past are integrated deeply into awareness.

This mythically re-visioned theology calls for relinquishment of the certainties offered by dogmatically assertive technologies and theologies. At first it may seem that giving up fixed notions about reason or God or faith is an abandonment of the essential core of Christian life and faith. But in the long tradition of Christianity, faith has seldom meant merely or primarily "giving mental assent to propositions."[42] From a mythological point of view, faith suffers a far greater danger when it becomes identified with a single and literal idea than when it remains open to continuous penetration of the mystery that always newly summons the faithful.

Chapter 1

What If...? Imagination and the Imaginal Realm

Starting womb-time,
I imagine I imagined,
"Well, it sure is comfortable In Here;
but What If I have to leave?
What might it be like Not In Here?"

So I've wondered into being
a place which remains both
Here and Not Here—
by imagining
first Not Here joins There,
then discover a world that's both
Here and There
between the two:
shared experience called relation;
not just sort of,
but a real third place,
and not because I imagined,
for it's been there all along.

"What If..." in *Entering the Mystery*
by Douglas C. Vest

This mythic re-visioning toward an imaginal, erotic soul begins with an in-depth look at imagination and the role it has played and can play in Western culture and Christianity. This and the next two chapters briefly explore problems arising with the mythic dominance

21

of the rational heroic ego and then examine in depth the mythic alternatives embodied in the image of the imaginal, erotic soul. To move to the mythic level is to draw out implicit assumptions that form the symbolic background framework of contemporary Western culture and to consider whether those one-dimensional and now rigid assumptions serve society and theology well. At the mythic level it becomes possible to re-vision a more balanced and flexible symbolic substructure capable of revitalizing culture and theology.

Recent years have seen a flurry of new books declaring the old idea that God is dead. If one asks, what is the nature of this dead God?, the answer is likely to be the narrow and precisely defined God of Aquinas—immutable, immovable, eternal—with its specific, fixed, and authoritative features taken as literal. In the emerging post-Enlightenment period, that vision of God remains too remote from the secular and scientific advances of these centuries to be believable. But a re-visioned mythology, coupled with the powerful work now happening in parallel disciplines, offers ways to embrace other, and now more credible, notions of a divine presence that continues compassionately to intersect human life.

In particular, imagination is an important means of experiencing God. Philosophy, religion, and psychology all attest to the fact that in disciplined imagination, persons encounter something beyond their own present knowing, something that seems oriented toward their wholeness. The process of engagement with that something beyond may require a loss of certainty and a willingness to be open to a new way of being in the world. But the gift of a more meaningful life is often received by those who persist. The nature of the reality encountered through imagination is ambiguous; but that is always characteristic of genuine encounters with divinity in myth and religion. This chapter demonstrates that many different modes of thought record the human value of mature imagination, and of an imaginal realm enfolding the life of the present moment. Imagination and the imaginal realm are a crucial first lens for an effective mythic re-visioning of theology.

INCLINATION TO DISTRUST

The status of the human imagination has been ambiguous throughout Western cultural history, largely because of the positivist and rationalist philosophies about reality that shape the dominant worldview. Western culture tends to see things largely as ego or other, causing or caused, subjects or objects, based on strict interpretations of natural and physical laws.[1] A suspicion exists that the imagination is unreliable, the source of private fantasies somehow dangerous to those reasonable standards by which people consent to live in society. This epistemology, this theory about how the world can be known, excludes information that in other times and places has been considered central to human life. Standing outside that perspective, this viewpoint can be understood as a relatively narrow mode of experience, minimizing as it does images and myths.[2] Rational modes of perception are squeezing out mystery and imagination, which are atrophying for lack of attention.

In addition to a scientific bias toward the rational, Western religion colludes in the distrust of imagination as at best a fanciful distraction, and at worst a potential temptation to error. Theological precision contributes to the reluctance to employ imagination, and pastoral guidance often seems unwilling to entrust imagination to ordinary devotion. Yet if imagination is understood as bringing to mind in the present something that is absent, then image and symbol are part of all religious thought that roots belief in something that cannot be directly shown.[3] In the absence of ongoing imaginative interplay, religious symbols tend to be taken literally, seen as superficially containing sacred truths instead of being pointers toward deeper mysteries. The devaluation of the imagination "is related to the devaluation of the soul, [...reducing soul] to an interchangeable rationality."[4] Without a lively and credible role for imagination, religious vitality suffers.

In general, Western theories of knowledge tend to regard the realms of human consciousness as consisting of sensory perception on the one hand, and of intellectual abstraction on the other. Sometimes the imagination is seen as having a middle space between the two, but often this is viewed as an inferior faculty and is subordinated either to perception or reason. Today, even though Western culture is inundated by images, the faculty of imagination and its corresponding realm of the imaginal are so collapsed that they are seldom even experienced.

In contrast, imagination is central to the integrative model framing this book, re-visioning rooted in epic myth. To re-vision involves imagining a different way of looking. To narrate the epic mythically involves a destabilizing leap of metaphor that opens up hitherto unknown possibilities within old stories. Imagination raises questions central to myth and religion: what is truth? Is truth something revealed unambiguously by data or dogma, or is it an eternally mysterious reality continuously revealed within and around data and dogma? The restoration of imagination and the imaginal realm to Western Christian thought gives access to sacred material otherwise out of reach and contributes toward an overall environment more supportive of soul and theological work.

PHILOSOPHY'S RICH CONTRIBUTION TO IMAGINATION

What can be known? And how can it be known? These questions of epistemology (the study of knowledge) have preoccupied Western philosophy in recent centuries, and the search for answers unleashed the scientific revolution. Beyond the epistemological questions are the ontological questions (reflection about being itself): what kind of a being is the human, especially in relation to the essence of being and to the world? And what are the responsibilities or obligations of the human person to others and indeed to life itself (ethical questions). All three types of questions are directly related to issues of the imagination, and because of the complexity of the issues, simple definitions are elusive.[5] No doubt any concept that touches on such important issues as truth, being, and ethics will have a controversial pedigree, and that is true for imagination as well.

Philosopher Edward Casey warns that the starting point for any description of imagination "lies in an initial recognition of the phenomenon's inherent ambiguity, its tendency to invite opposite evaluations."[6] Some of the confusion lies in the many ways the term is used, including four distinct usages:

1. The ability to evoke absent objects that exist elsewhere, without confusing these absent objects with things present here and now.
2. The construction and/or use of material forms and figures such as paintings, statues, photographs, etc., to represent real things in some "unreal" way.
3. The fictional projection of nonexistent things as in dreams or literary narratives.
4. The capacity of human consciousness to become fascinated by illusions, confusing what is real with what is unreal.[7]

Given this range of possible meanings, it is no wonder that confusion and anxiety exist about imagination's value, especially in religious contexts. Nevertheless, imagination does have a central role not only in the way the human-divine connection is understood, but in rites and worship as well.

Philosopher Richard Kearney offers a definition, identifying a central trait in "all the various terms for imagination—*yetser*, *phantasia*, *eikasia*, *Einbildungskraft*—they all refer, in their diverse ways, to the human power to convert absence into presence, actuality into possibility, what-is into something-other-than-it-is."[8] Imagination is the capacity to consider things other than in their immediate self-presentation. While such a definition includes the use of imagination to mentally escape from a troublesome situation, it also suggests the essential role of imagination in envisioning and planning for new possibilities or exploring how to live into relationship with the inherently unknowable holy. From the religious perspective, imagination links what is known by sensation and intellect to what is known by faith.

Philosophy plays a crucial role in creating and supporting the mythic framework in which people live. Several key movements in Western philosophy demonstrate the role imagination plays (and does not play) today in the cultural experience of Western Christianity and reveal emergent sources for a more substantial and fruitful place in the present historical moment.

Hebrew and Greek Beginnings
in Myth and Philosophy

Kearney observes that both of the "founding narratives" of Western culture, that of Adam and Eve in biblical literature, and that of Prometheus in Greek myth, reveal the power of imagination as coterminus with the origins of humanity, and as potentially dangerous.[9] The ability to see things as other than they are is the basis of the choice by Adam and Eve to eat the forbidden fruit revealing the knowledge of good and evil. The capacity to ask "what if…" is also the basis for Prometheus's decision to take (steal from the gods?) the gift of fire to share with humans for warmth and food.

The primary Hebrew word for *imagination* is *yetser*, a word that derives from the same root (*yzr*) as the term for *create* (*yatsar*). The parallelism of the words suggests that God created Adam and Eve in God's own image, intentionally risking that they might set themselves up as rivals, endeavoring to supplant God in the order of creation.[10] Thus one lesson of the Garden of Eden, a founding myth of Western religion and culture, is that while imagination is gift, it is also dangerous and possibly the basis of human pride, that most dangerous sin.

This lesson is confirmed in the Greek myth of Prometheus. Prometheus's name means "foresight," designating "the power to anticipate the future by projecting an horizon of imaginary possibilities."[11] Prometheus stole fire from the gods and bestowed it on humans, for which Zeus delivered eternal punishment. In this myth too, imagination is understood as potentially leading to an act of rebellion against the divine, an effort by humans (or in this case, titans) to take something reserved for the gods. Mythically, imagination is an act marked by essential ambiguity, both blessing and curse.

Although these two founding narratives are more myth than philosophy, Plato and Aristotle soon shift reflections on imagination to a more philosophical plane. Plato's philosophy reflects repugnance for the rather emotional tone of mythic narrative (*mythos*), and a move toward the more reasoned approach of *logos* (reasoned, logical thought). Plato's philosophy elevates the original forms of pure being into a transcendental realm of ideas, setting them above the imperfect and transitory realm of the created world of becoming.[12] He does see the created world as itself dynamic, penetrated at every point by the realm of the forms that offer the models from which the world of matter is copied.[13] It is this concern for copying, or imitation, which is central to Plato's opposition to imagination, for he sees it as inevitably mimetic, or merely a copy of the fundamentally real. Note however that even in his description of the realms of being and becoming, Plato is making a great imaginative leap as he describes the origin of things in a philosophical way, a radical new departure from the creation stories of his age.[14]

Aristotle's philosophical system includes a specific place for imagination, seeing the image as serving "as a mental intermediary between sensation and reason."[15] Imagination is a link between inner and outer, between the mind and the world. Whereas Plato sees images as imitations (*eikasia*) of eternal forms, Aristotle sees them as copies of sensation (*phantasia*), that is, as pictures created based on something actually seen, linking imagination to sensation or the physical world. Aristotle's philosophy expands the role of imagination in three ways beyond Plato: first, in envisioning imagination's work as an interior work, often of memory; second, in believing the image to be a precondition of all rational thought (whereas Plato's eternal forms need not be expressed in images); and third, in the possibility that imagination may lead to truth and not just illusory imitation.[16]

Aristotle establishes a special role for imagination in relation to art, where it is identified "with the positive capacity of art to portray the universal meaning of human existence."[17] Aristotle's *Poetics* describes the intention of poetry as "an imitation of an action that is serious, complete, and of a certain magnitude."[18] This imitation is quite a different notion of *mimesis* than Plato's, for it is not simply the imitation of a pure form, but is rather the unfolding of the "why" of the dramatic poem, the play of unconscious forces with consciousness that intentionally evokes "pity and fear effecting the proper purgation of those emotions."[19] Here Aristotle reveals the link between imagination and myth's concerns with the search for meaning.

Philosophers of the Enlightenment

Descartes

It is tempting to assign responsibility for the contemporary disregard of imagination to the influential seventeenth-century philosopher René Descartes, as Hillman does: "Basic to this modern view of persons is the psychology of Descartes; it imagines a universe divided into living subjects and dead objects. There is no space for anything intermediate, ambiguous, and metaphorical."[20] Certainly there is justification for this assertion. With Descartes, the world is separated into a dualism of mind and body in his move toward the reasoning subject as the sole source of knowledge. Descartes defines *substance* as that which is the cause of itself, something self-sufficient and needing nothing else to exist. Then he asserts that only two things in human experience count as substances, one of which is mind (*res cogitans*—the thinking thing) and other of which is matter (*res extensa*—the thing with extension in space).[21] These definitions definitively separate mind and matter, since a substance by definition is self-sufficient and freestanding. The primary faculty of mind is thought, and everything else flows from that: *cogito, ergo sum* (I think, therefore I am) becomes the watchword of the new paradigm. "The project is to build the entire world from the thinking self," detached from history and tradition.[22] Descartes embodies the portal into the new scientific worldview, with its emphasis on the rational (rather than the imaginal) faculty and its claim for knowledge creation solely from the thinking mind (rather than myth or revelation).

It may be a caricature, however, to attribute to Descartes sole responsibility for the momentum of the Enlightenment, with its preferences for the autonomy of the subject, its confidence in reason as the only necessary instrument of truth, and its emphasis on logos to the exclusion of mythos and imagination. Theologian Edward Farley notes that "Cartesianism" has been a frequent target for criticisms from both the left and the right in recent decades, and he urges a more nuanced view of the philosophy and the period. Farley's insight is that secularization was one of the principal effects of the Enlightenment, and that its spokespersons, like Descartes, needed to frame a bold and credible principle to confront "the authoritarianism and supernaturalism of the religious establishment," which included the intertwined issues of "monarchy, class hierarchies, jurisprudence, cosmology, and education."[23]

A balanced view suggests that the emergent disciplines of humanism and science, which offer such great benefits in today's world, were blocked from development under the controlling religious authority orientation of the late medieval period. Controlling institutions tend to be convinced of their modes of certainty (now often limited to the empirical and logical) and are accordingly adverse to imaginative challenge. At the time of Descartes, essential new scientific advances improving the quality of life for many people were made possible by the critical and investigative reason inaugurated by his philosophy. However, by the early twenty-first century, some of those scientific and rationalistic advances had developed their own sets of controlling institutions, including links with religious ones. It could be said that Descartes rightly analyzed the implicit mythic background of his time and effectively initiated a re-visioning of its central presuppositions. Descartes may have been no less essential to the emergent gifts of the Enlightenment than is a restoration of the role of imagination today.

KANT

From the point of view of imagination, Immanuel Kant both furthers the Cartesian paradigm and dramatically changes it. Like Descartes, Kant accepts the central role of the human subject in the perception and assessment of experience, with both of them challenging the authority of "definitive" dogma. Each individual human now is the hub of experience and thus of knowledge, while information is to be gathered inductively, by aggregating specific experience and drawing conclusions from the data. In the previous period, a deductive process governed, whereby constituted authority delivered truth based on its formal existence in religion or philosophy. With Descartes and Kant, the fountain of all knowledge is experience, consisting of external sensible objects perceived through the reasoning operations of the human subject.[24]

Kant, however—unlike Descartes, whose focus is solely on reason as the faculty of knowledge—includes an important role for imagination within his initial schema. With Kant, "the *mimetic* paradigm of imagining is replaced by the *productive* paradigm."[25] Imagination is no longer just a faculty for copying either the forms or the physical world; rather it becomes an active participant in bringing reason and sensation together. Kant even introduces the idea of a transcendental imagination, where imagination mediates between sensation and intellect, because he sees it as the common root of both forms of knowledge and thus able to synthesize them. For Kant, transcendence refers not to God, but to the ability to go beyond the ordinary. However, Kant is having it both ways, both centering the world in the human subject, *and* invoking something beyond that unites the previously separated pure subject and pure object.

However, although Kant describes imagination as having a central role in the first edition of his *Critique of Pure Reason* (1781), he becomes alarmed by its possible implications and considerably waters down his claims in the second edition, published 1787.[26] For while Kant's emphasis on the knowing subject is compatible with the philosophical rationalism at the foundation of the Enlightenment, the place he assigns to imagination threatens to undermine that rationality. In his later work, Kant retains an emphasis on the human subject, while accepting but marginalizing the transcendental imagination. By implication, a collective philosophical "stew" might equally well consist of different proportions: philosophy might emphasize imagination while minimizing the role of rational subject (one that is always seen as *other* than an "object" to be perceived, analyzed, or projected).

The overall momentum of Enlightenment philosophy implies that "the authority of State and Church, objective metaphysics and ontological knowledge" are no longer necessary.[27] Metaphysical propositions, such as that "the soul is immortal, substance is permanent, God exists...can be derived neither from experience nor from logic."[28] The next obvious philosophical step is that divine cause or first principle itself will be seen merely as a projection of the knowing subject.[29] At that time, most philosophers are not quite ready to go so far as to speak of that inevitable conclusion to their theories, but subsequent philosophy will have no such compunctions. In any case, Descartes and Kant saw the

Enlightenment as the human's emergence from self-inflicted immaturity—from reliance upon external authorities and reluctance to depend upon personal rational understanding.[30]

This new state of affairs evokes both an exhilarating freedom and a painful anxiety. The momentum of ideas cannot be stopped—too much rides on the shift of authority from powerful central institutions toward the individual's freedom to perceive and to assess. From Locke's statement that the grounds of civil society rest in the informed consent of each citizen to Luther's insistence on the necessity for every Christian to be able to read the Bible in the vernacular, the unquestioned credibility of the old feudal institutions is disintegrating. In retrospect, the work of Descartes and Kant may seem like a smooth transition from one dominant philosophy to another, although it seems likely that a "considerable level of anxiety fuels the Cartesian search for order."[31]

The decision of the philosophies of the Enlightenment to emphasize the human subject and by implication to depreciate concepts of divine being cannot be overestimated. These Western philosophical assertions about knowledge and being not only establish the foundation for scientific empiricism; they also profoundly influence Western concepts of religion and faith today. But an opening for alternative conceptions emerges once myth and imagination are brought into play. If imagination is understood to have a central role in human knowing, possibly philosophy need not focus on the human side of knowledge, but might potentially shift focus back to a concern for divine being. The section below on Sufi mysticism demonstrates the latter choice—an emphasis on imagination located in a theory emphasizing the being of God as it is poured out into the world. Possibly an appreciative critique of Enlightenment philosophy might reveal new possibilities more appropriate for the theological and soul needs of this time.

Phenomenology

Husserl

A third important movement in philosophy from the point of view of the imagination is the development of phenomenology

31

—with its explicit intention to give attention to the phenomena of life—inaugurated by Edmund Husserl with his *Ideas* in 1913. As noted above, Enlightenment philosophy takes the view that the basic act of consciousness is simply that one is conscious, without any necessary reference to the world. A primary philosophical emphasis on the knowing subject risks not only a sense of disconnection with divinity but also with the physical world. The substantial quality of mind in Descartes does give a kind of freedom to manipulate sensory experience, to master matter, as it were, with the greater strength of mind. But because Descartes's mind is primarily rational, although he sees the soul as belonging to the mind, soul tends to be marginalized. And because the substance of mind is strictly separated from the substance of body, the mind's connection with the physical world begins to seem insignificant. The clear separation of subject and object creates a situation in which "impersonality has become the mark of the truth of the known."[32] To a self as singular subject, everything becomes an object.

However Husserl, working a couple of centuries after Descartes, is not satisfied with the method of Enlightenment induction (working with objects of empirical experiments) or with that of medieval deduction (defining reality based on logical presuppositions). Rather he seeks "freedom from empiricist and rationalist premises," which he finds in a focus on intentionality, or consciousness *of something*.[33] Previous treatments of the imagination often confused images with thoughts or perceptions, making it difficult to identify imagining as a distinct activity of consciousness. But image is not perception, nor is it a purely sensory content; rather imagination is a particular *kind* of consciousness.

Observing himself imagining, Husserl sees there is a difference between the act of imagination (the *noesis*) and the object of imagination (the *noema*), two elements that overlap but are distinct when "the mind directs itself onto and absorbs itself in a specific content."[34] Husserl sees that imagination involves a conscious relationship with an image, a kind of intentionality toward an "other." Consciousness is always consciousness *of* something, and this means that the reality of the life-world exists independent of human subjectivity.[35]

Acknowledging both that the world exists and that human consciousness structures what is seen, Husserl seeks a philosophical way to restore a connection between the human subject and the depth of things. After affirming the subject's intentional relationship to the image, he then suspends the subject's intentionality in order to be present to things as they are.[36] This suspension (sometimes also called *epoché*) is "a leading back to (*re-ducere*) the essential structures of phenomena."[37] Although Husserl's "phenomenological reduction" might seem to be a move away from the world, it is intended instead to be a move away from the subject's unconscious entanglements with the world, so that a person can see more clearly both the world itself and the nature of personal assumptions about it. This step is similar to the work of mythic re-visioning, as an effort to gain enough intellectual and affective distance from the background mythological presuppositions of one's own culture to see it clearly and disentangle some of its strands. A high degree of self and other awareness is necessary even to attempt such a suspension or reduction, as well as an appreciation for the inevitable limitations of any single perceptual stance.

In making the reduction or suspension, the goal of phenomenology is the disclosure of essences. Essences (from the Greek *eidos*, meaning image) are disclosed, Husserl says, "when they are grasped not only in their actuality but also in their possibility—the latter being the special preserve of imagination."[38] The essence of something includes not only what is, but also what might be, the potential of the thing. Reason and logic can only go so far in anticipating potential; imagination must also be employed (a fact discovered as well by creative scientists and lovers of God).

Imagination thus plays a crucial intuitive role in Husserl's philosophy. If one brackets or neutralizes the normal perceptual relation to things, imagination or intuition moves forward into a central position to "reveal the life of human consciousness to itself."[39] Imagination is uniquely able to help a person withdraw from a normal attitude toward something, stand back and reflect on it, and observe the essence (actual and potential) both of the world and of consciousness itself.

But just how are these essences revealed? Does consciousness discover an essence through the subject's own creative imagination, or is consciousness engaged in a mutually influential relationship with something beyond itself? Does phenomenology really transcend the self-enclosure of the knowing subject? What guarantees that the phenomenal essence is not merely a projection of the observing subject? Paradox if not ambiguity pervades phenomenology, and it lends itself to multiple corollaries.

Still, Kearney affirms three decisive claims made by phenomenology:

1. Imagining is a productive act of consciousness, not a mental reproduction in the mind.
2. Imagining does not involve a courier service between body and mind but an original synthesis that precedes the age-old opposition between the sensible and the intelligible.
3. Imagining is not a luxury of idle fancy but an instrument of semantic innovation.[40]

Possibly the human observer never attains an objective understanding of the phenomenal world, but imagination still serves consciousness in the cocreation of genuinely new possibilities. When imagination can claim an active role of its own, a true partnership with sense and intelligence to articulate not only the present reality but also the possible future, it has moved a long way from delusion and hallucination, and established its relevance on a radically new footing.

BACHELARD

The philosophical moves explored so far have emphasized the knowing self, the human subject in a world of objects. With Gaston Bachelard a radically new perspective appears, something he calls a poetic imagination of the material world. Essentially, Bachelard explores the possibility that consciousness is not just a human faculty, but that the physical world itself bears a kind of consciousness, a consciousness that can be explored in a poetic manner through imagination. Bachelard had spent the early part of his life as a professor of the physical sciences, but, increasingly influenced by Husserl's work in phenomenology, embarks in the later part of his life on a project concerning "the imagination of matter—that is, the imagination of the four elements which philosophy and the ancient sciences...have regarded as the basis of all things."[41] He writes that "it is matter that governs form" and "matter is the unconscious of form."[42] This perspective reverses Aristotle's physics where form is the organizing principle for matter, since Bachelard's desire is to get a sense of the material world through the imagination, letting the formal properties fall into place afterward. He feels a need to approach the natural world differently than modern science, intuiting that the natural world is not inert matter but somehow enters human life spontaneously at an imaginative level.[43]

Although Bachelard is interested in the human subject, he "conceives of the human being as a de-centered subject nourished by a poetic power which transcends its control."[44] His starting point is not human consciousness but the imagination of matter, and he aims to bring them together. Bachelard reconnects psyche and matter in two ways. First, he works with the four elements (earth, air, fire, water—the subjects of his books) to take matter out of its inert state into a kind of sentience accessible to humans. Second, he defines poetic temperament as an extension of human consciousness whose character is to reach out into the surrounding world, thus challenging the notion of an isolated conscious ego.[45] His poetic sensibility rejoins psyche and nature and creates a sense of materiality accessible only through imagination.

Bachelard urges, "The imagination is not...the faculty for forming images of reality; it is the faculty for forming images which go beyond reality, which *sing* reality."[46] Images are productive of something beyond present reality, something that connects also with heart and soul rather than merely with mind. Not surprisingly, such images "harbor within themselves a certain diversity or contradictoriness;" they resist being confined to a single, simple meaning and they function dynamically in human experience.[47] Bachelard specifically connects images with archetypes, suggesting a link to Jung's work on psychic contents that emerge from a collective matrix and are capable of manifesting in a variety of specific forms.[48] Bachelard does not confuse the imaginative and the real, but he sees the imagination as "surpassing the real towards a renewed reality."[49] In other words, he proposes that rationality alone is incapable of perceiving the full spectrum of reality.

Bachelard perceives that image and imagination are not confined to the sense of sight only, for he often speaks of poetic imagining as a linguistic phenomenon.[50] He notes that in his books on the material imagination, "I have restricted my inquiry to the literary imagination [...because] literary expression enjoys an existence independent of [visual] perception."[51] Nor is image confined to that substantial mind separated by Descartes from the body and the physical world: Bachelard definitively restores the body-mind connection in his poetical and phenomenological reverie with the four constitutive elements of the physical world.

Reverie is central to Bachelard's method. He values both dreams (*rêve* in French) and *rêverie*, but he particularly values rêverie as "a spiritual phenomenon which is too natural—and also too useful in psychic equilibrium—to be treated as a derivative of the dream."[52] The practice of rêverie opens one to a world of simplicity and serenity that helps balance the demands of daily life. When an image rings true, then "how simple it is to discover one's soul at the end of rêverie!"[53] This quotation suggests how different Bachelard's approach is from that of mainstream philosophy, which he describes as going through tedious "steps taken to constitute a stable world after a thousand readjustments make us forget the brilliance of the first openings."[54] Bachelard dramatically shifts the locus and practice of the imagination in Western philosophy.

Reflections

These explorations of the status of imagination in the West suggest several key issues. Philosophy, of course, has taken additional turns beyond those indicated in this chapter during its postmodern phase, and those are discussed in subsequent chapters. But this chapter's concern has been with three central movements that influence the status of imagination in Western culture today: Greek and Hebrew beginnings, the Enlightenment period, and modern phenomenology. One recurring issue is the contrast between a view of imagination as having an active and productive role in consciousness versus an imitative and reproductive role. A way through this apparent opposition is suggested in Aristotle's use of the term *mimetic* for imagination's work in poetry, a term combining both active and receptive qualities. A second issue that surfaces repeatedly is whether the human subject is enclosed by personal subjectivity, and if not, what role imagination might play in essential engagement with "otherness," including even the relative otherness of the human body. Related to this aspect is the potential link of the imaginative capacity to possible worlds—situations and possibilities that do not presently exist in human experience but that might be brought into being through an imaginative connection to them.

A third issue is the relationship of the faculty of imagination to the transhuman, as well as to the physical world. One aspect of this issue is the ambiguous relationship to "divine being" revealed in the West's earliest mythic stories, and whether the "danger" dimension of imagination has a tendency to override the "opportunity" dimension in theological theory and practice. A fourth and related issue is the three-part division among sensation, imagination, and intellect, and the question of whether these are equal or hierarchical faculties, with implications of each position for soulful dimensions of human and earthly life. This issue is discussed further in the section on imagination and religion below.

None of these issues is resolved, but to surface them is to suggest the possibility of alternatives for a philosophy of imagination, as it might contribute to a mythic re-visioning of theology in the contemporary world. A robust concept of imagination reveals its power to restore mythic balance to the contemporary tendency to perceive "reality" as pertaining only to the (subjective) rational/conceptual and sensate realms of consciousness.

FROM A DIFFERENT ANGLE: THE IMAGINAL IN SUFI MYSTICISM

Why focus on Sufi mysticism in considering the imagination in religion? While much might be said both about the theology (or lack thereof) of imagination and about its practice in Christianity, this chapter takes a different approach, suggested by an anecdote. Years ago, I asked a wise old monk friend how best to come to know the city of Jerusalem. After thinking a few moments, he responded, "You need to return to the city many times from different directions." That answer provides the model for this book's re-visioning work—it circles around the subject, stopping here and there in several locations and returning to the center each time from a new viewpoint.

Sufism (Islamic mysticism) is of special interest for several reasons. First, in Sufism and especially in the twelfth-century thought of Sufi sages Suhrawardi and Ibn 'Arabī, an intentional effort is made to integrate sensation, intellect, and imagination as coequal human faculties. The concept of the imaginal realm in Sufism has been taken up by depth psychology and becomes a central theme in archetypal psychology. Second, Sufi thought views the relationship between the imagination and divine being differently from most of Western philosophy. Recall that while Kant suggests an integrative role for the imagination, his philosophy remains centered in the power and work of the rational human subject, that icon of the Enlightenment. However, Sufi mysticism suggests that an emphasis on the faculty of imagination need not imply a focus on the human subject. In Sufi mysticism the divine one is central, and imagination is the divine gift that enables the human to be in relation with God.

Third, while Islam as a monotheistic and Abrahamic faith shares the heritage of the Garden of Eden story with its warnings about imagination as the prerogative of God, Islam develops quite a different philosophical-religious history than the West. Consider that the "golden age" of Islam was coterminus with the Dark Ages of the Christian West, and Islam's philosophical and religious grounding was well under way before the empirical and experimental focus that emerged in the West with the Enlightenment. The tradition of Islam "has not undergone the same changes related to the spread of humanism, rationalism, empiricism, historicism and positivism which, since the Renaissance, have deeply affected Western scholarship in all domains including religion itself."[55] For example, the philosopher-mystic Suhrawardi describes his method by saying that his material "has not been assembled by thought and reasoning: rather, intellectual intuition, contemplation and ascetic practices have played a large role in it."[56] Sufi insights about the imagination,

38

though they are articulated by Islamic philosophers, are specifically religious insights, having to do with spiritual practice.

Up to this point, the human faculty of imagination has been the focus, and the possibility of a place in which that faculty is uniquely exercised has not come up. However, the concept of an imaginal place is central to Sufi thought. While Western Christian mystics tend to describe their experiences of God primarily in terms of relationship, Sufi mystics describe encounters with the holy as happening in a particular place or realm of experience, the *'alam al-mithāl*. As we shall see below, this place of correspondences has considerable implications for imagination, especially the religious imagination.

Islam's Golden Age

The context for the thought of Sufi scholars Suhrawardi and Ibn 'Arabī is the great Islamic cultural flourishing of the ninth to eleventh centuries, its golden age.[57] Amazingly, Islam is only three to five centuries old at this period, but it is geographically and linguistically secure enough to express strong interest in the pre-Islamic intellectual sciences, including philosophy. In 799 CE, the Abbasid dynasty brought the center of the Islamic empire to Baghdad, and by 810 a new city with a population of over one million people emerges between the Tigris and the Euphrates. Scholarship is encouraged, and the several schools of philosophy welcome people from all over the known world to their "houses of wisdom."[58] The writings from "the school of Alexandria, which itself was the meeting place of Hellenic, Jewish, Babylonian, and Egyptian cultural currents, were translated into Syriac and transplanted to Antioch and from there, farther east" and were finally brought to Baghdad.[59] All these sources of wisdom and others from Persians and Romans, Hebrews and Buddhists, are translated into Arabic in a great intellectual ferment, with many debates and commentaries. Suhrawardi and Ibn 'Arabī represent the epitome of Muslim scholarship emerging from this period.

SUHRAWARDI

Suhrawardi, who was born in 1153 and died in 1191 at age 38 while imprisoned by enemies jealous of his brilliance, is "master of the philosophy of illumination."[60] While he prefers symbolic and mystical narrative, his philosophic system unites "discursive reasoning and intellectual intuition, both formal training of the mind and purification of the soul" in a tradition called *Ishrāq*.[61] For Suhrawardi, God is light, and all reality possesses various degrees of light depending on its nearness to God. "The ontological status of a being depends on the degree to which it is illuminated or veiled."[62] The emphasis in Suhrawardi is not so much on knowing (epistemology) as rather on being (ontology). Between humans and God exists a vast hierarchy of lights, which Suhrawardi calls angels.

Each human has his or her own guardian angel. "Upon entering the body, the soul, or its inner center which is its immortal, angelic core, is divided into two parts, one remaining in heaven and the other descending into the...body."[63] The idea is that the angel helps each soul become unified in the divinized self it is intended to be, through interior work that occurs in the imaginal world, where both parts of the soul are periodically united. There is not one single set of answers or template for all human beings, but each being has his or her own particular self to become, through the mediation of the angel helper in the imaginal world.[64]

Whereas generally speaking, Christian theology emphasizes God's descent to humans in Jesus Christ, the Islamic approach tends to be in the opposite direction, that is, the ascent of the human to receive the fullness of God.[65] The two movements are complementary in both religions, however the emphases vary. Sufi philosophy is acutely aware that the glory of God is well beyond what humans can experience or imagine, and its cosmology emphasizes the mystery of divine being. Yet even with this vast distance, the Sufi mystic can be understood as seeking union with and in the divine mystery. The place in which the human soul is shaped for that union, which is to say, shaped for the wholeness that is the completion of human life, is the imaginal world, a concept developed especially in the writings of Ibn 'Arabī.

IBN 'ARABī

Ibn 'Arabī was born in southern Spain in 1165. A great Sufi sage and saint, he was also a prolific writer on subjects ranging from metaphysics, cosmology, and psychology, to Quranic commentaries. Seyyed Nasr says of him, "his greatest 'masterpiece' was his own life," not only because of his prayer and contemplation, but also because of his visions of the spiritual world.[66] Ibn 'Arabī is absorbed in questions concerning "a real *theoria*, or vision, of reality, the attainment of which depends upon the practice of the appropriate methods of realization."[67] Michel Chodkiewicz observes that "it would not be far from the mark to say that Ibn al-'Arabī never writes about anything except sanctity, its paths, and its goals."[68] The discussion below of the imaginal relies chiefly on Ibn 'Arabī's thought, though he himself is aware of, and builds on, Suhrawardi's ideas.

The mystical system that Ibn 'Arabī articulates "is generally designated by the term *wahdat al-wujūd*, 'unity of being.'"[69] The Arabic phrase is difficult to translate into English because it refers both to unity in God and wholeness in all reality. William Chittick emphasizes that a correct understanding of the phrase emerges from a primary question, "How can I find God?"[70] For *wujūd*, usually translated "existence" or "being," can also be translated "finding," so that *wahdat al-wujūd* can also mean "oneness or unity of finding." Islamic mysticism scholar Annemarie Schimmel observes that for Ibn 'Arabī "everything gains its *wujūd*, its existence, by 'being found,' i.e., perceived, by God."[71] Ibn 'Arabī uses the term not only as a concept about reality, but primarily as a pointer to an experience of finding and being found by God.

However, paradox is involved, because while reality is one, God is beyond all manifest qualities. "The concept of *wahdat al-wujūd* does not involve a substantial continuity between God and creation."[72] Although nothing exists except as a manifestation of God, creation is not God. The divine being is both hidden and revealed, and humans know God only through God's desire to be known, that is, by revelation. God is not real in any way that can be proved in time by sensory evidence. At one level nothing can be said about God, a reality made explicit in the Arabic script for God, which can be roughly translated into the consonant sounds for "the, nothing, mystery."[73] In the hidden essence, nothing is known of being, except "only one thing: precisely the sadness of the primordial solitude that makes Him yearn to be revealed."[74] Central to Sufi mysticism is the frequently repeated *hadīth*, or "sacred saying," translated by Stanizai as, "I was a hidden Treasure, and I loved to be known, so I created the Cosmos." Ibn 'Arabī adds to this [...I created the Cosmos] "in order to become in [humans] the object of my knowledge."[75] God is the treasure, who reveals Godself in creation, and additionally becomes Godself within loving humans, completing the promised wholeness or unity. Unity begins with love or longing, because God longs to be known, and the mirroring response of creation is its yearning for God.

Ibn 'Arabī uses the image of a mirror to suggest the Sufi mystic's desire "to overflow, to pour out the latent realities within," of that mutual relationship whereby God continually becomes manifest in creation.[76] Yet God remains inviolate mystery, even as "it reveals of itself in us."[77] The revelation of God's being occurs when the mystic is so transparent to God that God is manifest in him or her. And this work of cocreation is accomplished in the imaginal world, through the faculty of the active imagination.[78]

The Imaginal Realm

The imaginal realm is embedded in the Sufi vision of the cosmos, which includes three heavenly orders and three earthly ones, each of which is veiled from the others. Within this overall cosmology in general use by Sufis, Ibn 'Arabī's insight is to suggest that it makes sense to hypothesize an additional sphere linking the three heavenly orders and the three earthly ones, a sphere that he calls 'alam al-mithāl, "the imaginal world."[79]

The goal of the Sufi mystic is to engage in the responsive movement toward God so completely that the human is divinized, filled up with God. When the human becomes perfectly transparent to God, then God's being is manifested or mirrored perfectly in creation. Despite the vast cosmic distance between God's essence and humankind, the human being is the "link or medium between the two poles of Reality."[80] The theomorphized (God-embodied) mystic or saint is called "the Universal [Hu]man," one who reveals "the whole of the Universe in its oneness as 'seen' by the Divine Essence."[81] This is the model of the Sufi spiritual life, and its "privileged myth."[82]

In the transforming work of imagination, the human being is conceived as the isthmus, or *barzakh*, between God and the created world, transmitting to the created world the light and truth of God, while also communicating the twinkling reflections of the created world back to God.[83] The concept of the *barzakh* also applies to the imagination in general:

> A *barzakh* is something that separates two other things while never going to one side, as, for example, the line that separates shadow from sunlight....Any two adjacent things are in need of a *barzakh* which is neither the one nor the other but which possesses the power of both.... The *barzakh* is something that separates a known from an unknown, an existent from a nonexistent....It is called a *barzakh* as a technical term, and in itself it is intelligible, but it is only imagination. For when you perceive it and are intelligent, you will know that you have perceived an ontological thing upon which your eyes have fallen. But you will know for certain by proofs that there is nothing there in origin and root. So what is this thing for which you have affirmed an ontological thingness and from which you have negated that thingness in the state of your affirming it?[84]

Ibn 'Arabī goes on to say that imagination is neither existent nor nonexistent, emphasizing that its reality is not the same as sensory reality, nor the same as a reasoned reality. It is, however, intelligible to the educated heart, to the person who is a *barzakh*, an isthmus or mediator. Imagination is the ideal faculty to perceive the cosmos as it is—that is, as an ambiguous reality. "Ambiguity is an ontological fact, inherent in the nature of the cosmos. Nothing is certain but Being Itself, yet It is the 'coincidence of opposites.'"[85] The nature of profound truth in religious teachings requires imagination in this sense.

Imagination is practiced in the realm of the imaginal. As a realm, the *'alam al-mithāl* is the world of similitudes. *Mithāl* means likeness or image, being formed from a root word meaning to resemble, look like, imitate, or appear in the likeness of. Its cognates appear often in the Quran.[86] The translation of *'alam al-mithāl* as "imaginal world" comes from Iranian scholar and friend of Jung's Eranos Institute, Henry Corbin.[87]

Corresponding to the three faculties of sensation, reason, and imagination, Sufism envisions three corresponding realms: the sensory realm of sight, hearing, taste, touch, and smell; the intellectual realm of reason, conceptual thought, and abstraction; and the third realm of "the imaginal."[88]

> For them [the mystics] the world is "objectively" and actually threefold: between a universe that can be apprehended by pure intellectual perception (the universe of Cherubic Intelligences) and the universe perceptible to the senses, there is an intermediate world, the world of Idea-Images, of archetypal figures, of subtle substances, of "immaterial matter." This world is as real and objective, as consistent and subsistent as the intelligible and sensible worlds; it is an intermediate universe "where the spiritual takes body and the body becomes spiritual," a world consisting of real matter and real extension, though by comparison to sensible, corruptible matter these are subtle and immaterial.[89]

The imaginal world is as real as the sensate and the conceptual worlds, while different from either. It is beyond the realm of sensible experience, yet it is a "place." Corbin observes that this notion is not easy to comprehend for those accustomed to think only in terms of physical reality. The imaginal world is "visible" to the disciplined and devoted imagination, having "extension and dimension, figures and colors" that are available to imaginative perception.[90] The concept of extension in the imaginal world suggests a reference to the Cartesian *res extensa*; in a similar but not identical way to the body's extension in sensory space, the imaginal realm has "extension" that cannot be measured with the five senses. Corbin suggests that the ʻalam al-mithāl can be thought of as a place of archetypal images.[91]

The intermediary function of the imagination between the conceptual and the sensual is what stabilizes it and gives it reliability as a true source of knowledge. Such knowledge is not, of course, the kind of knowledge that is produced by empirical experiments or logical deductions, but it may offer knowledge closer to the truth of being of the cosmos. It is the kind of knowledge that enables the "hidden treasure" lovingly to be known.[92]

Reflections

Sufi mysticism as an example of imagination's role in religion offers interesting possibilities. Imagination, when practiced in the context of Sufi cosmology, does not reinforce the problematic isolated subject of modern Western philosophy, but on the contrary contributes to healing the Cartesian subject-object split. A mystical imagination challenges the mainline philosophical tradition of the West because it "breaks through the mutual isolation of consciousness and its object, of thought and being; here phenomenology becomes ontology."[93] Because of its intermediary role, a mystical or spiritual imagination exists within and cocreates an in-between place, a place where not only does dialogue occur between apparent opposites but also the presence of a "third" exists. That third is not only formed by the interaction of two apparent "others" but also enfolds them in a dynamic presence previously unknown.

This concept shows how imagination can be suitably restrained by its relationship to the corollary faculties of sensation and intellect, not as a subordinate faculty, but rather because constant interaction with the other faculties gives credibility to its witness. Imagination is not viewed as private or unreliable fantasy for two reasons. The practice of spiritual imagination occurs in the context of a disciplined search for the beloved, consisting of guidance from a wise friend or mentor, renunciation of all superficial distractions, watchfulness of one's thoughts, patience, gratitude, and complete trust in and surrender to God.[94]

The spiritual imagination of the Sufis is understood as a personal path or *tarīqua* (a pattern of spiritual practice) that is a branch of the main road of whole Islamic tradition, the *sharīà*. The personal practice "does not abolish the rites of the general tradition, but interiorizes them."[95] The mystic's path is firmly rooted in the basic elements of the Islamic faith. Certainly there are stresses at times between the radicalism of the Sufis and the relative conservatism of mainstream Muslims, just as there are between Western mystics and mainstream theology. Yet at a theological level, both those who practice personal disciplines and those whose faith is expressed primarily in communal worship understand their need for one another.

Spiritual imagination offers an answer to the question emerging from founding myths of the Abrahamic religions, whether imagination presents a danger of "stealing" prerogatives intended only for the gods. The Sufi concept of the goal of human life as *theomorphization*, embodying the qualities of God so that God can be better known in the cosmos, is a brilliant response. No doubt it is easier to state than to live, but theoretically it offers a remarkable way to integrate dedication to divine being with freedom for creative human imagination. The Sufi emphasis on being instead of on knowing shifts the center of discussion from the fact of the human subject to the orient or direction of human life, the possibility of and path toward abundance in human existence. This will not produce a universal dogma, because each person bears a different responsibility and a different way of bringing the divine presence to bear in this world. From this perspective, the secret of human life is not what one knows, but how one participates in the wider life around one—whether that wider life is called god or cosmos or life itself.

The Sufi imaginal realm has been adopted by archetypal psychology as one of its primary foundation stones. An important question for the next and closing section of this chapter is whether a psychology, even one that intentionally deals with "soul," can adequately appropriate a concept that may be essentially a religious reality, rooted in a concept of wide and mysterious being that is beyond the human while profoundly shaping human experience.

SOUL-WORK: PSYCHOLOGY AND THE IMAGE

The Greek word *psyche* means "soul," and a *psycho-logos* is the study of soul. Henri Ellenberger's comprehensive history of depth psychology traces its roots through ancient ritual, exorcism, magic, and temple healing, as he pursues the notion common to all such practices that disease is fundamentally caused by a loss of soul, while treatment is intended to restore soul. Ellenberger explores depth psychology's development through imaginal means and observes, for example, that the Renaissance term *"imagination...*held a much broader meaning than it does today and included what we call suggestion and autosuggestion."[96]

In the early twentieth century Sigmund Freud makes a startling contribution to the depth of psyche, with his imaginative inference that there must be an unconscious element corresponding to consciousness in human beings, because many events that cannot be explained by conscious intent (such as slips of the tongue and forgetfulness) nevertheless have a certain logic in them. Freud sees that sometimes the surface self-presentation is actually a mask for intentions of the unconscious, and he finds ways to understand meanings hidden behind immediate consciousness. However, Freud is very concerned to establish his work as a "science," and thus he minimizes its imaginative aspects. "Freud brilliantly represented a brilliant culmination of the Enlightenment project, bringing even the human unconscious under the light of rational investigation [while he also] radically undermined the Enlightenment project by his revelation that below or beyond the rational mind existed an overwhelmingly potent repository of nonrational forces."[97] Using imagination and intuition, Freud establishes what he calls a new field of natural science.

Jungian Psychology

C. G. Jung, who was Freud's colleague and early disciple, takes the same reality from a different point of view, seeing imagination as fundamentally linked to the interpretative and the creative work of the psyche. In his "Forward to Suzuki's *Introduction to Zen Buddhism*," Jung asserts that "every psychic process is an image and imagining,"[98] thereby asserting that an image is not simply a picture or memory but is something creative and productive, derived "from poetic usage, namely a figure of fancy or fantasy image."[99] Jung begins his career working in a psychiatric asylum, where he is surrounded with "the voices and visions of patients' psychoses. Rather than relegating the experience of imaginal figures to the limbo of pathology, he [Jung] actively sought his own voices."[100] In this way, Jung comes to postulate that images and imaginal figures are not solely to be interpreted reductively (as evidence of something hidden and hallucinatory) but can be seen as autonomous personalized figures symbolizing an idea not yet consciously known that may open new possibilities.[101]

As the nineteenth-century industrial revolution begins to shape not only human work but human environments (e.g., larger cities), human instinct becomes increasingly repressed. Depth psychologist Glen Slater observes that in this context nature no longer seems alive and religious sensibilities do not hold the same central place in the psyche.[102] Jung realizes that the energy and flow of the instinctual life is pressed "underground," that is, into the unconscious part of the psyche where instinct can be expressed in the form of images and symbols. He wonders if psychological disturbances might be a psychic move to retrieve the flow of instinctual life pushed away by directed rationality, and begins to explore this possibility in his patients and in his own experiences. "In human beings instincts express themselves in the form of unreflected, involuntary fantasy images, attitudes, and actions, which bear an inner resemblance to one another and yet are identical with the instinctive reactions of *Homo sapiens....*Like the instincts, these images have a relatively autonomous character; that is to say they are 'numinous.'"[103] Jung identifies instinctual forces in the unconscious that increasingly appear to be common to all people, and observes that these forces seem to bear an almost religious energy in their autonomy and personalism, often taking the form of images when they express themselves in dreams and imagination. Jung calls this formal aspect of the instinct an *archetype.*

An archetype is not easily defined, because above all it "represents a profound riddle surpassing our rational comprehension."[104] Jung says of them:

Archetypes are, by definition, factors and motifs that arrange the psychic elements in certain images, characterized as archetypal, but in such a way that they can be recognized only from the effects they produce. They exist preconsciously, and presumably they form the structural dominants of the psyche in general.[105]

We know the archetype only from its effects, and its effects generally are expressed in psychological complexes, or "feeling-toned groups of representations in the unconscious."[106] When an instinct is unable to find expression in consciousness, it turns to the unconscious and lives in semirepressed feelings, being fed by memories, reactions, and behaviors. When affect-laden instinctual energies form a constellation, they become so influential in the psyche that Jung calls them a *complex*. But complexes are not always negative or problematic energies. Two different kinds of complexes develop within the psyche, one linked to personal difficulties and painful experiences, and another that relates to nonrational matters that seem somehow to come from outside the self.[107] Jung associates the latter type of complex with the collective unconscious, calling it an archetype and inferring that it arises from universal images connected to a deeper and wider mythological substratum of human experience.

Jung explores these psychic structures and dynamic patterns in detail while paying attention to his own psychological process. Shortly after his break with Freud, Jung enters a personal period of inner uncertainty that he calls a "state of disorientation...[feeling] totally suspended in mid-air, for I had not yet found my own footing."[108] He says:

> I lived as if under constant inner pressure....Retrospection led to nothing but a fresh acknowledgment of my own ignorance. Thereupon I said to myself, "Since I know nothing at all, I shall simply do whatever occurs to me." Thus I consciously submitted myself to the impulses of the unconscious.[109]

Jung's need to be attentive to unconscious impulses is "painfully humiliating," and it draws him into a period of several years of imaginative play and dark dreams.[110] In the midst of this period, World War I breaks out, and Jung sees that to some extent his own experience "coincided with that of mankind in general."[111] But throughout this period, he says "there was no doubt in my mind that I must find the meaning of what I was experiencing in these fantasies....I had an unswerving conviction that I was obeying a higher will."[112] He adds, "To the extent that I managed to translate the emotions into images—that is to say, to find the images which were concealed in the emotions—I was inwardly calmed and reassured."[113]

As Jung continues this work, he finds semipermanent fantasy figures emerging from his own unconscious, figures with whom he dialogues. One of the most important of these is an "Elijah figure" Jung names Philemon, who appears first in a dream. Jung paints his dream-image and begins to have imaginal dialogues with this wisdom figure. Reflecting on these dialogues, Jung observes: "Philemon... brought home to me the crucial insight that there are things in the psyche which I do not produce, but which produce themselves and have their own life. Philemon represents a force which was not myself. In my fantasies I held conversations with him, and he said things which I had not consciously thought....It was he who taught me psychic objectivity, the reality of the psyche."[114]

Jung's psychic work bears some similarities to Ibn 'Arabī's encounters in the imaginal world, and Jung is not unaware of the parallel of his inner life with religious experience. He says:

> In antiquity when a man had to direct a prayer to the statue of the god, he stepped upon a stone that was erected at its side to enable people to shout their prayer into the ear, so that the god would hear them, and then he stared at the image until the god nodded his head or opened or shut his eyes and answered in some way. You see this was an abbreviated method of active imagina-tion, concentrating upon the image until it moved; and in that moment the god gave a hint, his assent or his denial or any other indication, and that is the numinosum.[115]

Active Imagination

Eventually Jung translates his own operational method dur-ing the time of his psychic crisis into a more structured process at the heart of his psychological method, calling it the practice of *active imagination*. A person is encouraged to invite images from his or her own archetypal complex into dialogue, forming a conscious relationship with inner feelings and symbols. The practice involves "a state of reverie in which judgment was suspended but consciousness preserved...note what fantasies occurred...and let these fantasies go their own way without interference."[116] The figures that appear are regarded as if they were real, because they have an imaginal reality.

During this process, the person is not focused on immediate interpretation or meaning of the figures, but rather is curious about them, watching and asking what is of interest to the figures or images themselves. The purpose of the conscious dialogue between ego and archetype is to release and transform otherwise blocked psychic energy "with full participation of conscious understanding."[117] In normal life, conflict exists between the conscious and the unconscious, "due to the fact that the unconscious behaves in a compensatory or complementary manner toward the conscious."[118] Whenever there is one-sidedness in consciousness, the unconscious sends up signals requiring attention in order to bring the psyche back into balance. When the need for rebalancing is signaled by an emotional disturbance, one can deal with it best "not by clarifying it intellectually but by giving it visible shape" in the method of active imagination.[119]

The emotions can be painted, or inner images produced, or voices heard. Body movements can help as can work with moldable materials. All these practices evoke information from the unconscious to work with. In such methods, "consciousness puts its media of expression at the disposal of the unconscious content."[120] The ego must be careful not to exert too much influence at this time, but as far as possible to let unconscious associations take the lead. Furthermore, the ego must be willing to engage disagreeable materials, for generally the unconscious holds materials that were repressed because of their "unwelcome, unexpected, irrational contents."[121]

Once the unconscious material takes form in image, "the question arises how the ego will relate to this position, and how the ego and the unconscious are to come to terms."[122] The opposite positions must be brought together, acknowledging the integrity of each "for the production of a third: the transcendent function."[123]

It is precisely the authentic engagement of two that releases the mysterious third. However, at this stage, "it is no longer the unconscious that takes the lead, but the ego."[124] Jung emphasizes that the ego position is of equal value to the unconscious position, and there is no hierarchy here, no agenda of submission on either part. Both must respect the other. Perhaps it is a bit like befriending a wild animal. After a person sits down to await the animal's visit, the initiative must be left with the animal, whose wariness of humanity shapes its own pace of gradually coming closer and closer until it reveals itself. But once the animal has drawn near, then the human must take the initiative in befriending the wild creature, remaining itself but softened and opened to allow the other to enter its heart.

In the practice of active imagination, persons sometimes wonder if they are making up the images and dialogues, but so long as they are in a state of deep reverie and willing to stay in the attitude of fair witness, the images and conversations that emerge will normally be, using Jung's language, revelatory of "things which I had not consciously thought," that is, things emerging spontaneously from the nonconscious part of the psyche.[125]

Slater observes that Jung believes that the face we show to the unconscious is the face it shows back. If the unconscious is respected, it is respectful too, whereas if the ego tries to control it, the unconscious becomes antagonized and causes angry eruptions, such as acting out, illness, depression.[126] On the other hand, a certain ego strength, stability, and consistency, are needed to confront the unconscious, although ego flexibility is more useful than ego rigidity. Active imagination can be blocked or misdirected if one starts out with a particular agenda (with the ego seeking to be in control) or identifies with the archetypal figures (with the unconscious building a psychic inflation). Genuine dialogue is blocked if the ego is alienated from the unconscious and hence from the imaginal figure, or if the ego identifies with the archetype rather than retaining the ego's own unique position in the dialogue.[127] When fear causes the ego tensely to "cling to its habitual state of consciousness," reconciliation between unconscious and ego is stalled and psychosis may result.[128] Active imagination involves a delicate dance between two equals, sometimes taking a long time, and "demanding sacrifices from both sides."[129] When an authentic engagement occurs between ego and complex, both are inevitably changed. The ego loses its old and narrower identity in favor of an expanded and more balanced wholeness, and the complex is resolved, that is, raised to consciousness, resulting "in a new distribution of psychic energy."[130] The authentic confrontation of the two positions "generates a tension charged with energy and creates a living, third thing...a living birth that leads to a new level of being."[131]

Archetypal complexes inevitably carry an opportunity for personal transformation. It is not by accident that Jung's description of active imagination occurs in his essay "The Transcendent Function."[132] The transcendent function might be considered as Jung's terminology for the process of profound inner transformation, or in religious terms, for *metanoia* (conversion of heart). For Jung, the union of conscious and the unconscious together introduces the transcendent function into the psyche.[133] An experience of new life and a new sense of personal wholeness result from practicing active imagination. In certain respects, attentiveness to the unconscious in imagination is an expression of taking the religious or soul side of life seriously. For in the process of claiming personal wholeness in active imagination, one also participates in the creation of an expanded experience of being in the greater psyche, soul itself.

Active imagination is founded in a witnessing, a willingness to be open to something of which the person is not yet aware. This process is a qualitatively different approach to psyche than that of developmental theory and other more scientific psychological methods, for its orientation is not toward adjustment to reality, but rather support of the increasing autonomy and discrete identity of psychic imaginal figures as a route to greater psychic wholeness.[134] Its orientation is to the imaginal as an essential nourishing ingredient for the soul of the world. Jung's work suggests that not only is the psyche bigger than personal consciousness, it is also bigger than the personal *un*conscious. Psyche includes the *collective unconscious*, which links the person to the wider world of bios, cosmos, god. In short, psyche is soul.

However, although Jung's orientation toward the collective unconscious connects the psyche to a wider world than individual consciousness, and although his understanding of the imaginal world suggests a kind of reality independent of individual fantasy, Jung shares Freud's desire for his work to be considered scientific. Despite Jung's willingness to speak of the numinous quality of figures from the collective unconscious, he insists "I am dealing with [religion's psychological aspect] from a purely empirical point of view, that is, I restrict myself to the observation of phenomena and I refrain from any application of metaphysical or philosophical considerations."[135] Jung comes right up to the edge of claiming a theological dimension in the way active imagination functions, but ultimately he balks. "Depth psychology had perhaps rendered a deeper inner world for modern man, but the objective universe as known by natural science was necessarily still opaque, without transcendent dimensions."[136] Jung's psychology raises the question of whether a psychological approach by itself can genuinely address the transcendent dimensions of human experience, no matter how expansively the term psyche is used.

James Hillman and Re-Visioning toward Soul

James Hillman tends to follow Jung's emphasis on an operational, empirical approach to psychology in founding the field of archetypal psychology.[137] Yet as he works with the material, Hillman moves away from the scientific bent toward a more artistic one: "archetypal psychology's first links are with culture and imagination rather than with medical and empirical psychologies."[138] Archetypal psychology is not easy to characterize, because it avoids positivism and linear thought, moving instead with images in a cyclical pattern. Archetypal psychology may involve retracing one's steps following a different route, throwing up many meanings rather than seeking a single fixed one, staying in the shadows. Hillman chooses the term *archetypal* because it is not directly associated with a mode of problem-solving and analysis, instead moving toward soul, imagination, and myth, toward something that transcends the human psyche and the human ego.[139] He says the word archetypal is "the result of an operation, given not with the image but with what happens with the image— a function of *making* rather than a function of *being*."[140] Hillman is interested in the poetic (*poesis*, or making) and disinterested in rational philosophy (with its desire to find and fix meaning).

What is the connection between archetypal psychology and soul? Hillman observes that "a passion to cage the invisible by visible methods continues to motivate the science of psychology.... When the searchers failed to find the soul in the places where they were looking (e.g., body parts and systems), scientistic psychology gave up also on the idea of soul."[141] In response to this loss, Hillman believes that the contemporary "job of psychology is to offer a way and find a place for soul within its own field."[142]

Hillman argues that the myth of the rational heroic human ego is the primary psychic metatheory of our culture, a theory that carries a one-sided pattern destructive of soul. Archetypal psychology endeavors not to be drawn by the centripetal force of that theory, instead honoring images emerging from psyche/soul that would restore wholeness to person and society. This involves playfulness, chaos, "underworld" thinking. Acknowledging that "re-visioning" is more than simple adjustment of details, Hillman proposes a fundamentally new way of thinking about what psychology is, requiring an emphasis on soul-work. Correspondingly, he de-emphasizes the normal model of seeing one client in a consulting room with the goal of adjustment to the positivist assumptions of the culture's hero metatheory. Hillman seeks return to *psyche-logos*, a deliberate (if also nonlinear) attentiveness to those aspects of soul that are avoided if not discarded by psychology's current orientation.

Hillman distinguishes between spirit (an emphasis on "peak" experiences and self-actualization) and soul (attention to the valleys of lonesomeness and depression). He attributes this basic distinction to an observation made by the Dalai Lama, "I call the high and light aspects of my being *spirit* and the dark and heavy aspect *soul*."[143] So Hillman attends to black, to the underworld, and above all to pathology—all ways he believes the soul is finding expression in the world today.[144] *Pathologizing* is one of the primary moves in Hillman's re-visioning, because his instinct is that soul is more likely to be found in the dark and heavy aspects of life than in the artificially bright and perfect faces the world so often expects.[145] An environment with no room for betrayal, failure, illness, aging, and death, even if that environment is only the interior one of the ego's posturing to itself, is alien to the authentically human and soulful.

Hillman extends his view to the culture and the soul of the world, believing that psychology must concern itself with the larger sphere. The human being is not the center of everything, not the purpose of evolution, not entitled to be the subject of natural objects. "Man exists in the midst of psyche; it is not the other way around. Therefore, soul is not confined by man, and there is much of psyche that extends beyond the nature of man."[146] Accordingly, soul-making is called *dehumanizing*, a deliberate shift of the human subject out of the center of things.

Hillman does not ignore the connection between theology and psychology, because he sees that soul is the single source of both, and he views himself as working toward a "nonagnostic psychology."[147] However, his own theology is polytheism, which he insists is essential to the soul's development, and he is often hostile toward religion in general and the Judeo-Christian tradition in particular.[148] Yet polytheism does not seem essential to Hillman's theories, only a willingness to be open to ever-new possibilities. In my view, the basic orientation of archetypal psychology toward soul and mystery suggests the value of a Christian exploration of its themes. Indeed, Hillman himself admits to seeking "a style of consciousness where psychology and religion are not defined against each other so that they may more easily become each other."[149] In ancient times the loss of soul meant that "a man is out of himself, unable to find either the outer connection between humans or the inner connection to himself....Without this soul, he has lost the sense of belonging and the sense of being in communion with the powers and the gods."[150] At present, loss of soul may be a condition affecting not just isolated individuals, but perhaps a whole culture. Soul has metaphysical and religious dimensions, as it "makes meaning possible, turns events into experiences, and is communicated in love," and these are precisely the problematic aspects of life in Western culture today.[151] Archetypal psychology takes as its concerns such diverse topics as cityscapes, ceilings, transportation, and bread, all symptoms of the loss of soul in the world.[152]

Two aspects of Hillman's re-visioning of psychology relate specifically to image and imagination. Hillman postulates: "If, as

Jung says, 'image is psyche,' then why not go on to say, 'images are soul,' and our job with them is to meet them on that soul level."[153] Images are central to *personifying*, because to personify (to give personality to) is to imagine things. ("Imagining" is Hillman's subtitle for the chapter on personifying in *Re-Visioning Psychology*.) Imagining "becomes crucial for moving from an abstract, objectified psychology," toward one in which dialoguing with an imaginal person is a primary method of soul work.[154] This does not mean affixing a literal meaning to a single image, but opening a poetic fantasy that involves a relationship, or dialogue, with a given image. For example, retreat work might involve a time to discover or select an object such as a tree or a rock, begin with appreciation for the precise sensual reality it is (touch, smell, weight, possible history, etc.), then dialogue with it about the nature of its life, and finally ask whether—based on its experience—it might have any wisdom to share.

In order to meet soul in the image, Hillman adapts and extends the notion of active imagination with the aid of Corbin's insights on the imaginal world, calling Corbin "the second immediate father of archetypal psychology."[155] Hillman calls for a witnessing attitude that avoids immediate interpretation (which automatically separates the image as an object to be "managed"). Instead one "talks" with an image and allows it to talk back, for example through word play (making nouns into verbs or adjectives, reversing relationships between parts of the image, dissolving time, and so forth).[156] One watches the behavior of the image and watches its ecology, what analogies arise and what they suggest.[157] Hillman's mantra is "Stick with the image!" because he believes that everything that is necessary for soul work is contained within images themselves as they arise in dreams or waking visions.[158]

Hillman's method is a combination of elements of phenomenology as well as mythic method. "Phenomenology and archetypal psychology need each other. Phenomenology needs the sense of mythic structures in the background and their deep values; archetypal psychology needs the de-literalizing, sometimes humorous, sense of metaphor in the foreground."[159] Archetypal psychology is rooted in the mythic and depth perspective, and benefits from the respectful distancing of phenomenology in its attentive curiosity about the world. And both are linked to an intangible network of relationships in the visible and invisible world. Hillman believes that our imaginal personifying is a response to living in a mythical consciousness, where imaginal persons are simply given spontaneously.[160]

Hillman's final major move in re-visioning, called *psychologizing*, is seeing through images, that is, not taking them literally but allowing metaphor to guide exploration of the images. Not only psychology, but also religion and myth, can suffer from too literal an interpretation, too quick an assumption that the meaning of a thing is clear-cut and already known. What psychologizing seeks is the depth native to the soul. Time and space are intentionally set aside to engage one's soul in profound reflection about nature and destiny. The soul engages what Hillman calls "psychological ideas" (or what here would be called "mythic ideas") such as the soul's relation with death, with virtue and beauty, with power and future.[161] Psychologizing is a special way of seeing, rooted in the Greek word *eidos*, which originally meant both "what is seen" (the image) as well as "the ability to see." Psychologizing gives us a soulful way to "see" the image. Hillman urges that the psyche "wants to find itself by seeing through...*by seeing through itself*" toward soul transparency.[162]

Depth psychological or archetypal ideas, like mythical fantasies, are a mirroring or reflecting about the depths of the soul. From this perspective, imagining is a way of seeing through problems or conflicts by forming stories or narratives about them, trying on possibilities that connect one's stories to those of others, living into alternatives that may seem strange. Such a metaphoric or mythic approach may seem not rational enough to be helpful, but imaginative means are often more successful than direct assaults in escaping the confines of old and enchaining mental patterns, both for individuals and for societies. The nature of the archetypal imagination means that "our archetypal fictions keep their mythopoetic, their truly fictional, character beyond what we do or say about them. We can never be certain whether we imagine them or they imagine us."[163] In the imaginal world, more is always there than meets the eye.

Hillman's re-visioning project brings into play a number of elements beyond the norm in contemporary psychology. As he integrates religion, philosophy, and theology with psychology, he endeavors to be faithful to the call of the soul in these times. And the imagination is central to the soul's health.

Reflection

Jung and Hillman both bring together traditionally religious themes with psychological issues, restoring soul to the concerns of psychology. Both are reluctant to identify with traditional religions, but they offer much of value for theological consideration. Jung's description of the process of transformation offers a model for how to work toward a re-visioned Western Christian theology. He advises letting go of old certainties and willingness to experience the pain and emotions connected with the loss of a cherished way of being, while also retaining the strength of an ego position seeking the attainment of some sense of meaning in apparent chaos. Jung emphasizes that psychic health and wholeness is often achieved by active engagement with imaginal figures from the collective unconscious. In his theory, the imaginal is a reality with profound psychic benefits, evoking the numinous, the awe-inspiring sense of the presence of something sacred. The process of transformation he envisions inevitably involves the inclusion of a mysterious "third," the transcendent function, whose origin and characteristics Jung leaves unspecified. For Christians, this might suggest the Holy Spirit, or perhaps better, the inevitable unknowability of God and the nature of a divine-human relationship built on continual openness to the possibility of new transformations.

Archetypal psychology makes clear that the restoration of imagination and the imaginal world is necessary for a soul-filled world. The move is away from the controlling ego and toward passionate engagement in an animated world. Its practice of imagination is a move toward the mythic cultural substratum, bringing messy energies to the fore that a light-blinded culture prefers not to acknowledge, aware that the meta-theory of the rational heroic human ego is a strong centripetal force that will absorb and render ineffective any new line of thought without constant vigilance.

Yet even while Jung speaks of the numinous and expansive quality of psyche and Hillman calls for a style of consciousness uniting religion and psychology, both psychologists are so uncomfortable with religious language—if not at times actively hostile to it—that they ultimately do not carry the implications of their theories into theological territory. This book begins and calls for further movement toward that work, building on the significant insights of depth and archetypal psychology, especially regarding the role of the imagination in assisting the human psyche's movement toward what has traditionally been understood as religious experience.

ANOTHER REALM OF EXPERIENCE

The aim of bringing all these points of view into conversation is to delve into imagination as an interpretive lens, capable of bringing new wisdom to theology and especially to Western Christianity. So where has this journey through philosophical, religious, and psychological theories of imagination brought us?

Each of the three interpretive lenses in my proposed theological re-visioning is at present relatively uncommon in the Western worldview, yet fully congruent with the foundational religious experiences of Christianity. The reason for beginning with philosophy is that Christianity in Western culture today remains mythically rooted in the worldview of the Enlightenment: confidence in reason applied by the knowing human subject. At the time, Enlightenment philosophy brought a major shift in theories about how truth can be known. Truth begins to be defined as that which can be known by the human subject, in the context of empirical tests. Knowledge is gained by the human subject from the rational intellect on the one hand, and sensory data on the other, with experience that fits neither of those two categories pushed to the margins. In that context, both theology and imagination suffered.

Imagination offers a powerful challenge to the knowing subject as the center of philosophy or religion, isolated from a world of objects and distinctly divided between sensation and thought, with no room for soul. Although the Enlightenment worldview is being challenged on many fronts today, rationality has not yet relinquished its mythic power to dominate and coopt alternative values. Re-visioning at a mythic level is required effectively to challenge inadequacies gradually being revealed about the older myths' relevance for the emerging period. Re-visioning from the point of view of imagination involves philosophical, religious, and psychological dimensions.

A robust concept of the imagination finds inadequate a definition of a world divided between mind and matter as the only forms of the real. From a theological point of view, imagination offers a way to restore soul to self-awareness and to deepen possibilities of experiencing and understanding the holy as engaged, multifaceted, and dynamic. Imagination can link disciplined spiritual practice that does not depend on a literal faith view with belief in something sacred and mysterious beyond the consciousness of enclosed human self.

Imagination can be understood philosophically not as fantasy or as the superficial proliferation of images, but as an experience of depth, "the ability to evoke absent objects which exist elsewhere, without confusing these absent objects with things present here and now."[164] Jung and Hillman show that psyche links the human to the cosmos through imaginative practice, and they offer a map suggesting that the route through suffering and darkness often is the way to wholeness. The Sufi experience of the imaginal realm shows specifically how such psychic, imaginative procedures can function in an explicitly religious environment, where deepening relationship with the holy is the goal. These religious and psychological approaches reveal that imagination is not so much "stolen" from jealous gods, as rather the means for human connection to the sacred.

The re-visioning of a metatheory about the world might also be called a hermeneutic perspective or an interpretive lens. "A metaphysics of the imagination," proposed by humanities scholar Adriana Berger, articulates a hermeneutics—or method of interpretation—useful for all the humanities, especially theology.[165] Her method is participative, in that it deemphasizes the separation between subject and object, inviting not merely objective analysis but sympathetic engagement. The central postulate of such an approach is that spiritual essence is revealed when "immediate experience is perceived intuitively on a prescientific ground."[166] In other words, the very distinction so foundational to the Enlightenment between subject and object, or thought and sensation, itself creates a barrier to experience of a spiritual connection. But when an intuitive encounter occurs between self and other without such a preconception, something additional, a spiritual essence, has opportunity to arise in the encounter. An "essential community between the visible and the invisible...can be grasped intuitively, as it restores the common ground lying between the physical and the spiritual. That common ground is the imagination which bears both a poetic and a cognitive function."[167] For Berger, imagination is the key to a restored sense of the nearness of the sacred in human life and interaction.

Berger's proposal for a hermeneutics of the imagination is a strong claim, yet one that is a logical extension of the sources reviewed in this chapter. An imaginative hermeneutics is suggested especially clearly in the philosophy of Gaston Bachelard, who "provided the epistemological basis for drawing up a statute of the poetic as opposed to the positivistic mind, [...re-establishing] the importance of both reverie and the dreamer, placing them on a level equal to that of the scientific approach."[168] Although today there is an increasing move toward participatory experience in humanistic and social science studies, the role of the imagination has not been fully appreciated in its mythic implications for Western Christian theology. Chapter 3 on the philosophy of Paul Ricoeur supports the value of a move to an imaginal, participatory hermeneutics.

Philosophy, religious experience, and psychology all contribute to a concept of disciplined imagination leading to an encounter with an "other" that potentially brings greater wholeness. The details of the encounter tend to be ambiguous, as encounters with divinity tend to be, yet they can be highly creative and beneficial, not only for individuals but for society. This chapter shows that many different modes of thought record the human value of mature imagination and of an imaginal realm enfolding the life of the present moment, crucial to this mythic re-visioning of theology.

Chapter 2

Thinking Otherwise:
A Feminist Vision

Life's no head trip—
if Descartes so thought!

So whence enters I-am-ness?
I'll call up feelings:
Admitting nowness,
whether of joy or of fear.
From knowing I'm loved.
Attuned with nature.
Affirming things spiritual.
Sensing I matter—
one of six billion!
Caring for others, letting
their needs touch my heart.

In short, my is-ness
embraces universes
far beyond thinking.

"Being, Ergo Thinking," in *Homes for the Heart*
by Douglas C. Vest

MARGINALIZATION

Theories about the nature of God are closely linked to assumptions about how human affairs are to be structured. Feminist theology starts with concern that the Western Christian God seems

63

exclusively portrayed as male. Yet feminist theological concerns soon broaden to include a multifaceted mythic template, linked closely to other implicit assertions about the created order. The composite feminist vision presented here challenges many elements of the heroic mythic template while it searches for a more adequate understanding of divinity and humanity.

On the surface, no responsible theologian today asserts that God is male, since by definition God can never be known directly— only by analogy and revelation, and then only provisionally on the basis of human interpretations.[1] Nevertheless the strong weight of tradition, language, and practice in Western Christianity affirms God's maleness.[2] Correspondingly, Western Christianity tends to regard those elements in creation deemed unlike God—femaleness, nature, the body, and so forth—as second-class things to be transcended in a mature spiritual life.[3] Five mythic assumptions about the created order are closely linked to the primary assumption of God's maleness. These are: (1) that created matter, sensory experience, the body, nature, and Earth are impediments to relationship with God that need to be transcended in maturity; (2) that hierarchy is a necessary and accurate description of the great chain of being connecting God to the world; (3) that the free development of the individual spirit is weakened by attachment to others and/or society; (4) that might is a reliable indicator of right; and (5) that because God is utterly other to the world, human experience involves inevitable polarities such as spirit/body, light/dark, and so forth.

This set of assumptions form a mythic network in contemporary Western culture and society that I call "heroic." The mythic substratum of culture is not primarily a collection of stories, not even necessarily a conscious awareness. The maleness of God and its corollaries form an interwoven archetypal complex deep in the Western psyche, influencing the whole culture. An archetypal complex is hidden in the unconscious and lives in semirepressed feelings, being fed by memories, reactions, and behaviors. When those semirepressed energies form a constellation, they become so influential in the personal or communal psyche that Jung calls them a complex. The archetypal complex of the hero is a mythic constellation, functioning as a tacit background behind Western assumptions both of God's maleness and of normative expectations for many dimensions of human experience.

For well over a generation, many feminist theologians have endeavored to explore this archetypal complex, challenging what I'm calling hero-centered theology by asking whether such a view of divinity and humanity is healthful and fruitful in today's world. Beginning with the issue of God's maleness, a feminist vision spirals again and again to interrelated issues, all intrinsically related to a more holistic and healing understanding of God's nature, humanity, and creation. Feminist theology urges a shift in thinking not only about God, but also about knowledge construction and the relations between self, other, and world.

However, the insights and ideas of feminist theology are consistently edged to the margins, having very little impact either on the academy or popular culture. The advantage to marginalization is being able to see clearly how power is being used in the center. The disadvantage is being unable to be heard by the community at large, whether because of "deafness" or because the ideas "don't make sense" when the hero complex so strongly influences even the formation of thought.

Given the high quality and liberating potential of the work of feminist theologians, it seems evident that ideas associated with feminist scholarship and theology become rapidly contained and discounted by a complex-opposing mythic field. Among the components of my mythic re-visioning, a feminist vision seems to be the most controversial. I believe controversy arises in part because initially feminism in general seems more familiar than the other two themes of imagination or Paul Ricoeur's philosophy. (People hold widely varying interpretations of what feminism is, but at least the word is known.) But perhaps the major reason for the controversy is the depth and power of the tacit archetypal complex of the hero.

I intentionally choose the word *erotic* as a contrast to *heroic* in order to evoke the emotional voltage of myth. Erotic in the United States tends to mean genital activity at best and pornography at worst. Yet the Greek root of the word (*eros*) means "an embodied form of loving, passion for life, strong emotional engagement." The heroic model is centered in an ideal of someone with the physical strength and mighty power who dashes into danger to win victory over a defeated enemy. In contrast, the erotic model is centered in a sensual appreciation of the world and an empowering willingness to be "foolish" in order to become friends with so-called enemies. It is a measure of the potency of the heroic myth that the erotic model is so distorted, or so quickly dismissed as fantasy.

I ask simply to engage these ideas as a fair witness, listening before judging. My aim is not to destroy the hero myth but to place alongside it, with fully equal standing, an alternate ideal for divinity and humanity. Language about God does shape the way the world is perceived, because "the symbol of God functions."[4] Theologian Elizabeth Johnson observes that language about God is "the ultimate point of reference for understanding experience, life, and the world."[5] A person's or society's understanding of the nature of divinity, even if more or less unreflective, shapes that person's or society's sense of itself and its sense of what is to be valued in the world. The inverse is also true: a person's or society's experience of itself and its values shapes concepts of God.[6] The two are inseparable. Feminism is concerned that an exclusively male understanding of the nature of God has infused the culture at large with a disregard, if not oppression, of the feminine and related values.

Before proceeding further, it may be useful to define feminism. Author Carol Flinders suggests it may be as deceptively simple as "belief in feminine strength and dignity," even as she admits that her neighbors insist, "Feminism just puts up walls....Even the *word's* divisive."[7] Theologian Rita Gross observes that "The most basic definition of feminism is the conviction that women really do inhabit the human realm and are not 'other,' not a separate species," though she adds that "Fully internalizing that statement involves a subtle and profound *change of consciousness* for both men and women."[8] The term *feminism* was "coined by Alexandre Dumas in 1872 to describe the emerging movement for women's rights, especially the vote, and equality with men."[9] Thus, modern feminism has political roots, which may contribute to its controversial status. But definitions change as usages change, so that now Benedictine scholar Joan Chittister urges an awareness that

*"Feminists...*come in two genders: female and male."[10] Observing that the word *feminine* is a term applying to the female gender involving traits structured by society, she defines femin*ism* as a point of view that "looks with new respect at values traditionally held by women or called feminine, whether, as a matter of fact, anything can rightfully be labeled specifically feminine or not."[11] Feminism is not about men or women, but is rather about mythic or tacit attitudes held by either or both.

Since deconstruction and postmodernism have permeated the academy, there is a reluctance to fall into what is considered the trap of "essentialism"—that is, of attempting to make universal claims about the essential nature of anything, including "the feminine." Recent scholarship challenges initial American feminism's characterization of the feminine in terms that applied mainly to white, North American, educationally and economically advantaged ladies.[12] In the early 1970s, Jungian feminist theologians such as Ann Ulanov unqualifiedly applauded the value of Jung's "new and fundamentally important point of view: a study of the symbolic meaning of the feminine and its role in psychic functioning."[13] Ten years later, Ulanov still appreciates this point of view, but nuances it carefully, characterizing the feminine as (1) being at the core of oneself; (2) being one with another; and (3) possessed of a personal continuity.[14] It is not easy to articulate qualities that express the values of feminism, while not claiming universal applicability of those qualities to all women's experience (nor universal absence from men's experience). Most feminism today is not antimale, but is focused on remedying structural issues in society that result in systematic domination of some of its members.

Although feminist theologians tend not to "name" specific values of feminism in order to avoid essentialism, I propose that by exploring the constituent mythic themes basic to both the heroic and erotic mythic archetypes, one can articulate elements common to each archetype and thereby identify their respective values. Obviously this task involves making generalizations—with its consequent dangers of exaggeration. Each of the themes below indicates an intention or tendency of the mythic archetype and should not be understood as applying to every specific situation. An archetype is not so much a precise and universal description as it is a bundle of energies emerging sometimes in one form and sometimes in another, but generally following a common pattern.[15]

Feminism is a loaded word, as is *erotic*. Yet there are no other words so capable of illuminating the contrast between the pervasiveness and destructiveness of the unchallenged hero myth, while revealing that human life does embody alternatives. A brief outline of each mythic archetype follows for both the heroic and the erotic models, along with narratives that embody each mythic stance.

MYTHIC MODELS AND NARRATIVES

The Heroic Mythic Model

The heroic model begins with the assumption of a male God of power and might who fights to win victories on behalf of his people. This apparently simple and obvious statement includes five core assumptions that I argue damage the world and distort the heart of Christian theology when they are presumed to be the only, or even the best, ordering for human affairs. The five (generally unexamined) assumptions are these:

1. Created matter, sensory experience, the human body, nature, and Earth are impediments to relationship with God. Beginning with Plato and Greek philosophy, the soul is understood as having three parts, one involving lust, one involving anger, and one whose function is to contemplate God. The third part, the *nous* (usually translated into English as "mind") is to be the charioteer whose job is to govern and contain the other two dangerous parts, represented as horses that need to be bridled.[16] The early Christian philosopher Augustine of Hippo reveals his conviction that chastity is essential for faithful discipleship in his *Confessions*, while other Christian theologians of the time view women's bodies as objects representing the most dangerous of temptations.[17] Monastic life has long been regarded as a superior form of Christian life, largely because of what is perceived as monastic escape from worldly matters. Nature itself is often viewed as matter requiring human management, a view that has supported the exploitation of natural resources for centuries.

Even prayer is frequently taught as something requiring withdrawal from nature and embodied matters. Susan Griffin elaborates this theme in *Woman and Nature,* where she both personalizes and makes omnipresent this mythic theme with the frequent phrases "It is said," or "It is decided."[18]

2. Hierarchy is a necessary and accurate description of the great chain of being connecting God to the world: God is above humans, humans above animals, and so forth. Therefore society itself will naturally involve hierarchical relationships as an extension of divine authority. Relationships are quite naturally ones of dominance and submission. The great cathedrals of Europe are models not only of skillful art and craft, but also of the "natural" separation of laypeople (who stand or sit in the nave, separated from holier places by a rood screen), the chancel (where the more highly trained monastics or boys' choirs sit in elaborately carved choir stalls), and finally the altar itself (where the sacred mysteries are celebrated by those holy enough to be priests).

In the culture at large, decision-making is assigned to a few at the top of the hierarchy. One evidence of this mythic assumption is the widespread conviction that all human communities will be "ruled" by a dominant "boss," whether named king or CEO; thus when the possibility of female leadership is considered, it is generally called matriarchy (mother rule or mother right), meaning that even in such societies, dominance of a few over many will be the way of life.[19]

3. The free and full development of the individual spirit is always and everywhere the source of creativity in society. Such individual development is weakened by emotional attachment to others and by too many demands from society. Reasonable individuals choose where and whether they are dutiful, rather than accept mutual responsibility as part of membership in a community. Society should be structured to allow individual freedom the maximum play, limited only by the freedom of other individuals' right for their private quests. This theme tends to arise most powerfully with the sixteenth- to eighteenth-century Enlightenment, whereas the first two heroic themes go back much farther in time; thus individualism as described here has not always been characteristic of Christian theology and practice. However, the Protestant

Reformation ushers in a period of heightened emphasis on the free expansion of the individual hero/spirit and emancipation from society and its demands. Now the spiritual life is viewed as essentially a solo act, and commitment to Christ is not inherited but considered to require a personal decision. One expression of the value given to personal choice is the multiplication of Christian denominations, a group manifestation of the cultural pressure toward individualism. Increasingly faith is privatized, and discipleship is measured by the statements to which one assents rather than by commitment to others in need. A sense of community is so rare that the phrase "the common good" comes to have little or no meaning.

4. Might is a reliable indicator of right: those who are winners—physically, economically, militarily—are rightly judged the most able. This theme appears when churches compete with each other for the largest number of worshippers and the biggest budgets. Competition is an obvious means to assure that the best qualified and most fit people naturally rise to the top, where financial and other rewards are signs of their favor with God. The measure of rightness with God seldom involves moral character or action, but is rather focused on sheer power, whether the power of money or popular opinion. A corollary to this theme is the curious and completely unproven notion that when all else fails, fisticuffs or wars can solve any conflict. In truth, might never solves anything; it merely postpones the next emergence of an old conflict. The potency of the heroic model in theology is visible in the paradox that reliance on forceful power as final arbiter of rightness (articulated, for example, in just war theories) is strangely at variance with the life of Christ, whose birth and death speak far more of vulnerability than of might.

5. Dualism and polarity accurately describe reality: just as God is utterly other to the world, human experience inevitably involves oppositions such as spirit/body or light/dark. Christian liturgies often emphasize light as opposed to darkness or the delights of heaven above as opposed to exile on earth below. Christians often ask, "But is this my will or God's will?" as if there were an absolute difference rather than a mutually interactive process. Depth psychology enshrines a contrast between a

masculine animus and a feminine anima as well as a struggle between consciousness and the unconscious. In daily life, frequently a choice is presented that includes one thing at the necessary cost of excluding another. Sometimes opening one door does require closing another, but many times both/and solutions exist that can be revealed with sensitive, mutually honoring reflection. An expectation of inherent dualities inevitably involves a judgment that one of two choices is superior, dividing the world into eternally alien forces.

This interwoven set of core assumptions forms a mythic network in contemporary Western culture and society that I call a heroic archetype, centered in a fixed notion of a kingly, triumphant God. To summarize, the primary ingredients of the heroic complex are: (1) that physical matter, especially nature and the human (especially female) body are impediments to relationship with God; (2) that the great chain of being connecting God to the world means that hierarchy is the best way to order human affairs; (3) that the free development of the individual spirit is dangerously constrained by society's demands; (4) that power and success are reliable indicators of righteousness; (5) that just as God is Other to creation, all human experience involves inevitable polarities such as spiritual/material, male/female and so forth; and finally, (6) that God is a lordly male.

Taken together, this overlapping set of assumptions describes a mythic substratum so prevalent and influential in Western theology and religious practice that it is scarcely noticed day to day. Nonetheless, the heroic model profoundly shapes even the possibilities for thinking about God, self, and world. I urge mythic attentiveness to the appearance of any one of these assumptions, because each is closely linked with the others, and in their current complex form, they circumscribe a closed system that is unhealthful both to women and men, though it continues to draw Western society and theology unthinkingly into its complex constellation.

Feminist theology assesses serious psychological and social consequences especially, though not exclusively, for women when dominant mythology conceives divinity in exclusively male terms. Rita Gross describes her personal encounter with "the most serious blind spot of contemporary scholarship, not only in religion, but also in all humanistic and social scientific disciplines:" the absence of women as subjects and the disregard of women as having sacred, adequate religious lives.[20] She distinguishes between feminism as an alternative social vision to patriarchy and women's studies as the scholarly pursuit of "exposing and critiquing the androcentrism that underlies most traditional scholarship."[21] Androcentrism collapses the male norm and the human norm and sees them as identical, treats women's religious lives peripherally, and assumes that the generic masculine also covers the feminine.[22] While at first such a notion may seem self-evidently inadequate, Gross nevertheless underscores that it is so deeply embedded in contemporary Western institutions that "nothing less than a paradigm shift in our model of humanity will remedy these problems."[23] A look at a heroic narrative will deepen comprehension of the current embeddedness of the heroic model.

A Heroic Narrative

Probably the best known theological expression of the heroic archetype as expressed in these six themes is the narrative set in the Garden of Eden, in the first chapters of the Bible. The narrative in the Bible (Genesis, chapters 2 and 3) unfolds like this:

> The Lord God made the earth and the heavens, causing a mist to rise up and water the ground, whereupon he formed clay out of which he made man and breathed life into the man's nostrils. The Lord God then planted a garden in the east where he put the man. In that garden were placed every tree for beauty and for food, as well as the tree of life and the tree of the knowledge of good and evil.
>
> A river flowed out of Eden to water the garden, and it divided and became four rivers, two of which were the Tigris and the Euphrates. The Lord God told the man to till the garden and keep it, saying, *"You may freely eat of every tree of the garden; but of the tree of the knowledge of good and evil you shall not eat, for in the day that you eat of it you shall die"* (Gen 2:16–17).

God decided the man should not be alone, so he made helpers for the man—beasts and birds he told the man to name. Yet among these was no helper fit for the man.

So the Lord God put the man into a deep sleep and took one of his ribs from which he made a woman and brought her to the man, who said: *"This at last is bone of my bones and flesh of my flesh; this one shall be called Woman, for out of Man this one was taken."* (Gen 2:23). The two became one flesh and were naked and not ashamed.

But trouble appears in paradise. *"Now the serpent was more crafty than any other wild animal that the Lord God had made. He said to the woman, 'Did God say, You shall not eat from any tree in the garden?'"* (Gen 3:1). The woman told the serpent they were allowed to eat the fruit, but not the fruit of the tree in the middle of the garden, lest they die. But the serpent challenged her, saying they would not die if they ate that fruit, but would have knowledge of good and evil. The fruit began to seem desirable to the woman to make her wise, so she ate some and gave some to her husband. Then they knew they were naked and made clothes of fig leaves for themselves, and hid from the Lord God.

But God called out to them, and the man confessed he was afraid of the Lord God because he was naked. God asked the man how he knew that he was naked, and the man said, *"The woman whom you gave to be with me, she gave me fruit from the tree, and I ate"* (Gen 3:12). When God turned to the woman, she said, *"The serpent tricked me, and I ate"* (Gen 3:13). So God punished the serpent by making him to be hated by all creatures, the woman by pain in childbirth and making her to be ruled by her husband, and the man by the need to wearily till the soil all the days of his life. Then the Lord God said, *"See, the man has become like one of us, knowing good and evil"* (Gen 3:22). And for fear he might also eat of the tree of eternal life, he drove out the man from the garden and set a flaming sword to prevent his return.

This mythic story has been enshrined in art and narrative throughout Western culture to the extent that it is almost unthinkingly accepted as the way things were "at the beginning." Although today few people would claim the literal truth of the story, it does still reign as the founding mythic archetype, influencing many dimensions of Western culture and theology. Let's test it against our six themes of the heroic archetype.

(1) Clearly God is male here: the word *Lord* and all the pronouns (except the last one, which is plural) for God imply maleness. (2) While at the beginning of the story, earth seems pleasant and abundant, once the man and woman have the knowledge of good and evil, they know to be ashamed of their nakedness, and they are exiled from any bounty the earth might offer. (3) Not only is God clearly the man's boss, the man is clearly boss over the woman and all living creatures, having the sole power of naming, and being assigned responsibility for earth's domain. (4) The man is clearly alone, even though he has many creatures to enjoy and befriend; but he is an individual, personally responsible for how things happen, with little or no support. The support may actually be there: the snake, at least, is able to communicate to the humans, and presumably other creatures might also be able to share their wisdom, such as it is; but the man is an individual first and foremost, and he is deaf to whatever community might exist. (5) God has the power and thus God makes the rules. The question is never raised whether God's action is appropriate, fair, or moral, in threatening man and woman with death if they share knowledge and eternal life, because he has the might. (6) While the tree presumably contains the knowledge of both good and evil, on the whole, the situation contains a great many oppositions: abundance/misery, pleasure/shame, obedience/exile, eternal life/death. If the single right choice is not made, disaster will follow. The best thing is to learn how to be on the good side, however good is defined.

At first glance, this may not seem to be a hero myth, and God is not portrayed as fighting for his people here. But this myth does set up many of the elements contained in the mythic hero archetype, and its effect is to set that archetype with its male God in the center of conscious and unconscious collective memory. The Genesis myth certainly has been used historically by Christian theologians to distort and diminish the full humanity of women. Early Christian theology often uses the Garden of Eden narrative as the basis for a conviction that women are the source of sin and should therefore be full of shame, consenting to be ruled by men. In the fifth century, John Chrysostom warns, "The woman taught once and ruined everything. On this account...let her not teach."[24] And more strongly, the second century Tertullian writes to a woman's community: "You are the devil's gateway....How easily you destroyed man, the image of God. Because of the death which you brought upon us, even the Son of God had to die."[25]

Yet a careful look reveals that this Eden myth, so central to Western religion, is an entirely constructed account. So far from being original, it is derivative from other, older creation stories. The Genesis account of the Garden of Eden concerns a woman, a tree, and a snake, elements that had already appeared in many mythologies in the Fertile Crescent of the ancient world, but initially the story usually conveyed quite a different intent and outcome. Joseph Campbell begins *Masks of God: Occidental Mythology* with these provocative words:

> No one familiar with the mythologies of the goddess of the primitive, ancient, and Oriental worlds can turn to the Bible without recognizing counterparts on every page, transformed, however to render an argument contrary to the older faiths. In Eve's scene at the tree, for example, nothing is said to indicate that the serpent who appeared and spoke to her was a deity in his [sic] own right, who had been revered in the Levant for at least seven thousand years before the composition of the Book of Genesis.[26]

Wendy Doniger observes, "other tellings of that myth cast it differently (a benevolent Goddess in her form of life-giving serpent and tree, giving the blessing of the fruit of useful knowledge that makes human life possible)."[27] This founding Christian myth seems deliberately to distort the themes present in older goddess-centered myths that honor women and nature, now interpreting them in such a way as to discredit previous symbols and tradition. The mythic, male-dominated theology emerging from this Eden narrative seems aimed at dishonoring not only women, but many elements of older sacred narratives. "On the symbolic level, the Genesis story tells us that the Mother of All the Living, the Sacred Snake, and the Sacred Tree are the source of suffering."[28] The woman's acceptance of the fruit from the snake signals a radical reinterpretation of divinity and humanity, with the older sacred symbols now signifying humanity's fall from grace and the original sin of the human race.

The symbol of God functions, meaning that all the qualities listed above in the model and myth associated with the male hero God reign unchecked in many contemporary social and institutional contexts. Effects of the hero model and narrative are expressed sociologically, psychologically, and in religion. Feminist theologians today often focus their work on the actual life possibilities of those who suffer most from the mythic hero complex of hierarchy and dominance. Johnson describes the goal of feminist religious discourse as "pivoting in its fullness around the flourishing of poor women of color in violent situations."[29] Rosemary Reuther claims the critical principle of feminist theology as "the promotion of the full humanity of women. Whatever denies, diminishes, or distorts the full humanity of women is, therefore, appraised as not redemptive."[30] And Fiorenza writes the term *wo/men* "not only to indicate the instability in the meaning of the term but also to signal that when I say wo/men I also mean to include subordinated men [...and to challenge] those kyriarchal structures [of dominance] which determine wo/men's lives and status and *also impact* the lives and status of men of subordinated race, classes, countries, and religions, albeit in different ways."[31] There is evidence that sexual violence in Euro-American societies may be linked to the superior value given to the male and the inferior value to the female where male God imagery is united with patriarchy.[32] Throughout the world women and especially girl children are the poorest and apparently most expendable of resources, as well as the primary noncombatant victims of the brutality of war. The close identification of Christianity with a particular image of God's heroic maleness and a corresponding power structure has produced and is producing, in Reuther's language, a "denial, diminishment and distortion" of the full humanity of women and men.

Psychologically, exclusively male language about God can cause women to feel they have no part in divine being. A woman may feel she has no basis for valuing and affirming herself as made in the image of God, or that her own experience can never reveal God's qualities and activities. She may even be alienated "from her own experience when she presumes that 'the holy' cannot be like her."[33] The cry of Ntozake Shange's protagonist at the end of her Broadway play resonates through feminist literature: "I found God in myself and I loved her fiercely!"[34] It is an experience that women seldom have in hero-dominated religions. "Religions centered on the worship of a male God create 'moods' and 'motivations' that keep women in a state of psychological dependence on men and male authority."[35] The symbols of religion have a powerful influence on inner development and spiritual maturity, amplifying complexes at the depth psychological level of the personal and collective unconscious.

It is not only women who suffer from the hero complex. Men often experience tremendous pressure to be strong, repress emotions, and carry heavy burdens of responsibility alone. Men may have difficulty forming friendships with other men because the male norm of competition tends to override cooperation. The hero complex asks a great deal of men, and generally isolates them from a community of support. The image of Christ as always wise and in control, taking care of others and ignoring self—that image (however misguided) is a tough one to emulate.

The mythic effects of hero imagery of God extend to religion as well. Mary Grey observes that "perhaps the strongest conviction" emerging from the first thirty years of the feminist theology movement is that the traditional symbolism of God the Father functions to exclude women not only in church leadership but also in society.[36] "Throughout history this has meant that justification for the leadership, authority and participation of women in society has had almost no theoretical underpinning."[37] Further, images of God such as lord, judge, and king legitimize power structures of unchecked dominance.

Interpretation is pivotal. The founding myth of Genesis can be understood in many ways. William Paden observes that "the words of the Bible can be read to support any philosophy or theology....

Is the Garden of Eden story to be read as a sexist message about the subordination of women, expressing the demotion of Eve from her original status as a goddess, or as a conventional parable of disobedience? Is it a mystical allegory of the fall of consciousness into the separate world of opposites, or is it a literal account of real events that happened at a real time and place? Is the serpent good for bringing about self-consciousness, or evil for bringing about sin?[38]

There are many ways to understand the Garden of Eden, and truth no doubt resides in a composite and open-ended understanding. However, my argument is that the dominant mythic substratum of Western society has so distorted the core of truth residing in the original Eden narrative that it is draining life and health out of the faith. I propose that the continued vitality of Western Christianity is linked to a radical re-visioning, a profound mythic shift, that begins to separate core Christian values from the dominant hero archetype. A feminist re-visioning of the nature of God and its corollary principles addresses the oppression of women and suppression of options for full human flourishing by mythically reclaiming an erotic model.

The Erotic Mythic Model

An erotic mythic model offers contrasts to the heroic one, in five interrelated themes, and a mythic narrative demonstrates that erotic archetype. The final portion of this chapter explores how to speak of God (the sixth, or primary, theme), considering alternative feminist theologies and ways to think about God. A mythic, erotic theological model begins with willingness to be confused about language for God and circles back again and again to the importance of five interrelated elements:

1. Respect for the body, the senses, nature, and Earth are central to the work of soul. An erotic approach to theology affirms the close affinity between the elements of the physical world and God's very presence. Nature is seen neither as "tooth and claw," nor is it sentimentalized. Rather the rhythms of the

natural world are viewed as gifts, as signs and symbols of the pattern of life, death, and renewal that are given with life and consciousness themselves. Respect for the human body offers many insights and experiences, from the marvel of healing that the body is capable of, to the ecstatic experiences of sexual union similar in many ways to the embrace of God. Death is not to be feared, but to be celebrated as a necessary part of the ongoing cycle of regeneration seen everywhere in the world.

"Embodied thinking" endeavors to "enlarge experience through empathy."[39] Meaning is formed not only in relation to tradition, nature, and so forth, but also in relation to one's "deepest and nonrational knowledge," or the sacred erotic in contrast to "the flattened affect of asceticism."[40] Because God is creator, every element of the physical world is permeated with God's presence, inviting deeper attention and response. When the material world is distorted or abused in any of its aspects, God also suffers the pain of that violation.

2. A shared mutuality is the basis for religious and social life and decision-making. When insights and decisions are open to engagement from everyone who has an interest or stake in the issue, often solutions surface that are far more comprehensive than is possible from only one point of view. The process of engaging many persons in community life can be time-consuming. Yet such a process frequently results in better long-term decisions as well as providing openings for Holy Spirit or Holy Wisdom to bring to bear surprisingly new options.[41] Power-over suggests domination and coercion, whereas power-with suggests "cooperation, partnership and mutuality."[42] The most beneficial and creative ways to connect humans, divinity and the whole created order are within flexible circles, networks, or webs. Whenever any portion of the web prospers or suffers, the whole network does likewise.

3. A sense of community is valued equally with personhood. Both individual and community are important, and neither should always take precedence over the other. One of the greatest blessings life offers is the experience of genuine community, not always easy to create or sustain but very rewarding when received. Individualism is lonely, carrying with it a demand always to show

one's best face, and never really to be vulnerable to another. The creation and ongoing nurture of relationships with people, the world, and God are of more value than the creation and maintenance of rules setting boundaries between members, as suggested in the Old Testament's preference for covenant over contract. Even God is embedded in a web of relationships. As the African word *ubuntu* suggests, relationships form us, even to the extent that a person is a person through other people.[43]

4. Win-win solutions create long-term reconciliation. Conflict is inevitable in human and other affairs, but violence is an inadequate and foolish response to conflict. Physical force and economic bullying are expressions of desperation in humans lacking an inner core of integrity and faithfulness. The belief that conflicts are best solved by overpowering an opponent demonstrates ignorance of the web of interconnections comprising creation, a web that is ruptured at peril not only to individual persons but to a sacred whole. Many methods are emerging to practice cooperative ways of dealing with conflict oriented toward genuine reconciliation and shared power through spiritual strength.[44]

5. Diversity need not be expressed as oppositional. A nondualist mode of understanding diversity might be a dance of complementarities and paradoxes within a multifaceted whole. Paradoxes can point toward mysteries that invite a wider vision beyond literal contrasts. Listening to others may reveal complementary goals where only conflict initially appeared. Seeking *both/and* solutions to issues can override snap judgments based on appearances only.

I call this feminist mythic model erotic in contrast to heroic. Erotic as an alternative to heroic is intended to be a shorthand reference not so much to sexuality as to a vision of spirituality as involving a joyously creative relationship with the physical world. Because this book is primarily about issues in Christian theology, it may seem strange to think of applying erotic language to Jesus. Yet one could say with justification that the life of Jesus of Nazareth is far better described and imitated with these five erotic themes than by a pattern of heroic conquest and domination.

Many of these particular themes of the erotic mythic archetype are trickling into the culture with increasing acceptance, as "cracks" are increasingly being revealed in the heroic worldview. I've been fascinated to find responses to this list of themes such as, "Yes, I like and agree with all those, but don't change the language about God, or the way I think about God." I am endeavoring to demonstrate that an image of a male, kingly God bears the inevitable corollaries that together comprise the heroic model. The image of God does function, shown here as an interconnected heroic mythic archetype that dominates Western cultural and theological thought.

Taking seriously the alternative themes of the erotic mythic archetype involves a fundamental shift in thinking, not only about knowledge construction and a picture of self and world, but also about the very nature of God. Gross observes that one reason why many scholars resist the feminist paradigm shift is that "the information...cannot simply be added to the picture they already have. *In almost all cases, they discover that they have to repaint the whole picture.*"[45] Yet she says that in the absence of such a shift, not only does the scholar not have all the relevant data, but "we will not have accurate methods for organizing, understanding, and interpreting the data that we do have. Therefore, we will arrive at false or partial hypotheses regarding those phenomena."[46] Re-visioning theology from an erotic mythic perspective may challenge traditional affirmations of faith, but it also provides the possibility of deepening and broadening the mythic foundations of faith to heighten theology's relevance for women as well as offering a more graceful way of living for women and men.

Consider and compare the earlier heroic mythic narrative with an erotic mythic narrative set forth here that may make clearer the intimate connection between an image of God and corresponding worldview.

An Erotic Mythic Narrative

No single erotic mythic narrative prevails, nor is it set forth in any specific text, as was the Garden of Eden narrative demonstrating the heroic myth. Exploring alternative mythic patterns about divinity, feminists have searched the human past and present, looking for places and times in which divinity and society have been conceived differently than the heroic model. As a result, Gross affirms that "The most important and encouraging conclusion of feminist scholarship is that patriarchy is the cultural creation of a certain epoch in human history, not an inevitable necessity of human biology."[47]

Many scholars today agree that "the most ancient human image of the divine was female."[48] And Merlin Stone asks provocatively, "At the very dawn of religion, God was a woman. Do you remember?"[49] The theory of predominantly goddess worship in an era before written records are available is controversial, because it is both a scholarly hypothesis and a sacred narrative claimed by many feminists in popular culture. The lack of written records means that archeological and other scholarly assessments must inevitably include some interpretive schema (as is now recognized to be the case for any scholarly work). At present there are no commonly agreed upon methods to assess religion practices in prehistoric cultures. In addition, "the societies studied by these scholars have been patriarchal for so long and because these societies have become so dominant over so much of the globe, classicists and historians of religion often find the hypothesis of non-patriarchal social organization unbelievable."[50]

As many feminist scholars and others are asking today, is it possible even to imagine something different than the now dominant heroic culture? A fish swimming in water presumably cannot imagine an environment without water. This is the issue that a mythic critique addresses squarely. Inquiry at a mythic level suggests that, indeed, religious imagination seems to have been severely limited by the heroic mythic presuppositions dominant for much of recorded Western history. However, the mythic level is precisely where imagination can flourish, and a credible alternate sacred narrative has emerged in the last twenty or so years—a narrative that is not entirely scientifically based because it includes imaginative reflection. Even so, this alternate narrative is founded in careful study of ancient artifacts, and it presents an interpretive story bearing power to evoke strong and positive archetypal responses.[51]

Here is the basic erotic sacred narrative about prehistory.[52]

In the beginning, dating from about 30,000 BCE, human cultures tend to worship the divine feminine. This divinity is not so much singular as plural, taking many forms in many places, but fundamentally representing the energies of birth and death and regeneration that seem everywhere revealed in earth and its children. The fact that women can bleed and not die arouses astonishment, and when live children emerge from the maternal womb, it is counted miraculous. The miracle is not assigned to individual females, but to the fecundity of earth that surrounds and supports small tribes. Mountains represent the breasts of mother earth, and caves are understood to be womblike (both are sites containing many sacred artifacts, evidences of early worship). Throughout the fertile crescent, Europe, India, and other places of early human habitation, one of the most ubiquitous images found is of a woman holding open her labia, inviting entry into the goddess' womb of life and death and renewal. These images are called "Sheila-na-gigs" in Europe and Lajj? Gaur? figures in Asia.[53]

Over twenty times more female than male figurines have been excavated from European sites thus far, strongly suggesting that the sacred images of these cultures are theacentric, or goddess-centered. Theacentric cultures seem particularly to value (and often assign to the goddess's own form) the symbols of the bird and the snake. Birds and especially water birds are seen to move smoothly and comfortably between the primal elements of water, earth, and sky. And snakes are at home both on earth and below it, in caves and tunnels. The ability to function equally well in multiple environments is seen as a symbol of the trickster, the surprising goddess who moves where and how she will. The snake in particular is known as a canny and wise creature. Because of the snake's ability apparently to die and be reborn in the sloughing of its skin, serpents are associated "with life, rejuvenation, fertility, and regeneration, [and are] a symbol of immortality."[54] In many theacentric cultures, the snake is often portrayed with goddess as a symbol of her own mysterious and regenerative powers.

The cultures and indeed civilizations that form from about 6500 BCE to about 3500 BCE develop the arts of pottery, spinning and weaving, cooking, and agriculture. Sometimes living in cities of up to ten thousand residents, these civilizations are able to support artisans who design jewelry and figurines not only in clay, but in gold and copper as well. Towns are not built primarily in defensible locations, but rather in places offering good water and soil. Strangely for modern thought, there is little evidence of fortification walls or defensive weapons from this period.

Religion seems as integral to these cultures as breathing, with many homes containing ritual centers or altars, as well as larger temples for common worship. Figurines suggest that worship and political affairs generally involve women in leadership, although men also seem to have positions of influence. Temple and ritual dwellings contain objects of highest quality marble and ceramic items, objects that stay with the ritual dwellings rather than being buried with those who die. Burials are often in common graves, without high status symbols buried with leaders, and without distinction between men and women. Bodies are shaped into a fetal position for birth into whatever follows this life.

The preferred term for these societies is not matriarchal (suggesting hierarchy), but matrifocal, meaning a society centered around worship of the divine feminine and guided by influential women, but nonetheless egalitarian, with shared leadership including both sexes.

Before assessing this erotic mythic narrative, consider how it corresponds to the erotic model above.

1. Worship is primarily immanent rather than transcendent, more earth-based than heaven-centered. Earth itself is the source of awe and wonder, as it moves through relatively predictable cycles of day and night, in the seasons of spring, summer, fall, and

winter. Mystery surrounds the ordinary where people do not take for granted the unfolding of life and death. Especially the female body is honored, and divinity naturally is seen to take the form of fecundity, though not exclusively fertility, for goddess is known to be dispenser of death as well as life. Living in a world seen as having cyclical rhythms rather than linear movement, death is understood as prelude to further mysteries.

2. Leadership is shared at every level. When goddess is worshipped in a specific image, there is no competition with another image. Goddess's abilities are not distributed as in the Greek pantheon, with each goddess having specific functions; space exists for many different approaches to the mystery surrounding life. The divine is primarily involved in domestic matters rather than in territorial wars, so she need not insist that one form is more powerful than another. Power arises from cooperation among many strengths. (Note: Given that the societies now under discussion had no written language, we cannot prove that leadership was shared. However, in some places such as Crete, a goddess-centered society similar to the erotic narrative did continue into the historic period. And the point of this erotic narrative is that it is a mythic reality, consistent with archeological discoveries, yet interpreted outside the frame of the contemporary mythic, that is, heroic stance.)

3. Even critics of the erotic sacred narrative agree that the primary form of consciousness in these cultures was communal rather than individual.[55] Life depended in many ways upon other persons with whom one lived. It was obvious to all that humans were vulnerable and needed one another. Alone even as a single family, it was nearly impossible to survive and manage the range of needed tasks, such as hunting and gathering food, remaining safe from the predations of large animals, creating shelters, making fires, and even cooperating in daily life, including the necessity of having several women together to weave large tapestries for warmth and beauty. People knew themselves primarily as members of a specific community, and experienced their lives as formed in essential relationships. In this state of mutual vulnerability, a sense of the sacred was very close, and goddess was known in the midst of the web of life.

4. No doubt there were conflicts even in these prehistoric communities. But since they were built without defensive walls, and since the artifacts do not depict the physical fights of battles so characteristic of art in later periods, the conclusion must be that people learned to deal with conflict without resorting to violence. Since the society appears not to be hierarchical, there would not have been a chief who could squelch conflict with a stern look of authority. So what methods did they use to negotiate conflict? We don't know, having lost contact with these cultures with the invasions of sky-god warriors in the second and third millenniums BCE.[56] Certainly methods of negotiation must have been highly developed. No doubt sometimes punishment was required, such as perhaps temporary or even permanent banishment.

5. Obviously these societies understood diversity, given their awe for creatures that were at home in diverse environments. It seems likely, however, that with their perspective of cyclical rhythms in life, they saw everything as interlinked in a great web of life, rather than as polar opposites requiring judgments and choices. The relatively familiar Latin word *hostis*, meaning "enemy" or "stranger," is derived from an older Sanskrit root form *ghos-ti*, meaning "someone with whom one has reciprocal duties of hospitality."[57] In English those linguistic roots can lead to two words, both "hospitality" and "hostile," suggesting that there is a choice whether strangers may be welcomed as friends or received as enemies. An intention of hospitality toward another with whom one has conflict can go a long way toward resolution.

The archeomythological basis for much though not all of this narrative is based on the work of respected archeomythologist Marija Gimbutas, although other scholars also contribute to the unfolding of this erotic narrative. Gimbutas's vision of the characteristics of a matrifocal society centering in worship of goddess is controversial, and Lucy Goodison as well as others have challenged its authenticity. Among other challenges, Goodison is concerned with Gimbutas's insistence that it is not possible to understand the prehistoric period without considering the religious dimension (worship of goddess) as central to all the culture's sociological functions. While Goodison acknowledges that "the contribution of the Goddess movement needs to be recognized as both spiritual and archaeological," she also observes that archaeologists are reluctant if not negative about "the possibility of effectively studying religion through archaeological materials."[58] That particular criticism of the erotic sacred narrative suggests the importance of the imaginal methodology of archetypal psychology discussed in chapter two of this book, as a means of imaginative yet authoritative study of issues related to the human soul and its yearnings. When evaluation of the erotic sacred narrative is conducted at the imaginal or mythic level, the limitations of an academic method with no capacity for understanding religion or the spiritual life are obvious.[59] Thus another reason to take seriously the erotic, sacred narrative is that it reveals the tendency toward secularity implicit in the standard rational heroic ego archetype.

In order to assess "the Gimbutas paradigm," philosopher Mara Keller explores Plato's *Republic* for its approach to "the complex, interconnected epistemologies of both science and mythology."[60] Keller describes Plato as acknowledging four levels of truth-seeking, each with its own hermeneutics or interpretive scheme. First, *eikasia* is taking sense perceptions at face value, a kind of conjecture based on common thinking; second, *pistis* is direct sensory perception of empirical facts; third, *dianoia* is discursive reasoning, deducing conclusions from accepted principles; and finally *noesis* is a reconsideration of first principles based on direct apprehension or intuition.[61] Noting that much contemporary archaeology is empiricist, Keller observes that such a perspective "cannot logically believe it possible to have any probable knowledge of the mind-states or spiritual experiences of ancient peoples."[62] To such empiricists, she raises the question, "how does one construct a highly probable interpretation of symbolic meaning from material objects, images and signs?"[63] Keller recommends the method of *noesis* as a response, a method very similar to imaginal interpretive method.

Whether or not such a sacred narrative can ever be demonstrated to be accurate history (a concept which itself is questionable in a time when scholars know that history is always shaped by an interpretive frame), from a mythological point of view this narrative is important as an articulation of a feminist theological mythic archetype. The idea of an egalitarian society that finds ways to resolve conflicts without mass violence, lives cooperatively in a fashion that honors the community as well as the individuals comprising it, and finds no rigid separation between the body of earth, humans, and divinity, represents a mythos worth articulating. An important part of this narrative is the explicit recognition of a female body and spirit as bearer of divine energy. This need not mean the exclusion of male body and spirit from divinity, but rather that neither image is an exclusive picture of the holy. This sacred erotic narrative stimulates the imagination to take seriously the possible ongoing connections between a theology of the feminine in God and an anthropology of feminine elements in the sacred created order. This vision of a prehistory of goddess worship at the center of a whole sacred circle of life is a powerful mythic erotic archetype.

Reflection

This description of two different mythic models and narratives presents a clear contrast between a heroic and an erotic understanding of God and human life. The goal is not to succumb to a dualism that merely supplants one dominant myth with another, but rather to exchange a model of dominance for one of equality. Under the sway of the dominant heroic model, a temptation exists to discount any other mythic model as unrealistic or fantastic. This discussion is intended to broaden a sense of the options available for human life, society. and the sacred. In particular the unchecked heroic myth has destructive effects on the treatment of women and other marginalized people, and our world can no longer afford unthinkingly to dismiss the potential contributions to our common life of over half the world's population.

This is a theological re-visioning project, yet much of this chapter so far has related to the human side of the God-human relationship. The point is, as previously stated, the symbol of God functions to affect and influence the acceptable range of human behavior, and this section has endeavored to show how differing views of God correspond to differing views of human life. Now the discussion turns to re-visioning the nature of God, exploring in some detail the contemporary theological work of several feminist theologians whose goal is to stay within the Christian tradition, honoring Christ and the tradition's core values, while moving toward a conception of God more congruent with an inclusive sense of the web of life.

THE NATURE OF GOD: THE CONTEMPORARY CONVERSATION

Feminist Christian theologians are those who affirm a basic compatibility between the core of Christian faith and feminist values, even as they struggle with language for and about God. Rosemary Reuther affirms that "once the mythology about Jesus as Messiah or divine Logos, with its traditional masculine imagery, is stripped off, the Jesus of the synoptic Gospels can be recognized as a figure remarkably compatible with feminism."[64] However, in an effort to make clear that language about God must extend beyond male gendered words, Reuther chooses to write the God/ess, referring to "the primal Matrix, the great womb within which all things...are generated."[65] Similarly, Elisabeth Schüssler Fiorenza writes the word G*d, which she roots in orthodox Jewish custom that not only works in a language without vowels but also regards the name of Yahweh as unspeakable. Fiorenza calls her term a "broken way to emphasize the inadequacy of language to speak about the divine."[66] I prefer to spell the word *Godde* (and will do so for the balance of this book), as the Old English way of writing the name of God. The word *Godde* is spoken in the same way as God, but in reading it, the mind lingers a moment with the possibility that the infinite being that Christianity names Godde is not limited by maleness.[67] Such small shifts in language may have little weight against the prominence of male language in the scripture and tradition of Christianity, although within and outside major religious traditions, feminist scholarship has considerably expanded "the possibility of feminine symbols of the divine."[68]

Lucy Tatman describes the "classical Christian paradigm" of Godde as found in the writings of Augustine, Aquinas, Luther, and Calvin this way: "God is a wholly other, transcendent, omniscient, omnipotent, absolutely sovereign deity."[69] This concept clearly suggests a great gulf between Godde and humankind. While Tatman's is generally a fair summary of the classical description of Godde, Melissa Raphael observes that feminists have a tendency to overstate their case, creating a sort of parody of a "masculine sky god, detached from (or transcendent to) the natural cycles he created, demanding absolute obedience from his creatures, and leading history towards a pre-determined purpose."[70] Of course, the core elements of Christian faith do not require that Godde be limited to such qualities, although existing Western mythology may obscure genuine and faithful alternatives. In addition, the limits of the classical view reduce its capacity to speak meaningfully in a postmodern environment, much less to the hearts of contemporary women. This is the dilemma that Christian feminists face in their endeavor to speak of the nature of God.

Several contemporary feminist theologians have undertaken credible and sensitive forays into alternative understandings of Godde, congruent with the proposed erotic mythic archetype.

Sallie McFague

In keeping with the commitment to reflexivity or self-disclosure valued by feminists, McFague identifies herself immediately as a white, middle-class, Protestant feminist, teaching at Vanderbilt Divinity School in Nashville, Tennessee.[71] Her methodology emerges as reflective construction based on scripture.[72] She values the importance of metaphor, an emphasis emerging from her focus on the parable, which she calls "a prime genre of Scripture and certainly the central form of Jesus' teaching."[73]

McFague believes that language is at root metaphorical and so too is shared human knowledge."[74] Metaphor is especially suited to religious language because while Godde is inherently unknowable, humans desire to know Godde, and metaphors have a unique ability to create meaning by *the stretching of the whole creature beyond itself into the unknown.*"[75] Metaphor does this by using words "*in*appropriately,"[76] that is, it speaks about something unfamiliar by reference to something familiar, thus creating a tension "by the relation of similarity and dissimilarity."[77] Metaphor does not produce absolute or final dogmas, but it is capable of bearing an essential tension and finding fruitfulness in what might ordinarily be seen as destabilizing. McFague justifies her "as if" theology in the fact that Christian scripture and tradition are themselves reliant on metaphor and a certain ambiguity.[78] She points out that even in scripture, God is more than can be said, both "unlike as well as like our metaphors."[79]

Metaphorical theology as a strategy "encourages nontraditional, unconventional, novel ways of expressing the relationship between God and the world not because such ways are necessarily better than received ways but because they cannot be ruled out as better unless tried."[80] An emphasis on metaphoric thought in theology also serves as a guard against dominant Christian metaphors and models becoming either idols or irrelevant.[81]

With this method, the theologian plays with possibilities, undertaking thought experiments with imaginative boldness. McFague's first major attempt at such play is to propose a threefold model—Godde as mother, lover, and friend—as a way to think of the Trinity as "God's impartial, reuniting and reciprocal love to the world."[82] After dealing with possible anxieties about Godde as mother related to sexuality (father is a sexual image too) and fear of being swallowed up (generated by an expectation of Godde as fierce judge over us), McFague points out that a profound and graceful shift in consciousness can come with thinking of mother-godde as giver of life itself.[83] "There simply is no other imagery available to us that has this power for expressing the interdependence and interrelatedness of all life with its ground."[84] In addition, Godde as mother forces a consideration of godly, *agape* love not as totally unmotivated, disinterested love, but as expressive of the "elements of need, desire, and mutuality [that] are evident in all forms of love."[85]

Godde as lover of the world "represents God as savior whose passion—both as desire for and suffering with the beloved—is oriented toward healing and reuniting all parts of the body."[86] McFague proposes that Jesus' love is not agape but *eros*, a passionate outpouring for the sake of the beloved.[87] Eros is the form of love to describe Godde's healing encounter with the world in

Jesus. Spirit as friend (rooted in the Greek *philia*, love) suggests the reciprocity of Godde's engagement with the world, a quality of interdependence. In summary, this form of trinity, based on various types of love, is rooted in response and responsibility, operating "by persuasion, care, attention, passion, and mutuality."[88]

As she moves more toward constructive theology, McFague shifts her focus to the universe as Godde's body. In a concern for ecology and an emphasis on embodiment, McFague writes of Godde "as the source and divine matrix of all that is, as the power enlivening and sustaining creation in all its diversity and intricacy—source, matrix, power."[89] She writes that humans are embodied organisms: "Whatever more or other we may be, we *are* bodies, made of the same stuff as all other life-forms on our planet."[90] Humans are not the only, and perhaps not even the most important, of earth creatures, but in Godde, a relational and participative universe of all beings comes to exist. Godde's body is no more purely spiritualized than human bodies. "God's body, that which supports all life, is not matter or spirit but the matrix out of which everything that is evolves....The world is not *ours* to manipulate for *our* purposes. If we see it as God's body, the way God is present to us, we will indeed know we tread on sacred ground."[91] Attentiveness to this earth opens humans to the mystery and wonder that are Godde.

Elizabeth A. Johnson

Elizabeth Johnson is a Roman Catholic religious sister and a faculty member of the theology department at Fordham University who lectures to Catholic audiences around the world. "Whereas McFague invokes the use of a newly constructed metaphor for getting at a radicalized understanding of the incarnation, Johnson returns to the traditions...to retrieve an image for addressing the incarnation: Wisdom."[92] Thus Johnson can be considered a revisionist theologian rather than a constructivist. Influenced by liberation theology and ecological concerns, Johnson undertakes the work of deconstructing the tradition to "unmask the hidden dynamic of domination in the Christian tradition's language, custom, memory, history, sacred texts, ethics, symbolism, theology, and ritual."[93] As already noted, Johnson is clear that the goal of feminist discourse "pivots in its fullness around the flourishing of poor women of color in violent situations."[94]

The question that shapes all Johnson's work is, "What is the right way to speak about God?"[95] Endeavoring to find answers to that question, Johnson turns to symbols, taking a position of symbolic realism, which she defines as the understanding of "religious symbols as non-literal representations of a transcendent reality, which so mediate reality that it is disclosed and communicated through the symbol and experienced in it."[96] Johnson affirms that a symbol carries a "surplus of meaning."[97]

Finding what might be called the "signature" of God within the created world, Johnson also turns to analogy. She points to a practice of early Christian theology speaking about Godde in "a threefold motion of affirmation, negation, and eminence."[98] The ancient theological practice is first to affirm something about Godde in analogy from nature, then to deny that affirmation because all language about Godde is inadequate, and finally to make a statement of faith even knowing that words are always inadequate. In this way, concepts and analogies from human experience about Godde go through a double negation, first denying or negating the capacity of any analogy to speak adequately about Godde, but then affirming that Godde is a reality truer than any negation, and making the choice to be open to the always unknowable but ever present one. This Christian tradition of threefold movement in analogy offers a clear contrast both with univocality (holding solely to one single meaning) or equivocality (claiming emptiness because Godde is always beyond ultimate human knowing). Johnson says the Christian analogical method establishes a "relationship of participation" through which "all creatures participate to some degree in 'being,' the very dynamism of existing which God in essence is."[99]

In one of her major books, *She Who Is: The Mystery of God in Feminist Theological Discourse*, Johnson seeks to articulate ways of thinking about Godde congruent with feminist concerns. Drawing on the resources of scripture and tradition, she names three primary qualities of "She Who Is" in Christian understanding. First, *Godde is triune*, not as traditionally stated "Father, Son and Holy Spirit," but rather as a being fundamentally in relation—

"not an isolated, static, ruling monarch but a relational, dynamic, tripersonal mystery of love."[100] As presently understood, the symbol of the Trinity is not only confusing, but is "used to sustain the patriarchal subordination of women" both in its male imagery and in its hierarchical pattern of relationship.[101] Observing that any symbol is analogical rather than literal, Johnson suggests that the symbol of Trinity is intended to affirm communion within unity in Godde's very being.[102]

The second quality Johnson names about Godde in Christian thought follows from the first: not only is Godde in relationship "interiorly," but also Godde is in genuine, reciprocal relationship with the world, in a "compassionate connectedness" that is collegial and empowering.[103] Johnson refers to the emerging experience of women of personhood defined "neither as a self-encapsulated ego nor a diffuse self denied, but selfhood on the model of relational autonomy."[104] By analogy to such experience, God's being can be seen to be relational by nature (and not by accident).

Godde is dynamic, relational mystery, namely "incomprehensible liveliness," that overflows so that "everything that exists does so through participation in divine being."[105] This quality of sheer liveliness in Godde is not well described by the classic notions of static substance, but is better expressed by Mary Daly's insight that Godde is understood better as a verb than as a noun.[106] Alternatively, John Macquarrie suggests that the dynamism of Godde's being is best expressed as "letting-be"—not in the sense of ignoring creatures "but by saying 'Let there be,' that is, by empowering, enabling, bringing them into being."[107] This overflowing relationality is freely chosen, a coinherence of Godde and the world, each enfolded in the other, "while each remains radically distinct."[108] This notion introduces the idea of deficiency in Godde in the form of interdependence, vulnerability, and risk implicit in any truly reciprocal relationship.[109] Such a concept is different both from traditional theism's unbridgeable gap between Godde and the world and from classical pantheism's notion of identity between Godde and the world.[110]

The third primary quality of Godde is *compassion poured out*. Classic theology describes God as "apathic," from the Greek *a-patheia*, meaning "no pathos or suffering." "Since suffering is a passive state requiring that one be acted upon by an outside force," it was thought that Godde could not suffer.[111] Johnson observes that the idea of the apathic God is shaped "by the patriarchal ideal: ...being in control, existing self-contained and self-directed, apart from entanglements with others."[112] The English word *compassion* is referred to as a translation of *hesed*, a Hebrew word literally meaning "womb-love."[113] The Latin roots of the English compassion reveal its meaning as "suffering with," so the feminist claim that Godde is compassion challenges traditional ideas of Godde as impassible and immutable. Johnson insists, "the idea of the impassible, omnipotent God appears riddled with inadequacies:"

> The idea of God simply cannot remain unaffected by the basic datum of so much suffering and death. Nor can it tolerate the kind of divine complicity in evil that happens when divine power is conceived as the force that could stop all of this but simply chooses not to, for whatever reason. A God who is not in some way affected by such pain is not really worthy of human love and praise....Such a God is morally intolerable.[114]

This is very tricky ground, for the feminist theologian does not want to suggest that suffering is a value in itself, nor that women (or any oppressed people) should emulate Godde's weakness or powerlessness. Yet it is essential to address the question of suffering and evil in the world.

Johnson urges stepping "decisively out of the androcentric system of power-over versus victimization and think in other categories about power, pain, and their deep interweaving in human experience."[115] She suggests that women may be truly in the image of Godde when they experience pain in childbirth, suffering and anger due to injustice, grief over unnecessary loss or harm, and personal degradation. The message of the cross is identification with human suffering and no easy escape from its darkness, yet it offers the mystery that suffering can be "overcome, from within through the power of love."[116] She is seeking "an understanding that does not divide power and compassionate love in a dualistic framework that identifies love with a resignation of power and the exercise of power with a denial of love."[117] Compassion is the strength that arises within suffering, especially in community, "a blazing fierceness, rather than an interior emotion, and it has an efficacy for transformation."[118]

Elisabeth Schüssler Fiorenza

Elisabeth Schüssler Fiorenza is professor of scripture and interpretation at Harvard Divinity School and past president of the Society of Biblical Literature. Like the other feminist theologians considered here, she is white and educationally/economically advantaged, but unlike them, she spent the early years of her life in Europe (Germany) rather than in the United States. Her primary interest and concern as a feminist is not systematic theology but scripture and its interpretation, so her work generally proceeds from biblical texts. She does this in a way that radically diverges from what she calls "malestream theology."[119]

To set her work in context, it is useful to know that the emphasis in New Testament studies for at least the last century has been what is called the "quest for the historical Jesus." For some time it has been clear that no consensus will be achieved in the quest, because the facts of Jesus' life are minimally corroborated outside the four gospels, which—written more than thirty years after Jesus' death—are themselves already interpretations and even inconsistent with one another. Fiorenza takes exception to "the scholarly claim to have produced a history or biography of the 'real' Jesus that, unlike theological-religious images of Jesus, is a truly scientific account of Jesus as he 'really' was," noting that "scholars inescapably fashion the Historical-Jesus in their own image and likeness."[120] She is particularly opposed to "a literalist dogmatic reading...that seeks to 'fix' the pluriform expressions...and ambiguous metaphors of Jesus Christ into a single, definite discourse of meaning."[121]

Instead of that pretense, Fiorenza proposes a feminist ideology critique, a mode of investigation "from a committed position within a social analytic whose legitimacy is argued for not on the grounds of its scientific Truth but on the basis of its explanatory power and its commitment to emancipatory social change."[122] Fiorenza stands all previous hermeneutics about Jesus on their heads, and stakes out a territory for her method that acknowledges she will construct interpretations (through imaginative play with scholarly investigation), and admits up front that the approach she is taking to the material comes from a commitment to liberation of women and other oppressed peoples. To begin this work, she coins the term *kyriarchy* to mean "the domination of the lord, slave master, husband, the elite freeborn educated and propertied man over all wo/men and sub-altern men."[123] She also invents the term *kyriocentrism*, to describe a point of view "which has the ideological function of naturalizing and legitimating not just gender but all forms of domination."[124] This is radical terminology, since some Christian theologians propose the Greek word *kyrios*, lord, to be the simplest possible formulation of faith in Jesus Christ as Savior.[125] In contrast, Fiorenza insists that domination, no matter how well intended, cannot be salvific.

One of the most problematic aspects of kyriocentric discourses is that they "function as ideologies, that is, they mystify the 'constructedness' of their account of reality."[126] In other words, since every scholar carries some point of view, and since many contemporary scholars are influenced by the rational heroic myth, the existing accounts of Jesus and his life and his message inevitably carry some bias, some imaginative leap. Unfortunately, too often those accounts purport to be the only possible way to understand the gospel. Therefore it is important for feminist Christological reconstruction not only to investigate texts about women and Jesus nor simply to focus on gender relations. Instead, the whole theological framework must be reconsidered, reconceptualizing "early Judaism and early Christianity in such a way that it can make marginalized wo/men visible as central agents who have shaped Jewish and Christian history and religion."[127] Fiorenza feels strongly that feminists must not relinquish biblical interpretation to kyriocentric discourse. Quoting E. Fox-Genovese, Fiorenza urges that feminists cannot afford

> to jettison all claims to the product and record of so
> many centuries of collective life. To the extent that men

have spoken they have done so on the basis of the privileged access to history and rule, not on the basis of
intrinsic personal or sexual merit. Their social representation and social institutions belong however to our
collective past. The lords of creation do not exist inde-
pendently of those they oppress.[128]

The goal is a model of scholarship that tests and evaluates
source materials able to transform androcentric history into a
common history. The feminist critical hermeneutic that Fiorenza
develops moves from androcentric texts to their social-historical
contexts, claiming "the contemporary communities of women
struggling for liberation as its locus of revelation...as well as
reclaiming its foresisters as victims *and* subjects participating in
patriarchal culture."[129] Fiorenza assumes that women were there
with Jesus, playing important roles, until it is proved otherwise.[130]
She is avowedly engaged in "an imaginative reconstruction of historical reality."[131] And the appropriate criterion for evaluating this
critical feminist theory of liberation is "not orthodoxy or doctrinal systematics but its ability to change religious structures of second-class citizenship in the academy and religion as well as its
ability to transform theological and religious mindsets of self-
alienation, low self-esteem and subordination."[132]

Fiorenza adopts primarily a rhetorical-emancipatory paradigm, including "not just a hermeneutic-scientific but also an eth-
ical-political turn."[133] She urges that exploration of biblical texts
involves awareness of how those texts themselves may dehuman-
ize people, in order that scholars and readers also notice and erad-
icate their own mindsets that internalize violence and prejudice. A
variety of exegetical and interpretive methods are employed in
Fiorenza's overall paradigm, including hermeneutics of experience, domination and social location, suspicion, critical evaluation, creative imagination, remembering and reconstruction, and
transformative action for change.[134] The goal of this rhetorical-
emancipatory paradigm is to "shift focus from the modern question, How can we believe in G*d? to the question What kind of
G*d do Christians proclaim? and Do religious faith and commu-

nity make a difference in the struggle for the well-being of all in the global village?"[135]

In *Jesus, Miriam's Child, Sophia's Prophet*, Fiorenza elaborates the concept of Jesus as "Sophia's prophet."[136] Scholars have long been aware that Jesus' understanding of the Messiah, that is, the Christ, seems markedly different from prevailing expectations in his world. Some suggest that Jesus may be modeling his actions on the "suffering servant" of the later books of Isaiah, and/or that the gospel writers saw this spirit in Jesus. As she searches the New Testament for clues to Jesus' vision of the Christ, Fiorenza finds that remarkably often, the words spoken by Jesus seem based on and parallel to the words of the figure of Lady Wisdom in Hebrew and intertestamental scriptures. (*Sophia* is the Greek translation of wisdom, whereas *Hokmah* is the Hebrew word.) Fiorenza suggests that Jesus can be understood as Sophia's prophet, proposing that "the earliest Palestinian theological remembrances and interpretations of Jesus' life and death understand him as Sophia's messenger and later as Sophia herself. The earliest Christian theology is sophialogy."[137]

Many books of scripture speak of Lady Wisdom or Sophia, revealing a multi-faceted figure with core features. Sophia is leader, preacher, architect of the world, called sister, spouse, mother, and beloved.[138] "She searches the streets for people, finds them, and invites them to her festive table. She offers life, knowledge, rest, and salvation to all those who will accept her."[139] Jesus Christ's way parallels that of Sophia, who was sent or came down to earth, found no place to dwell, and hence "returned to her place and took her seat among the angels."[140] Sophia expresses Godde's qualities as she "holds open a future for the poor and outcast and offers God's gracious goodness to *all* children of Israel without exception."[141]

Jesus as prophet of Sophia offers two Christological themes—one as "wise teacher, who in his concrete life relates to our ongoing quest for a gracious G*d"; and a second emphasizing that his teaching is "meant not only for hearing but for being acted upon."[142] Jesus is not solely or even primarily interested in being a wonderful preacher as much as in affecting people's hearts and actions, in giving them a new way to live in peace and love. In claiming Jesus as Sophia's prophet, Fiorenza does not want to emphasize Jesus as the superlative end of the wisdom tradition, but rather to suggest that he joins and shares with others an ongoing open tradition that Jesus "does not close but activates."[143]

Fiorenza insists that it is unwise to focus on Jesus as "the great charismatic leader or divine man," because this merely feeds into the hero mythology so intertwined with kyriocentrism.[144] More important than any single figure is the community of people who gather around Jesus and who together create the *basileia* of Godde. *Basileia tou theou* is a term central to Jesus' preaching, and is usually translated "kingdom of God." But scholars are not in agreement either about its translation or about its meaning. Fiorenza finds unacceptable a translation that places "an emphasis on G*d's kingly rule, often explicated in terms of domination."[145] She prefers the translation "realm" and understands it to mean "the praxis of inclusive wholeness."[146]

Seeking an image to convey Jesus' concept of *basileia* or "realm," Fiorenza focuses on the festive meal. "The power of God's *basileia* is realized in Jesus' table community with the poor, the sinners, the tax collectors, and prostitutes."[147] Indeed, some scholars are now naming this remarkable practice of Jesus' table fellowship at the center of the *basileia* as "open commensality."[148] Fiorenza observes that this fellowship suggests that God's presence and power are revealed in the people themselves, not as the holiness of the elect but as the wholeness of all. And for Fiorenza this corresponds to the voice of Sophia then and now—"a public, radical democratic voice rather than a 'feminine' privatized one."[149] The voice of the gospels is muted when it is insisted that Jesus alone carries Sophia's message; her message is birthed and transmitted within the context of the community of women and men who surround Jesus and who with him cocreate the *basileia tou theou* in the eternal present.

Finally, Fiorenza claims no interest in establishing definitive, closed readings of texts or theological issues. "Against the allurement of literalist certainty and the enticement of playful excess, I have argued that the road of a critical feminist christological inquiry must be variegated, inclusive, and open-ended but still remain engaged and committed."[150]

Reflection

Who is the Godde who emerges from these theological conversations? If these descriptions are compared with what might be called the classic paradigm of a kingly male God as "a wholly other, transcendent, omniscient, omnipotent, absolutely sovereign deity," quite a contrast emerges.[151] In general feminist theologians are not so interested in the nature of Godde as were classic theologians, perhaps because of the tentativeness with which any theory of "absolutes" must be held in a postmodern environment that values multiple perspectives more than any single theory. Recent descriptions of Godde are more tentative and less certain, and this quality itself is illuminating. The classic paradigm offered a God who was a firm and fixed guidepost that one could count on, no matter what. There was no change in such a god, no "give." On the other hand, there is something unsettling about a Godde of uncertainty—how can such a Godde be relied upon? Feminist thought definitely brings theology into a world of uncertainty, where Godde is so much engaged in the web of life as to be a fluid reality, so much a partner in human troubles that Godself may be influenced by shifts in the cosmic network. But perhaps it is more comforting to know we are companioned in whatever happens, than to count on a possible rescue.

An alternative approach to Godde's nature takes shape in feminist theology. Godde is understood by way of metaphors and analogies, which are inherently destabilizing—a reminder that Godde is always more than can be (directly) known. This is not to say that any metaphor or analogy will suffice to speak of Godde. However, the metaphors offered by feminist theologians present new ways of thinking about Godde—ways that both liberate women and other oppressed people and give reason to value the nonhuman world as an expression of Godde's body. Again and again, feminists return to love as an aspect of Godde's being, generally an embodied and even erotic love rather than an abstract and disinterested love. Feminist theologians like Johnson and Fiorenza find new ways of thinking about Godde within the tradition and scripture, moving away from a view of Godde as an absolute and contained self and toward a view of Godde whose strength is the capacity and desire to remain present in the midst of profound suffering, embodying even there the mystery of a love that leads toward wholeness.

Rather than allow themselves to be paralyzed by a postmodern emphasis on deconstruction, feminist theologians are using postmodern tools to chip away at viewpoints that have been taken for granted, such as dominance and dualism, while also exploring new viewpoints. Instead of a pluralism of voices leading toward fragmentation, the presence of many voices in feminist theology creates and honors interconnective webs where differences are honored while a sustaining network of relationship is claimed.

Finally, feminist theologians are using imaginative reconstruction to good effect. Refusing to accept a "common sense" approach to theology, they help to demystify the fact that even common sense is a construction based on a certain worldview. Drawing both from their own experience and from their commitment to liberate people from oppression, poverty, and violence wherever and whenever it appears, feminist theologians construct new ways of thinking about familiar Christian symbols that bring a breath of fresh air into theology and religion. The symbols of the cosmos as the body of Godde, Jesus as wisdom (Sophia), and open table fellowship are particularly potent in this new construction.

THINKING OTHERWISE

Theologian Catherine Keller offers a useful summary of the overall contributions of feminist theology to talk about Godde and religion.[152] She makes four points:

1. Feminist theology offers a willingness to be confused about language. As is obvious by the lack of common terminology even among feminists, language is still a problem, regarding Godde, gender, and sex. Contemporary Godde-talk still tends to be overwhelmingly male, with insistence on linear reason and achievement of certainty of content. In this context, feminist theology keeps pressing the fact that Godde is beyond language, that our existing language has become idolatrous, and that feminism can-

not and does not offer a single alternative. It is tempting to seek something certain, clear, and universal, even though in today's world, such notions are of dubious value. Feminist theology resists that temptation, instead urging that willingness to be confused is an appropriate response to an ever emergent mystery.

2. Feminist theology includes a conviction that divinity incarnated is not singular but pancarnal. That is to say that an embodied divinity reveals something about the nature of all reality, not only about Jesus Christ. The incarnation of Godde in Jesus points to the reality that Godde is embodied in all the flesh of the world. Divinity is in intimacy with all bodies, even sparrows. This is not pantheism, because Godde can't be reduced to the totality of bodies, and is not reduced or contained at all, even by our language. Fundamentally, Godde is possibilities seeking embodiment, and the optimum human response is to accept and enjoy the present (necessarily incomplete) forms of divine embodiment rather than waiting for some sort of final purity.

3. Godde is in personal relationship with embodied possibilities. The divine reality is not some abstraction beyond human reach, but in some incomprehensible way chooses to be in direct relationship with each and all in creation. This seems to insult our rational faculties, and is hard to think through, even by feminists. Yet even as certainty eludes thought, possibilities keep opening for relationship.

4. The goal of feminist theology is to continue liberating the eros, the erotic love of Godde, into a community of love that works for justice, creation, and abundance. The erotic love of Godde is beyond human capacity, but is nonetheless poured out whenever and wherever it is not blocked. Love does not ask reciprocity, but does ask action, generosity, and thankfulness.

Keller's observations expand and illumine the meaning of an erotic mythic archetype as foundational to feminist theology. They also raise a problem associated with that archetype. A culture steeped in scientism with its tendency to literalism is eager for proof; it wants certainty and clarity of thought. The erotic myth can seem a bit indecisive in its reluctance to make firm assertions about God and the "rules" of relationship with Godde. The fact is that, at the archetypal level, nothing is finally clear or certain.

There is no real proof for any of the central assumptions of the hero myth; and the central assumptions of the erotic myth actually encourage a movement away from certainty. If, as seems necessary by definition, Godde is always more than language can express or mind can encompass, the most appropriate way to relate to Godde is humbly and provisionally. Feminist theology is destabilizing, and intends to be.

Feminist theology is closely related to the movement of postmodernism, which is explored more fully in the next chapter. For feminism, the postmodern perspective brings both strengths and problems. Feminist theology rightly builds on the shifts in perspective brought by what Fiorenza calls deconstruction and postmodernism's "corrections" of modernity's reliance on reason and progress: (1) the aesthetic corrective stressing "experiential concreteness and intuitive imagination over rationalist abstraction;" (2) the cultural correction insisting on cultural autonomy with its corresponding valuing of the particularity and nonuniversality of any tradition; and (3) the political corrective asserting that reason is always shaped by position and perspective, that is to say, by power issues.[153]

However, as is true for any field of the humanities concerned with exploring alternative ways of thinking about possibilities for truth, deconstruction is ultimately not a satisfactory place for feminist theology to stand, because in itself, deconstruction has no tools to speak about values or ethics. Feminism, like postmodernism itself, tends to be stuck at the point of reconstruction. Reconstruction requires some concept of how to speak about values. It must move beyond the limits of a postmodernity that refuses generalities and emphasizes particularities, a philosophy that disregards unifying themes in favor of discrete and separated parts. How might feminism do this while remaining credible in the academy?

I propose that feminist theology be more explicit about the mythic erotic archetype undergirding its work, the archetype I call a feminist vision. The concept of myth as a people's tacit understanding of the sacred and the way ultimate truths touch human experience means that living myths are seldom visible to those who live them.[154] Bringing mythic material to the forefront of awareness may be painful, and taking seriously the need or desire to cocreate a new mythic vision may require a kind of dying to deeply cherished but no longer life-giving convictions. The myth of the hero is one of those once-cherished convictions, now deeply embedded in the archetypal levels of Western culture, to the extent that Christian theology has often been interwoven with this myth of the hero, identifying Jesus with an image of the rational heroic ego.

A mythic approach to feminist theology effectively strengthens theology's capacity to challenge the powerful but mostly unconscious cultural mythic hero archetype. At a mythic level, one can speak of truths deeper than facts, exploring alternative ways to know Godde and to structure human life. Such a challenge is not designed to produce new theological certainties, but rather to destabilize any concept of theological certainty and baptize imaginations to genuinely new possibilities for theology. Reconstruction in theology involves, if not requires, imagination, but as yet there is no adequate theory about what makes imagination a reliable communal process, and this is a concern both for feminist theology and for imagination as described above. In the quest for an adequate theory for credible constructive work, both feminist theology and imagination are also linked to the next chapter of this book. There the problem of whether and how it is legitimate to speak of values in a postmodern world is addressed in the philosophical work of the twentieth-century philosopher Paul Ricoeur.

Chapter 3

The "Open" Philosophy of Paul Ricoeur

Beauty appears—becomes!
Loveliness takes residence where mini-worlds combine.
At this moment in my garden, one rose enters my awareness.
"Lovely!" I exclaim spontaneously...
Maybe this petalled beauty offers up itself
in newly existing space
shared by a flower and me—
a space unprovable to those in whom a whiff of doubt objects;
yet in a realm that's very real—I dare be confident to claim—
as I let the universe expand beyond my centered self.

"Merging Worlds" in *Entering the Mystery*
by Douglas C. Vest

IS THERE SOMETHING BEYOND?

This book sets forth new foundations for theology in the present age, an age in which theology tends to be constrained by the dominant existing myth of the rational heroic ego. Imagination is offered as a mythic alternative to rationality, and a feminist vision as an alternative to the heroic. This chapter on philosopher Paul Ricoeur addresses the "ego" element of the dominant Western myth, by setting forth a credible place for "soul" in philosophy, theology, and myth.

If the issue of chapter 1 is how the human experience of Godde is shaped by a valuing of rationality to the exclusion of imagination, and the issue of chapter 2 is how that experience is deformed by a

106

predominantly heroic and masculine notion of divinity, the issue of this chapter is whether anything meaningful can be spoken or understood about Godde, soul, and human values. Or, in the terms with which chapter 2 ended, how can postmodernity get to reconstruction from its deconstructive beginnings.

Theology has always sought to make the gospel relevant to the contemporary world, which means today it must engage the postmodern world of uncertainty and ongoing change. Although the two previous components of this mythic composite lens, the imaginal and feminism, are emerging anew in a postmodern context, they rely on values that by their nature are synthetic and beyond the reach of empirical measurement, as of course does theology itself. If the aims are to talk about values, to bring meaning into dialogue with empiricism, and to develop a religious language that is relevant to Western culture, this will only be persuasive in the postmodern conversation with a sound philosophical foundation. Because philosophy is a way of talking about the basic structures that shape our human capacities to exist, to think, to know, and to interact with the world, it has no less importance in shaping human life and thought than scientific discoveries about the physical world.

Paul Ricoeur provides the essential philosophical foundation for theological reconstruction in a mythic mode. Ricoeur significantly advances theology's task by establishing a conceptual basis for continual renewal of imagination and the life-giving spiritual energy of eros in our world. His open philosophy, technically called phenomenological hermeneutics, is a credible and persuasive response to the deconstructive orientation of the postmodern worldview.

Postmodernity eludes definition, in part because it emphasizes fluidity in thought. Commentators may treat postmodernism as the source of all things problematic, or alternatively as the saving grace for the contemporary world. Essentially postmodernity emerges in reaction to the glowing expectations of progress and the confidence in reason and order characteristic of early modernity. The term *postmodern* was first used in Lyotard's 1984 book called *The Postmodern Condition: A Report on Knowledge*, in which he declares that all "master stories" have come to their end.[1] In particular, this declaration often takes the form given it by Langdon Gilkey: "God and metaphysics 'died' in the West in approximately the same half century."[2] Ontology, the study of being itself, tends to be eclipsed in postmodernity, because of wariness of making any generalizations about being, human or divine. Postmodernists tend instead to emphasize the study of knowledge (epistemology), endeavoring to determine how it is that we know anything.

Postmodernism is a diffuse scholarly tradition, arising from several fields, including literary criticism, art, and philosophy. One way to think of it is as a way of looking at the world that emphasizes playfulness and differences over rules and sameness; it stresses the metaphoric and slippery nature of language over the modernist, objective factual understandings of how communication proceeds; it addresses the manner in which meaning is not something possessed by a word, an action, or an object as much as it is the product of a series of relations that comprise the word or the object.[3]

Postmodernism can be characterized by at least three central features: the celebration of difference; the belief that many interpretations are possible, and that every interpretation serves a particular point of view; and the rejection of overall or referential absolutes in favor of an interest in the internal relations in a specific context, such as a sentence or a myth. To use Doniger's metaphoric images, postmodernism is more interested in the microscope than the telescope: "Through the microscope end…we see the thousands of details that each culture uses."[4]

The movement of the postmodern is away from (what is seen as artificially imposed) universalism and toward separation and fragmentation. This emphasis on detail characteristic of each culture or position does honor viewpoints that in the past have been muted if not muzzled, and the play of opinions is celebrated. But much of the energy of postmodernity to date has been focused on deconstructing the presumed overarching modes of order characteristic of modernity. The question for a re-visioned theology is how to honor what such deconstruction has attained while moving toward an affirmation of connectedness among disparate groups and different points of view. Richard Kearney observes the danger of a distinctly postmodern preoccupation with *alterity* (otherness) that is unable "to acknowledge a difference between self and other without separating them so schismatically that *no* relation at all is possible."[5]

Religion is particularly hard-hit by the challenges of post-modernity, not only because religious elites have used religious structure to further their own power positions, but also because the literal way many modern people seem to conceive Godde and faith is alien to postmodern sensibilities. Sigmund Freud is one of the first major figures to bring a serious deconstructionist challenge to religion, and Ricoeur views him as a founder of the "school of suspicion" in "opposition to a phenomenology of the sacred."[6] Suspicion is a useful tool for deconstruction, but a poor one for construction. Post-modernity brings significant gains to the search for wisdom, but overall it has been committed to an analytic and separatist perspective uncongenial to religion. In contrast, Ricoeur endeavors to balance the hermeneutics of suspicion characteristic of postmodernity with a reconstructive posture grounded in the multiple meanings of symbol and myth.

In his constructive philosophy Ricoeur does not tend to use the term *postmodernity*; more commonly he speaks of structuralism, deconstruction, or a hermeneutics of suspicion. His strategy in addressing these positions is consistently to take the insights seriously, to understand them as deeply and thoroughly as possible, to claim those insights as valuable in the goal of advancing knowledge. Ricoeur engages his "opponents" on their own ground, affirming the strengths they bring to the conversation, and only then moves on to consider and demonstrate what elements might be absent in the position he is studying. Thus his work advances by dialectical engagement with an apparently opposing point of view in a process whereby both positions (his own and the other) are changed or influenced in each engagement (which is a thoroughly postmodern method!).

In Ricoeur's twentieth-century philosophy, one consistently finds openness toward mystery and its ongoing role in human life. Ricoeur creates his philosophy poetically, that is, round-about, repetitively, using memory and imagination as tools, just as the deep psyche moves in its encounters with the sacred. Without limiting or literalizing the form(s) of mystery, Ricoeur offers a philosophical foundation always open to the presence of something mysterious and beyond human comprehension.

REFLECTIVE PHILOSOPHY UNDER CONSTRUCTION

As a twentieth-century Frenchman, Ricoeur works in the philosophical tradition emerging from Descartes's simple formula, *I think therefore I am.* "The separate self, conscious of itself and of its own distinctness from a world 'outside' it, is born in the Cartesian era. It is a psychological birth—of 'inwardness,' of 'subjectivity,' of 'locatedness' in space and time."[7] What is now usually considered the natural way to think of oneself and one's presence in the world—as a separate and enclosed mind aware primarily of oneself and connecting to other things only through reason and perception—was birthed in Descartes's seventeenth-century affirmation. Western philosophical thought in the centuries since then has largely expanded this basic notion of the centrality of the self as the subject of philosophical speculation, if not of experienced reality. Ricoeur calls this tradition the philosophies of the subject.

Reflective (or reflexive) philosophy focuses on human reflection on self and its relation to world, and is strongly skeptical about idealism or abstract and other-worldly propositions, in particular about the concept of a universal Godde. Although Ricoeur is a lifelong Christian, he commits to constrain himself "not to mix genres...adhering to the notion of a philosophy without any absolute."[8] In philosophy, he will not speak of or call upon any notion of Godde. He turns instead to a poetic mode, which may evoke mystery without the need to name or describe it.

I believe that the underlying issue that motivates much of Ricoeur's work is *the question of the subject,* or *of the self.* While Ricoeur often takes up a particular subject matter such as psychoanalysis or linguistic structuralism as the vehicle for analysis, he returns again and again to the implications for the cogito postulated by Descartes. Although that self will experience many changes in engagement with the challenges of the twentieth century, Ricoeur is not defensive as he engages questions to the reflective self. Acknowledging, for example, that psychoanalysis poses major challenges to the autonomy of the self, he responds: "reflective philosophy is invited, not to remain intact by warding off enemy assaults, but rather to take support from its adversary, to ally itself with that which most challenges it."[9]

Psychoanalysis

Ricoeur's engagement with Freud and psychoanalysis illumines both how he allies himself with adversaries and how the cogito-self of the reflective tradition is changed by that alliance. Ricoeur turns his attention to Freud because of his perception that psychoanalysis directly challenges the philosophies of the self in a displacement of the subject itself. Engaging this adversary, Ricoeur devotes himself to the study of Freud, approaching Freud's work with the view that the primary hermeneutical (interpretive) issue in Freud is "the relations involved between manifest and latent meaning."[10] Ricoeur has long been aware that language, symbols, and experience are characterized by multiple meaning possibilities, and thus always require interpretation. But Freud, Marx, and Nietzsche all take the position that illusory surface meanings are presented in order to hide deeper (and less noble) meanings. Freud proposes that the surface self is hiding its erotic desires; Marx that the surface self is hiding its greed for economic power; and Nietzsche that the surface self is hiding an emptiness where the soul should be by inventing a game about god. Exploring the range of these challenges, Ricoeur is troubled that "there is no general hermeneutics, no universal canon for exegesis, but only disparate and opposed theories concerning the rules of interpretation."[11] In particular, the hermeneutics of suspicion, an exercise designed to reduce data to its bare skeleton, takes up "the problem of the Cartesian doubt, to carry it to the very heart of the Cartesian stronghold. The philosopher trained in the school of Descartes knows that things are doubtful...but he does not doubt that consciousness is such as it appears to itself."[12]

Ricoeur engages Freud because he thinks it a mistake to consider only the negative impact of a hermeneutics of suspicion; he wants to assimilate its positive value for the art of interpretation

itself. Ricoeur sees the possibility of extending the notion of consciousness (beyond the immediate self) by taking Freud's suspicion
seriously.[13] So he divides his assessment of Freud into an analytic—
a close reading of Freud's work as such—and a dialectic, where he
endeavors to interpret Freud philosophically. Through the course
of three successive readings of Freud in the analytic, Ricoeur finds
that the conflict of interpretation between meaning and suspicion
is not as stark as originally presumed, but that in order to come to
common ground, each cycle of Freud's development must first be
considered separately to do justice to it.

THE ANALYTIC READINGS

The first reading of Freud intends a natural science and establishes the topography associated with the interpretation of dreams
and neurotic systems, a topography using the language of *unconscious, preconscious,* and *consciousness.*[14] Ricoeur explores how
these concepts gradually become a metaphoric or symbolic way of
describing inner psychic processes. Increasingly, psychoanalysis
focuses on deciphering symptoms that are presumed to be linked to
underground connections. This deciphering work is, of course, a
hermeneutics, an interpretive schema that Ricoeur calls a "seman-
tics of desire."[15]

As clinical practice reveals more dynamic aspects of the
"underground," Freud begins to use the term *unconscious* less as an
adjective and more as a noun.[16] The patient's resistance to material
emerging from the unconscious (a noun) suggests that becoming
conscious involves "a transgression, a crossing of a barrier."[17] The
sense of self-consciousness that philosophy has regarded as simple
self-awareness is understood in psychoanalysis as a complex play of
instincts and instinctual aims on the surface of consciousness.[18] This
forces Ricoeur's admission that *"The question of consciousness is
just as obscure as that of the unconscious."*[19] The implication is that
Descartes's cogito does not know itself as it thinks it does, but is perhaps merely engaged in a narcissism of self-delusion.

Ricoeur's second, deeper analytic reading examines Freud's
extension of his ideas to the sphere of culture. Here the earlier
language of unconscious and conscious is superseded by another

model, that of *ego, id, superego*. Ricoeur insists that Freud's engagement in culture is not accidental but a move that "shows the real intentions" of psychoanalysis as a scheme capable of interpreting culture at large.[20] The instinctual factor of the id is confronted by the superego whose province is culture's expectations internalized within the psyche, a province that Freud calls the "reality" factor. Psychoanalytic interpretive work becomes more complex, as it is required to deal with the interactions and confrontations of desire and authority *within* a person, or what might be called "the debate between the pleasure-unpleasure principle and the reality principle."[21]

The insight at play here is that the unconscious is not only the province of the repressed wishes of the id, but also of the repressed demands of the superego or the internalization of society's rules.[22] Elements of "morality" such as self-observation, conscience, and believed ideals are no less subject to the deformations of the unconscious and its defenses than are the pressures of sexual appetite. At issue is the ego's force or weakness and its formation in relation to what Freud calls "the harshness of life," a code phrase for the helplessness of the ego in its primal situation of subjection to the multiple demands of the unconscious.[23] The desires of the id, matched with the repressions of the superego, place the ego in a position of fear comparable with its position of desire, so that together fear and desire are the twin motives of psychic intention.

Religion in particular comes under attack in Freud's analysis of culture, for he defines it as a representation to which no reality corresponds, merely an apparent crutch or solace in the face of life's conflicting demands.[24] But Ricoeur sees the real issue as how religious ideas function (or do not) "in balancing the renunciations and satisfactions through which man tries to make his harsh life tolerable."[25] Ricoeur observes that the brilliance of Freud's system is also its limitation—it *is* interpretation from first to last, and Freud is disinterested in other possible interpretations, such as the possible positive functions of imagination.[26] In contrast, Ricoeur understands imagination not primarily as making present something absent or unreal, but more significantly as a means to make real truths normally hidden in the dream world and the cosmos.[27]

The third cycle in Ricoeur's analytic reading of Freud reveals the symbolic and mythological foundations in psychoanalysis itself, as Ricoeur examines the major revisions effected by the introduction of the death instinct. Death receives the mythical name Thanatos, and the id "changes meaning and receives the mythical name of Eros."[28] The reality principle unfolds "a whole hierarchy of meaning that goes under the equally mythical name of Ananke" (necessity).[29] Myths evoke their own allies, and the connections with Ananke as destiny in Greek theatre, as nature in Renaissance philosophy, and as "eternal return" in Nietzsche begin to open Freud's earlier formulation of the reality principle to new possibilities of wisdom.[30] Whereas Freud began with ideas about natural energy, it is clear that he is now working with interpretive concepts about meaning.

Freud's hypothesis of the death instinct sets limits on the validity of the pleasure principle.[31] The instinct toward death is revealed in inertia, the compulsion to repeat, and in destructiveness. The introduction of death as an "instinct" allows us to see its relation to necessity (Ananke), and to realize how profoundly Eros (life, sexuality) is the factor that resists death. Now psychoanalysis acknowledges a dualism of instinctual forces, overlapping each other and confronting each other at every turn.[32] Culture itself is situated between these two great mythic forces, Thanatos and Eros. But the death instinct is a problem for Freud, for it involves *direct speculation* about the instincts (rather than simply clinical observation of the effects of instincts). This shift to direct speculation is inherently mythical.[33]

Ricoeur is also interested in the reality principle and its role in psychoanalysis, because he sees it as a single function that is engaged both in reality-testing and in a process of becoming conscious.[34] In contrast with the relatively simple regressions of the pleasure principle, "the reality principle is the long and hard path; it entails renunciation and mourning over archaic objects."[35] This interaction of desire and a sort of reality "discipline" with its orientation toward the other and the world gives the ego an openness and possibility that are also found in the polyvalent nuances of language and myth.

Ricoeur frames Freud's conceptual structure as a way of posing "in systematic terms its central problem: how the sublime arises

114

within desire."[36] When a psyche moves from narcissism to subli-
mation, a new self-detachment is possible in relation to the world.[37]
The strength of the ego now can be seen not in its ability to dominate but to mediate, to effect conciliation or diplomacy among
competing claims, some of which may be progressive as well as
regressive. Ricoeur calls this shift in the functioning of the reality
principle a "prudence" principle, "opposed to the false idealism of
the superego, to its destructive demands" and names this emergent
prudence function "the ethics of psychoanalysis."[38] When the ego
functions in this way, it plays a very similar role to that of the ana-
lyst, not judging, but paying attention to and introducing interaction with the real world. Ricoeur observes that the suspension of
value judgments as the basic step toward self-knowledge is very
similar to the foundational principle of phenomenology.[39] The analytic has revealed the way in which the interpretive schemas of psychoanalysis and Ricoeur's open philosophy begin to converge.

DIALECTIC AND EVALUATION

However, there are divergences as well as similarities between
the two interpretive schemes, which Ricoeur addresses as he moves
to his dialectic and evaluation of psychoanalysis. Given his orientation to the cogito and the reductionist impact of psychoanalysis,
Ricoeur must address the question, What must the subject of
(philosophical) reflection be if it is likewise to be the subject of psychoanalysis? Freud himself is not interested in the philosophical
subject; in psychoanalysis "the *ego* of the *cogito sum* has escaped
each time."[40] But "psychoanalysis has in no way eliminated consciousness and the ego; it has not replaced the subject but dis-
placed it."[41]

After Freud, the subject can no longer see itself as innocently
as it once did; the task of self-reflection has become the necessity
of a long journey through self-awareness. The great value of psychoanalysis is to challenge the immediate consciousness of the
cogito. Freud has revealed that consciousness is not a given but a
task.[42] Ricoeur acknowledges:

> I understand the Freudian metapsychology as an adven-
> ture of reflection; the dispossession of consciousness is

its path, because the act of becoming conscious is its task. But it is a wounded Cogito that results from this adventure—a Cogito that posits itself but does not possess itself; a Cogito that sees its original truth only in and through the avowal of the inadequacy, illusion and lying of actual consciousness.[43]

Psychoanalysis has dealt a blow to the subject of reflective philosophy, but in a sense, it is a welcome blow, for it results in a more authentic self-awareness.

Ricoeur calls psychoanalysis an "archeology of the subject," acknowledging that this is not one of Freud's concepts, but that it forms the basis for Ricoeur's own understanding of Freudianism.[44] In Ricoeur's view, Freudianism is like an archeological project, and that metaphor for psychoanalysis clearly suggests that there may be other work to do apart from what is necessary to clear the ground. In suggesting what that work might be, Ricoeur compares Freud's insights with those of St. Paul, Luther, and others in their critique of "existence under the law."[45] The law, no less than the self, must be critiqued, because naïve idealism is a trap, and morality without self-reflection and compassion too often becomes mere self-justification. Human ideals, religion, the whole panoply of human aspirations—all these must also bear critique. Yet there is a difference between critique and dismissal. The human self cannot be separated from the search for meaning simply because it is sometimes self-deluding.

So Ricoeur matches Freud's archeology with what he calls a teleology. In other words, the "past" of the cogito is to be linked with its possible "futures." It is not enough for the subject to discover the inadequacy of its own immediate self-awareness, because the fullness of human being requires response to a sense of *telos* (purpose). "The subject must also discover that the process of 'becoming conscious,' through which it *appropriates* the meaning of its existence as desire and effort, does not belong to it, but belongs to the *meaning* that is formed in it."[46] Consciousness has a trajectory that is not limited to the experience of what the ego can construct. Despite discouragement and even failure, the human subject continues to be called beyond itself by the very nature of the process of living.

Even the move toward teleology or spirit requires a kind of dispossession of consciousness. New symbols and invitations continue to appear in subjective awareness that, when engaged beyond self-consciousness, lead finally to wisdom.[47] But it is not the ego, the will, or the grasping of some final content that animates this movement. The consciousness emerging from the teleological process that Ricoeur posits is not merely self-presence or an outside stability, but is rather a capacity to be in movement with and to some extent transformed by the spirit.[48] Ricoeur's unfolding construction of a new reflective philosophy involves an internal dialectic between what he calls archeology and teleology. It is rooted in the mystery of manifest and latent meaning inherent in language and symbol, as well as the necessity of sustained engagement with multiple meanings and interpretive strategies. Ricoeur's response to Freud's hermeneutics of suspicion honors its wisdom while extending it toward reconstructive work, expanding its capacity to speak for its values as well as against what it deplores.

Self, Symbol, and Metaphor

Acknowledging that the self, the cogito, is no longer innocent, Ricoeur sees that it is important to move more deeply into self-awareness, beyond superficial stories that cover deeper truths. At the same time, he shows there is more to the self than the reductions of the masters of suspicion; the human self is also an aspiration, always transcending itself. What the self hides is not merely its dirty little secrets, but also its transformative longings. Humans cannot be reduced to their failures and limitations and then be put back together again merely as the remainder of those reductions. Rather it is possible to move from a first innocence, through an awareness of flaws and inadequacies, as well as awareness of our aspirations, and thus to a "second naiveté," conscious and chosen.[49]

The possibility of a second naiveté rests to some extent on the way the world itself is constructed. The cosmos is not a closed system, with no new energy coming from outside. Ricoeur compares the cosmos to a poem, quoting Mallarmé's definition of a poem as "chance conquered word by word."[50] Continuing, Ricoeur says that "To understand a poem means for the reader to overcome in turn the fortuitous appearance and to rediscover, not necessarily by understanding but by poetic sensitivity, the 'spirit of the song beneath the text.'...the network of relations and correspondences which constitute the 'glitter beneath the surface' in the poem."[51] In light of that network of relations and correspondences, Ricoeur urges that the philosophical revolution centering the world on the cogito needs to be completed by displacing the center of reference to Transcendence.[52] The Cartesian phrase, *Cogito, ergo sum* (I think, therefore I am) is not a logical connection: "it is a paradox encroached upon by a feeling of mystery."[53] Transcendence and mystery are not to be understood as a fixed and homogeneous substance that can be known by philosophy.[54] Both emerge in relation to sensitive inquiry. Cosmos as well as consciousness is open to ever-new *possible worlds*, a term Ricoeur uses to refer to the "ensemble of references opened up by every kind of text, descriptive or poetic, that I have read, understood, and loved....What we understand first in discourse is not another person, but...the outline of a new way of being in the world."[55]

Ricoeur's confidence in these realities is expanded through his exploration of language and myth. From the beginning, Ricoeur has experienced reservations about the self-enclosure of the reflective tradition he inherits. His early work on human fallibility and evil causes him to "introduce into the circle of reflection the long detour by way of the symbols and myths transmitted by the great cultures....The critique of reflexive consciousness receives a compensation in the prospective function performed in all great cultures by the symbolic language of mythical narratives."[56] Ricoeur finds that he cannot speak of the self without considering mythic narratives and symbols that shape the culture in which the self emerges. In this assessment, he approaches myth very much as a depth psychologist might—that the great symbols and stories frame human culture and set limits on self-understanding. However, he finds that symbols and myths always bear a surplus of meaning, lending themselves to varying interpretations. Thus it is crucial to investigate these stories and symbols for their meaning-rich capabilities, if an adequate understanding of self and cosmos is to be found.

SURPLUS OF MEANING

Ricoeur realizes that *a reconstructive philosophy begins its work with the leftover surplus of meaning,* when a hermeneutics of suspicion finishes its work. Whereas some philosophers believe language and myth are self-enclosed, with no external reference, Ricoeur notices that when they complete their analysis, a residue of meaning remains containing ingredients that are dynamically present in the event of language or myth. Ricoeur observes that "In the phenomenon of the sentence, language passes outside itself; reference is the mark of the self-transcendence of language."[57] The reference or referential function of a sentence or a myth is the world that opens in front of it and is received by the reader or hearer of the narrative.

Ricoeur realizes that he is moving toward an integration of his phenomenological method with a hermeneutical (interpretive) approach. As with his work on Freud, Ricoeur acknowledges that in complex human culture, there will be an inevitable conflict of interpretations between several points of view. Ricoeur's aim is the development of a theory that will account for such conflicts while revealing a surplus of meaning that gives legitimacy to something beyond a reductionist approach. At this point he defines symbol and the art of hermeneutics in terms of each other. First, he defines *symbol* as "any structure of signification in which a direct, primary, literal meaning designates, in addition, another meaning which is indirect, secondary and figurative and which can be apprehended only through the first."[58] By definition, the symbol has a literal meaning *and* a meaning or meanings beyond the literal.

Then, Ricoeur defines the concept of *interpretation* as "the work of thought which consists in deciphering the hidden meaning in the apparent meaning, in unfolding the levels of meaning implied in the literal meaning."[59] The art of interpretation involves the recognition of more than one meaning, and an effort to unfold some of those meanings. These two definitions give Ricoeur the structure he needs in order to have a common playing field encompassing a hermeneutics of suspicion, a hermeneutics of linguistic abstraction, and a hermeneutics of meaning.

Further, this logic of surplus meaning enables Ricoeur to say that "Reduction is only the inverse, the negative side, of a wanting-to-say which aspires to become a wanting-to-show."[60] The principle of a logic of surplus meaning is incorporated within his reconstructed philosophy of reflection, although Ricoeur understands full well that there are consequences for the cogito. The graft of hermeneutics onto phenomenology "changes the wild stock!...By joining these multivocal meanings to self-knowledge we profoundly transform the problematic of the *cogito*."[61] Genuine reflective philosophy must be one of critique, not merely the naive acceptance of the vanity and emptiness of false consciousness. "The cogito can be recovered only by the detour of a decipherment of the documents of its life."[62] Now subjectivity must always be interpreted, both with suspicion and with respect for meaning. Interpretation necessarily involves an exploration of the narratives and myths not only of personal history but also of the culture.

SEMANTIC INNOVATION

As Ricoeur plays with the concept of language and symbol as bearers of literal as well as additional meanings, he turns to a particular kind of linguistic symbol, that of the metaphor. Metaphor is a semantic impertinence: it suggests a resemblance embodying a tension between identity and difference. Metaphor does the unexpected and the unsettling. For example, when Jesus calls Peter his "rock," it is initially startling, because Peter has been anything but steady and stable. The key to metaphor is thus not primarily its form or even its sense, but rather "the *reference* of the metaphorical statement as the power to 'redescribe' reality."[63] With its trajectory toward a reference beyond itself, metaphor introduces creativity into language. Ricoeur proposes a phenomenological principle here, that "the suspension of literal reference is the condition for the power of second-degree reference, which is properly poetic reference."[64] In other words, in order fully to appreciate the semantic innovation of metaphor, one must be willing temporarily to suspend or bracket literal comprehension. In the example of Jesus and Peter, Jesus is not literally saying Peter is a rock, but by offering the metaphor, he asks his listeners to look deeper, to push beyond literal comprehension to see what he sees in Peter, something deeper and more permanent than the obvious. Religious reference, like poetic language, relies heavily on metaphor, and the implication is that the full possibilities of such language atrophy unless one is able to suspend an impulse to remain at the literal level of understanding.

The suspension of the first, literal meaning is the springboard into another, qualitatively different, mode of reference. "Is not the function of poetry to establish another world—another world that corresponds to other possibilities of existence, to possibilities that would be most deeply our own?...The entire strategy of poetic discourse plays on this point."[65] Metaphor by its nature intends to disrupt the literal level of perception and communication so that innovation in meaning emerges. In a similar way, one could say that myth reveals truth deeper than any facts can convey. The natural surplus of meaning in symbol, language, and myth means potentially that new truths can be discovered each time such richly potent sources are re-visited. Something new comes into existence as one engages the metaphor—it can be said that the metaphor creates semantic innovation. Ricoeur's careful exploration of possibilities inherent in language and narrative supports an expanded and substantive role for the use of imagination, a feminist vision, and other dimensions of theological re-visioning. Ricoeur has indeed produced a credible way of thinking philosophically about interpretations that expand rather than reduce the evident and literal meanings of cultural and religious phenomena.

Even so, Ricoeur is aware that serious objections meet "the possibility that the metaphorical statement might aspire to truth value."[66] In a dense discussion of this problem, Ricoeur addresses issues that have arisen previously here, as for example in chapter one with questions about whether imagination is merely private fantasy. To counter that concern, Ricoeur proposes an alternative to "a romantic and psychologizing conception of hermeneutics."[67] Without a philosophical theory about the structure of physical as well as metaphysical reality, it can be easy to dismiss humanist theories. But Ricoeur cannot be satisfied with a permanent bracketing of external reality, for his philosophical community, now under the dominant influence of "scientific aims," can and will dismiss out of hand a romantic and psychologizing hermeneutics. Indeed, most fields of inquiry nowadays utilize this postulate to decide on the meaning of truth and reality: "there is no truth beyond the pale of possible verification (or falsification), and that in the last analysis all verification is empirical, as defined by scientific procedure."[68] So Ricoeur is at pains to show that semantic innovation does indeed refer to experienced possibilities in the common world. At stake is not only semantic innovation but any evidence of nontangible creative presence in human experience. Such innovations and experiences cannot be demonstrated in the form of rigid and absolute certainties that are immutable for all time, but do exist as genuine possibilities that can be embodied in the active lives of real people.

Ricoeur affirms, "we are allowed to speak of metaphorical truth, but in an equally 'tensive' sense of the word 'truth.'"[69] The secret to metaphoric truth is the maintenance of the tension between "is not" and "is." One must not naively fall victim to the uncritical assumption that the "is not" is absent. While such naiveté might seem to be the usual stance of faith, Ricoeur suggests that faith might be conceived less in relation to literal truth and more in relation to the nuances of mysticism, whose ecstatic visions are incapable of being rendered precisely in language. Metaphoric truth expresses an opportunity to "participate in the totality of things via an 'open communion,'" as distinct from adherence to once-for-all doctrinal statements.[70] Ricoeur uses the term *tensive aliveness* as a way of emphasizing the vital rather than the logical aspect of metaphoric truth.[71] He insists that tensive aliveness is an apt description not only of semantic innovation but also describes an ontological reality, the presence of being that nevertheless only reveals itself "partially, ambiguously, and through symbolic indirection."[72] Metaphoric truth leads both to discoveries of new dimensions of human being, and to encounter with the reality of being itself, not now conceived as substance but as dynamism.

A dialectic of metaphorical truth must nevertheless have a critical component. Here the work is not to mistake the metaphor for its reference. In a certain sense, metaphor is pretense, and if this is forgotten, the mask may be mistaken for the face. Critical vigilance is necessary, but it must be a certain kind of vigilance. Metaphor must be used consciously and reflectively. One must "include the critical incision of the (literal) 'is not' within the ontological vehemence of the (metaphorical) 'is.'"[73] Maintaining the tension that is inherent to metaphoric truth, Ricoeur suggests that both interpretation and ontological reflection (thoughts about Being itself) are expressed better in questioning than in asserting.[74]

Metaphor cannot be eliminated from language because "it is not in fact possible to present 'the literal truth,' to say 'what the facts are,' as logical empiricism demands."[75] Metaphoric language is precisely how one can speak of "those aspects of our being-in-the-world that cannot be talked about directly."[76] Indeed, Ricoeur postulates that poetic language may actually "break through to a pre-scientific, ante-predicative level, where the notions of fact, object, reality and truth...are *called into question*."[77] Openness to the fullness of life requires "a second naiveté beyond iconoclasm."[78] And this form of truth is equally as compelling as scientific truth, one that forms a basis for a constructive contemporary philosophy and theology.[79]

ONESELF AS ANOTHER

Ricoeur's philosophy gradually shifts toward ontology (being itself) and away from the epistemology (knowledge acquisition) that has so occupied postmodern deconstruction. Postmodernity is interested mainly in how things can be known, because it is primarily interested in identifying the loci of multiple viewpoints. This deconstructive work has been beneficial in revealing the structures of power that minimize or disparage other perspectives. However, in its focus on epistemology, postmodernism reveals its own single-minded perspective, namely that Godde and metaphysics are no longer subjects worth serious discussion. An analytical bias tends to disparage synthesis, that is, the collection of themes into what seems a common pattern. And postmodernism tends to avoid ontology, that is, conversation

123

about the basic structures of being in the world. As Ricoeur returns to the question of the self, he finds himself focusing on the interconnections among provisional structures of being, linking Godde and the individual, cosmos and bios. No longer is the cogito freestanding and isolated. Oneself is inevitably another.

Self as Problem

Ricoeur's reflective philosophy, his philosophy of the self, has engaged major adversaries that challenge it. Ricoeur has also elaborated a notion of metaphorical truth that is an opening to the mystery that surrounds and indeed summons human persons. But in the process, the self itself has been changed; it is no longer the immediate, transparent, "innocent" self of Descartes's cogito. Consciousness, as Ricoeur observes, is no longer a given, but is now a task.[80] The self is a discovery, made in a series of painful encounters with its own deceptive tendencies. And yet at the level of mystery and paradox, "I no longer appear to myself as a *task*, as a project. I am a *problem resolved* as though by a greater wisdom than myself."[81] Life itself nourishes the self beyond the capacity of its own willing.

Thus, Ricoeur comes back to the problem of self now as a question of the self in relationship, for in some respects the self is inconceivable except in terms of its embeddedness in life, in relationship, in encounter with mystery. In Ricoeur's *Oneself as Another*, his hermeneutics of the self is at an equal distance from those who would overthrow the cogito altogether and from those who would defend it, since one position undervalues and the other overvalues the cogito. In contrast to both, Ricoeur sets up a dialectic between self and other-than-self, with the notion that a certain kind of otherness "can be constitutive of selfhood as such."[82] This is similar to the African concept of *ubuntu* mentioned earlier, the idea that "a person depends on other persons to be a person."[83] In *Oneself as Another*, Ricoeur challenges the immediacy and independence of the cogito and its claim to be the ultimate foundation of certainty, turning Descartes on his head. He equally challenges the disintegration of the self "pursued mercilessly by Nietzschean (and other) deconstruction."[84] Here Ricoeur engages, beyond his usual adversaries, the field of action theory, including the ethical and moral determinations of action related to the categories of the good and the obligatory. In this new conversational dialectic, Ricoeur speaks now of the acting and suffering individual. He postulates an essential connection between autonomy of the self, solicitude for the neighbor, and justice for every person,[85] demonstrating the relationships between self and world, self and other, self and mystery (or Godde). These concerns are clearly central to theology and bear implications for its re-visioning.

Ricoeur formulates an ontology—not a mere epistemology, which can reveal a preference to chart the safe place of speaking comfortably about knowledge acquisition—but a philosophy revealing the fundamental characteristics of being and of value, insofar as a closely worked dialectic can reveal them. He does not speak of being as having "substance," as did Plato, but rather employs the mode of Aristotle's polysemy (multiple dimensions) of being. Even against the backdrop of a radical plurality rooted in the many meanings of being, it is possible to speak of human action as a fundamental mode of being, as act and potentiality.[86] Such an ontology does not claim the kind of certainty to which the cogito once aspired—the certainty of scientific verification. Ricoeur's truth here rests in a logic of attestation or testimony—an expression of trust in oneself as capable of saying, acting, doing, and the ability to recognize oneself as a character in a narrative.

Sameness and Selfhood

For Ricoeur, the problem of personal identity constitutes "a privileged place of confrontation between the two major uses of the concept of identity," that is, identity as sameness (idem) and identity as selfhood (ipse).[87] From my point of view, Ricoeur does not quite make the distinctions I expected between the two terms: he says that idem identity means sameness and permanence in time, but he insists that ipse identity also relates to another kind of permanence in time, which is self-constancy or keeping one's word.[88] Idem is about what Ricoeur calls character, that is, the "what" of identity, one's acquired dispositions. Ipse is about keeping one's word, the "who" of identity, the ability to say "here I stand" even in the face of recognition that time will change things. Although Ricoeur does not say so directly, I believe that with these two terms, he intends to introduce the kind of tension revealed in his study of metaphor—a quality of divergence and discordance in the ipse that dances in dialectic with the sameness and convergence of idem. Such an intention does seem to be expressed in the observation that "with the question "who?" ...the self returns just when the same slips away."[89]

The interaction of discordance with concordance is also suggested by Ricoeur's test for the truth of the assertion of selfhood as attestation—not as a test of verification or falsification, but as a test of another order.[90] "Attestation can be defined as the *assurance of being oneself acting and suffering*,"[91] an affirmation somewhat reminiscent of the feminist experience of "hearing each other into speech."[92] Here Ricoeur adds another test for truth, alongside the already established tests of scientific empiricism and the tensive truth of metaphor: the truth of attestation. But he still must engage the question of whether and how subjectivity can include value stances in a postmodern reconstructive world, a question with immediate relevance to theology.

From Self-Respect to Self-Esteem

Now Ricoeur enters the realm of prescribing, an entry he acknowledges is "a radical break with all that precedes only in the tradition of thought stemming from (philosopher David) Hume, for which 'ought' is opposed to 'is.'"[93] Ricoeur moves away from the self-centeredness of the question "who?" into the arena of the impact or effect of action on others, using language of duty (obligation) and the good. He makes this decision because his unfolding concept of the self in relation requires philosophical thought on the nature of the relationships. The subject of *Oneself as Another* is a speaking and acting being, who by definition is "accessible to *precepts* which, in the form of advice, recommendation, and instruction, teach how to succeed—hence how to do well—in what one has undertaken."[94] While precepts may be technical, strategic, aesthetic, or otherwise, they can also be moral rules.

Ricoeur distinguishes between ethics and morality, a distinction of his own making. *Ethics*, for Ricoeur, refers to the aim of an accomplished life, while *morality* refers to "the articulation of this aim in norms characterized at once by the claim to universality and by an effect of constraint."[95] Ethics is similar to Aristotle's teleological perspective, a kind of response to an inner demand for integrity, and thus ethics has primacy over morality. Morality, as the visible and common articulation of rules, may seem more important than ethics, but it does not reach to the essence of being. As response to externally imposed standards, morality can represent only a partial fulfillment of the ethical aim. The impact on selfhood of fidelity to morality is self-respect, whereas the impact of fidelity to ethics is self-esteem. Taken together, "self-esteem and self-respect together will represent the most advanced stages of the growth of selfhood, which is at the same time its unfolding."[96]

The *ethical intention* is defined as *"aiming at the 'good life' with and for others, in just institutions."*[97] The good is that which draws the self always toward that which is beyond reach, expanding the self's inherent capacity, even as it satisfies the present desire. In making choices that shape life ideals as well as particular decisions, the agent gains a sense of "being the author of one's own discourse...of judging well and acting well in a momentary and provisional approximation of living well."[98]

While subjective reflexivity can seem to carry the danger of turning in upon itself, Ricoeur's thesis is that the good life *necessarily* involves being with and for others in solicitude. "Solicitude is not something added on to self-esteem from the outside but it unfolds the dialogic dimension of self-esteem."[99] Ricoeur's self is not Levinas's ego defined by the condition of separation, but is rather a being whose life is centrally mediated by others.[100] Ricoeur challenges the concept of individual self at the heart of the so-called natural law theory—a concept that establishes the individual's preferential right to be protected by law without any inherent reciprocal obligations. The individual and the society cannot be distinguished or separated, because the good life at which the individual aims necessarily involves others—not merely as a moral or legal obligation, but because of the nature of being itself. Just as a human is embodied in a physical body yet indisputably in the world, so humans are embodied in the social body

yet indisputably unique. Ricoeur strikes at the root of the separatist individualism that has come to characterize life in Western
democracies by evoking Aristotle's concept of friendship as the
bridge between the good life and justice.

Certainly it is possible through law to insist that persons be
"summoned to responsibility" by the other.[101] But this constitutes
only the norm of morality and not the standard of ethics Ricoeur is
urging. Solicitude bears "a more fundamental status than obedience
to duty: ...that of *benevolent spontaneity*, intimately related to self-
esteem within the framework of the 'good' life."[102] A generous and
nonmandatory response to the other is essential to self-esteem, as
well as a willingness to receive generosity from others. "To self-
esteem, understood as a reflexive moment of the wish for the 'good
life,' solicitude adds essentially the dimension of lack, the fact that we
need friends....the self perceives itself as another among others."[103]

These ideas move the reflective self of philosophy far from
Kant's prideful "emergence from self-inflicted immaturity" that
sought to build the entire world from the thinking self. Without
abandoning the tradition of reflexive philosophy altogether, he is
nonetheless constructing a new paradigm, moving away from the
individual-dominant ego toward a communally-embedded soul.
Ricoeur is guiding reflective philosophy in the direction of a real-
istic awareness of personal need and limitation, not as something
to be ashamed of but as something that links us to others. Ricoeur
has engaged the hermeneutics of suspicion in such a way as to be
acutely aware of the illusions of the self, but that experience has
not destroyed his confidence in humanity or culture. Step by step,
he is constructing a way to engage worlds beyond the known and
familiar patterns of self-interest. That construction begins with
awareness that self and friend need each other.

It is not enough, however, to define ethical relation to others
merely in terms of face-to-face relationships, for justice extends to
the life of institutions. Solicitude must be completed by equality.
Ricoeur defines an *institution* as "the structure of living together
as this belongs to a historical community," and suggests that it is
fundamentally organized around a bond of common mores rather
than constraining rules.[104] He evaluates the ethical status of an
institution by marking "the gap separating *power in common* and

domination."[105] Institutions are ethical when those who have power exercise it in common. Ricoeur maintains that *"Equality is to life in institutions what solicitude is to interpersonal relations."*[106] An individual's self-esteem is finally constituted by employing ethical standards by solicitude in face-to-face relationships and by equality in institutions.

Ricoeur shifts to a discussion of morality and its corresponding self-respect. While both ethics and morality aim at establishing reciprocity where there is lack of it, ethics is the affirmation for which morality is the prohibition.[107] Morality limits one's freedom in the treatment of others, while ethics evokes care beyond what is required. In contrast to ethics, where equality is the standard, the norms of morality imply a shift in the status of participants, "a dissymmetry that places one in the position of agent and the other in that of patient."[108] Were it not for this dissymmetry, there would be no need for legal and other normative constraints. The problem of dissymmetry suggests that morality in laws and norms cannot cover every eventuality, so inevitably a morality of obligation *will produce* "conflictual situations where practical wisdom has no recourse, in our opinion, other than to return to the initial intuition of ethics."[109] Morality can never take the place of ethics. But one need not therefore disavow morality, which serves the useful purpose of occasioning those conflicts that remind the self of its ethical calling.

Conflict and Self-Constancy

Why does morality inevitably lead to conflict? Ricoeur answers by turning to myth, specifically the myth of Antigone, expressed as dramatic tragedy by Sophocles. The myth is a reminder of the discordance that is part of every life, the unexpected shocks "capable of awakening our mistrust with respect not only to the illusions of the heart but also to the illusions born of the hubris of practical reason itself."[110] The tragic wisdom of Antigone's myth tests moral judgment in the unexpected and unforeseeable situation of the irruption of archaic and mythical energies, and invites meditation on the inevitable place of conflict in moral life.

In Sophocles' drama, Creon is the uncle of Antigone and Polynices, unfortunate children of the union of Oedipus and his mother. Polynices leads an army contesting Creon's governorship of Thebes. Creon defeats and kills his nephew, exposing the corpse as carrion for birds and dogs and refusing to allow its burial because Polynices challenged the safety and sanctity of the city-state. Antigone pleads that family blood should allow some leniency, but Creon is not moved. Placing family values above the interest of the city, Antigone throws a handful of dust on her brother's corpse, only to find herself arrested and sentenced to a living death by her uncle through imprisonment in a tomb. At the last minute, Creon decides to let Antigone live, but he is too late; she has committed suicide and Creon's family is destroyed as a result.[111]

Within the realm of morality, there is no solution to this conflict. Ricoeur shows how both Antigone and Creon, claiming to be sole authors of their lives, passionately draw lines between family and city-state that admit of no nuances, no exceptions. Inevitable collisions result from this one-sidedness. The possibility of reconciliation "rests on an actual renunciation by each party of his partiality and has the value of a pardon in which each is truly recognized by the other."[112] Ricoeur observes that the dramatic form of tragedy cannot produce such reconciliation; however comedy can, because it offers a vibrant and "lucid witness to the nonessentiality of goals that are mutually destructive."[113]

From these observations, Ricoeur proposes a hypothesis: "The source of conflict lies not only in the one-sidedness of the characters but also in the one-sidedness of the *moral principles* which themselves are confronted with the complexity of life."[114] This is an astonishing statement, and might at first seem dreadful to a religious mind. Yet in a sense, this is where serious reflection on the complexity of postmodern life must lead—to the awareness that moral principles themselves can be one-sided, producing destructive conflict. Nevertheless, Ricoeur does not propose to abandon morality either to arbitrariness (the "anything goes" spirit of some postmoderns), or to univocity (the one-sided classic position that he has just demolished). In between these two, Ricoeur places conviction.

What Ricoeur is exploring is the nature of selfhood in an organic gathering of women and men, where power is not exercised as domination.[115] In a situation of full equal power for all participants, consensus may be an impossibility. Yet this may be beneficial, if handled rightly. Ricoeur proposes that "democracy is not a political system without conflicts, but a system in which conflicts are open and negotiable in accordance with recognized rules of arbitration."[116] Where there is always a plurality of preferred values, the realization of any one set of values will no doubt be at the expense of another set, so that any equilibrium can only be temporary. At its best, democracy is "the system that accepts its contradictions to the point of institutionalizing conflict."[117] There is a place for the maxims of morality, standards that can be universalized, but these can only be regarded as the upright beams of a structure, not as its foundation. For a system founded on the presumption of conflict to be effective, the foundation must be formed by a mutual commitment in which individual persons agree to commit themselves to a shared humanity that is more sustaining than any particular set of rules.

At the core of such a commitment is what Ricoeur calls "self-constancy," which he describes as the personal principle corresponding to the communal principle of justice.[118] Self-constancy includes both an "obligation to maintain one's self in keeping one's promises" as well as "the desire to respond to an expectation, even to a request coming from another."[119] Self-constancy includes elements of self-esteem as well as solicitude and justice. The fidelity to another implied in self-constancy is called by Gabriel Marcel availability (*disponibilité*).[120] This is not the same kind of thing implied in a legal contract, in which the other has a right to expect something of a person. The energy of availability is quite different; it emerges from the self who says "'You can count on me.' This *counting on* connects self-constancy, in its moral tenor, to the principle of reciprocity founded in solicitude."[121] This is not a naïve solicitude, but a critical one, having "passed through the double test of the moral conditions of respect and the conflicts generated by the latter."[122]

Morality often claims universality for its norms, but in a complex world of plural identities, that claim will be surely be challenged on the basis of a wider ethical context within which that morality originally was formed. Minority communities that have

"lost" the last round of value conflicts will inevitably seek to destabilize the system so that a new and different realization of values can
be created in the present. And that pattern is continuous. If the present "winners" and "losers" do not understand that their contemporary norms are set within the broader context of an ethics of human
equality, conflict will escalate rather than move toward the current
reconciliation. Ricoeur makes clear that the principle of autonomy
cannot be given priority over the respect owed to persons nor to the
principle of justice in institutions. Specifically, Ricoeur makes the
claim that "the category of the most disadvantaged has to be taken
as the term of reference for all just distribution, and...the one who
receives my action—its potential victim—has to be respected as an
equal of the agent I am."[123] In a community of justice, there is a preferential option for the poor. And not only that, but those who give
and those who receive are regarded equally. The vision of community that emerges from these reflections on selfhood represents as
great a challenge to the myth of the rational heroic ego as does the
erotic mythic narrative offered in chapter two.

Starting from Descartes's cogito, Ricoeur has made a long
journey through the dimensions of the self. Ricoeur has always
insisted that the immediate and naive cogito of Descartes must
take a detour through various objectifying procedures. "The self
could return home only at the end of a long journey. And it is 'as
another' that the self returned."[124] In *Oneself as Another*, the self
reveals itself in turn as self-respect, self-esteem, and self-constancy,
and in all these aspects, in relationship with others. In the process,
much is also revealed about the nature of the world in which self
acts and suffers, for there is, at last, an ontology implicit in
Ricoeur's hermeneutics. That ontology is expressed in the certainty
of *attestation*, referring to "a plane at once epistemological and
ontological....Attestation is the assurance—the credence and the
trust—of *existing* in the mode of selfhood."[125] And attestation is
fundamentally about relationship, fully expressed only in the
notion of soul. Throughout this long journey, Ricoeur affirms,
despite the odds, that human creativity and imagination flourish in
the world, and that isolation, temporality, and discordance are
continuously penetrated by mutuality, infinity, and harmony. His

philosophy is always open toward inbreaking mystery and newness of life, not without suffering, but always with hope.

OPENNESS TO MYSTERY

Ricoeur engages one of the basic issues for postmodern philosophy: is it possible to "acknowledge a difference between self
and other without separating them so schismatically that *no* relation at all is possible?"[126] When reflective philosophy emphasizes
the isolated cogito and postmodern philosophy emphasizes analysis of diverse things, "how can we justify the principle of universalization itself, which alone enables us to reach agreement
through argumentation on practical questions?"[127] This is particularly a theological problem because theology rests on the postulate of an inherent relationship between the human and the
transhuman, however the divine is conceived, and this implies
some form of universalization.

Recall that Aristotle presented the task of epic myth as revealing "what is possible according to the laws or probability or necessity."[128] Ricoeur's constructive task for reflective philosophy is
similar. As against the dominant strains of twentieth-century philosophy, he must present an approach to philosophy that is at least
equally credible with those on which the rational heroic ego is
based. He must account for dissonance and discordant elements in
his philosophical perspective as well as supporting the human aspiration toward transcendence. So Ricoeur will not claim the discovery of new *substances* with fixed forms, either for the self or for
Godde. Instead he sets forth a process of dialectical engagement
that can be applied in all situations of apparently conflicting interpretations, resulting in creative new concepts of "what is possible."

One of Ricoeur's aims is the reuniting of science and religion, which throughout the twentieth century seem increasingly
to be separated. Science, or perhaps better technology, is beginning to function more and more like a religion, increasingly insisting that its way of seeing and interpreting the world is the only
valid way to do so, advocating the belief that anything unable to
be analyzed and measured does not really exist. This is under-

standable, given that in its infancy, science had to fight against institutional religion's insistence on its way of seeing and interpreting the world, the belief that anything not revealed by revelation and church tradition does not really exist. These two points of view are indeed a conflict of interpretations. However, both science and religion/myth speak to and about essential elements of human experience, it is at tremendous cost to the inner integrity of human soul that either perspective is denied. Unlike the ego, the soul is more like the Sufi *barzakh*, a sort of isthmus between the elements of life that are tangible and those that are intangible. The soul is the receptacle for the hints and echoes of the "more than," the home of mystical yearnings that express themselves in awe and wonder, suffering and delight. It is nourished both in the physical world and the metaphysical one.

In the late twentieth century, scientific terminology (that of explanation) tends to be in vogue, so building a bridge between science and religion needs to start from the scientific side (largely as articulated by postmodernism), and any movement toward the sacred must be presented in terms that respect the validity of core postmodern perspectives. One of Ricoeur's contributions is to point out that "scientism" is in fact a point of view, and that there are other legitimate ways of thinking about issues.

Fundamentally, Ricoeur does accept postmodernity's viewpoint that neither "transparent, autonomous subjectivity" for the self nor absolute knowledge of the world or Godde can ever be achieved; indeed, in many ways Ricoeur himself is postmodern. "Only by recognizing the various obstacles and opacities which the project of self-understanding encounters, and by thus resisting the facile solution of some 'absolute synthesis' of knowledge which would contrive to resolve prematurely the conflict of interpretations, can we achieve an authentic grasp of the role of human creativity and imagination."[129] Ricoeur engages in ongoing dialectic with aspects of postmodern or scientific thought because what they have to say is important, and because he hopes to gain them as allies in a reconstructive engagement with mythic and theological themes.

How does this reconstruction proceed? Ricoeur often observes that, looking back over his works, "he has a personal impression of discontinuity, while his interpreters have centered

their efforts on bringing out elements of continuity."[130] Ricoeur
sees most of his works as arising from a "residue left" by a previous work that offers a new challenge.[131] But Ricoeur himself
teaches that the author's intention is not necessarily the only or
even the most important factor in a text's meaning. In a sense the
contemporary reader, with the whole collection before her, is able
to observe connections that were not visible to the author during
the individual crafting of each work, although without a doubt she
also imposes her own questions in the discovery of continuities.

A pattern exists in all of Ricoeur's inquiry that may offer
more benefit for a mythic consideration of the soul and theology
than any specific content. He calls it the *procedure of the dialectic*. Rather than identify the scientific position of explanation as a
polar opposite to the religious position of understanding, Ricoeur
prefers to see them as partners in a "complex and highly mediated
dialectic."[132] The dialectic procedure in fact expresses the whole
process that Ricoeur means by the word *hermeneutics*, a process
that unfolds, in front of the text, symbol, or myth, "the 'world'
which it opens up and discloses."[133]

Using any text for example, the first step is a good guess
about what is important to the reader, what is especially noticed.
However, the self-aware reader knows that the guess needs to be
critiqued, seeking something more than a mere projection of the
reading self into the text. The next step of critique is not merely
an effort to demonstrate the correctness of the guess, but rather
to set it aside in order to be open to other possible interpretations.

The second step is called *distanciation*.[134] Here the inquirer is
looking both for the sense (the evident) and the reference of the text
(the claim of the text to reach reality, its truth value). Ricoeur
believes that any discourse is the projection of a world; the questions are what world is projected here, and can the inquirer
acknowledge the gift of that way of seeing? This inquiry is not limited to the author's intention, but also looks to what the text might
reveal beyond what was intended. What world is envisioned, imagined, projected here? This second step involves explanation and critique, but also goes further to an exploration of the projection of
possibilities in the text, what Ricoeur calls the world in front of the
text, a proposed world that could be inhabited by the reader.[135]

The third step Ricoeur calls *appropriation*, his translation of the German term *Aneignung*, meaning "to make one's own what was initially alien."[136] Having explored the possible worlds of the text, the reader has two options, either to place oneself outside the text, as an observer, or to endeavor to actualize the potential of the reference in one's own life. The text is seeking to engage the reader; shall she or he participate in its meaning, placing himself "*en route* toward the *orient* (direction) of the text?[137]

It does not require a great imagination to envision how to apply this process to any conflict, whether interpersonal, international, or academic. The concept is that both parties, both text and reader, both science and religion, are genuinely changed by such a dialectic encounter. In Ricoeur's philosophical method, a genuine dialectical engagement of opposing positions can bring critique to conviction, and from there establish "a *reflective equilibrium*."[138] For Ricoeur, conviction and critique, or universalism and particularity, are complementary rather than oppositional.[139] Ricoeur speaks of having a twofold reference for his life, "two legs" expressing philosophy and religion, both of which have engaged him all his life. He formulates this as "the relation between conviction and critique...yet philosophy is not simply critical, it too belonging to the order of conviction. And religious conviction itself possesses an internal, critical dimension."[140] The interplay of critique and conviction frames much of Ricoeur's work, and while he doesn't tend to speak of soul, it is fair to describe the cogito as it unfolds in Ricoeur's hands as the self of soul.

The reconstructive position articulated by Ricoeur includes acceptance of a world of radical complexity and polyvalence. Many points of view exist and have validity. Furthermore, any generalization is necessarily provisional, because fluctuating issues and relationships may require it to be revised at some future time. But all statements are subject to appropriate forms of logic applicable to human interpretation, whether those logical forms are of empirical verification, of probability, discovery, or attestation. The provisional quality of generalization applies also to statements about the nature of human soul and of Godde, which are necessarily partial because human perceptions of the sacred can only be partial. Creative imagination plays a crucial role in semantic innovation, especially when disciplined by the logics of probability and discovery. Conflicting interpretations are inevitable, and reconciliation can only be the result of a commitment to dialectical engagement, in which each is genuinely open to the position of another, so that both are changed by the encounter. Tensive vitality is at the heart of such encounters. Unifying factors are those of process, mutual respect, and ethical commitment rather than of common substance or abstract conception.

Domenico Jervolino observes that Ricoeur's "'unquiet subject' is not a substance but a desire, a questioning and a hope."[141] Jervolino continues:

> In effect, the "question of the subject" means that the subject is called into question. The subject called into question is the cogito at its broadest and most dynamic, a plural, finite subjectivity, actuating itself as striving and as a desire for being, which is not behind us or beneath us as some sort of metaphysical substratum, but is rather a task for our praxis and our hope for the future. Thus understood, the "question of the subject" implies a relationship with its "other," i.e., with that which calls it into question and transforms its pure reflection, ever exposed to the risk of narcissism and metaphysical arrogance, into a questioning which generates "meaning" in the course of its searching.[142]

Ricoeur's self can never rest on its laurels, but it can count on a challenging and vibrant life. Ricoeur's philosophy of reflection is sustained by displacing the self from the center, observing that the wounded cogito is nourished "by recentering itself around its Other: cosmos, bios, or psyche. It finds itself by losing itself. It finds itself instructed and clarified after losing itself and its narcissism."[143] This soul is not isolated, but always called forth from its present partiality not only toward deeper self-knowledge but toward committed engagement with an expansive community of the world.

Conclusion:
A Bold Theology

If one assumes
the universe is closed,
the entropic message is
that all of this—
matter and energy alike—
inexorably becomes inert.

Science and religion haven't yet discussed
whether Godde is in
or outside the universe.
Let's hope in the right place!
free of the planetary puzzle,
ready to add another bit
of creation here and there,
and set the universe ajar—
if not fully opened.

"Entropy" in *Churchianity Lite*
by Douglas C. Vest

What is the nature of the universe? Is Godde inside or outside the universe? How do human beings fit into the scheme of
things? Or is there a scheme of things? These are fundamentally
theological questions. Theology's task is continuously to translate
the power of encounter with the holy into narratives and symbols
that speak to the contemporary world. Today that task is complicated by a double bind. Under the reign of a Western myth of the
rational heroic ego, theology has been pushed aside as increasingly irrelevant. In response to this trend, religious institutions

have tended to take a defensive posture against attack, becoming increasingly more dogmatic and literal. The interaction of these two trends creates an environment with little room for play and puzzlement, poetry and mystery, qualities arguably at the heart of the divine-human relationship.

The result of this double bind has been a lack of communication between the secular world and the religious one (if such a clear distinction can be made), and a growing sense that either religion or science must "win" and defeat the other. This impasse can be resolved by a mythic approach to theology capable of restoring theology's ability to reveal the vibrant mystery of the holy in a way that respects and is persuasive in the diverse postmodern world.

The theological re-visioning posed in this book challenges that state of affairs by moving toward a mythic viewpoint. Myth is the window into the ambiguous world enfolding this one. Myth directs attention to the implicit or tacit narrative underneath what a culture says about itself, revealing a depth psychological level of complexes that can hold a culture tightly in the past. With a mythic approach, Western's culture's attachment to the rational heroic ego is made visible as a stance that is preventing credible conversation about Godde in today's Western Christianity. When this stance is brought into the foreground for examination, gradually the rigid ties to Godde as self-contained hero can be loosened by exposure to possibilities embodied in an imaginal, erotic soul, released in favor of a new valuing of dialogue, mutuality, and the physical and imaginal worlds. Gradually the irrational attachment to rationality as a salvific perspective can be more balanced with a new valuing of poetry and imagination. The fixation on an enclosed and self-sufficient hero can be nurtured with mutuality and passionate engagement in the physical world. The ego can be strengthened by an understanding that soul is deepened when partial beings move toward wholeness in caring relationships with others.

EMBRACING CHAOS

Even the vibrant mythology of the imaginal, erotic soul is amenable to many interpretations and resists a single literal meaning. The flow of genuine mythology is blocked when it is confined, and its multiplicity can be welcomed as a continuous source of renewal. Myth teaches those who move more deeply into it and leads them forward into previously unimagined possibilities. What this might mean for theology was long ago suggested by a Christian theologian, Gregory of Nyssa, as he reflected on that curious passage in the book of Genesis where Moses asks to see Godde's face (Exod 33:17–23). Yahweh responds by telling Moses to hide in a cave, which Yahweh covers until he has passed by, and only then may Moses view Godde's back side. Nyssa ponders this image and concludes that there is some quality inherent in the holy that inevitably goes out before human understanding, drawing it always from one fulfillment by increasing its desire for yet more.[1] Nyssa points out that "if these things are looked at literally, not only will the understanding of those who seek God be dim, but their concept of God will also be inappropriate."[2]

The shift from literalism to a mythic view of theology is an uncomfortable one, although well attested even in Nyssa's fourth century of Christianity. The reason is that that shift is parallel to the epic, psychological, and spiritually formative work of disequilibrium described in the introduction. The task requires undergoing a period of intense disorientation while the old ways of thinking about and living new ways of being with Godde fall away. In effect this is a period in which the ego gives up control in favor of the soul's deepened trust in the always surprising and finally unknowable Godde. The lived space of an imaginal, erotic soul does involve something more like chaos than orderliness. While physics now reveals that chaos is more often the prelude to a new pattern of wholeness than a movement of entropy into death, living in chaos is challenging. My proposed approach to theology does require a kind of dying to what in the past has seemed comforting and orderly, so as to be open to new forms of being, both one's own and Godde's. Chaos requires confidence in the living Godde and a willingness to trust in what seems darkness while the new is being born in hiddenness. Uncertainty and ambiguity are inevitable companions of an imaginal, erotic soul, yet they can be highly creative.

This theological re-visioning intends to offer language and perspective about the seemingly chaotic periods (in personal and communal life) that will facilitate the ongoing creation of an open story, a story that is always renewing itself, always subject to creative disorientation. The story of the imaginal, erotic soul is never finished and lives continually in ambiguity, because it remains imaginative and thus capable of accompanying people and culture into the abyss. If all that happens is a substitution of one literal vision of a rational heroic ego with another literal vision of an imaginal, erotic soul, little will have changed theologically. Each of the elements of the re-visioning is selected in part because it bears a pattern of openness, a pattern of readiness to live in a continually shifting sacred story.

Each mythological shift proposed in the image of the imaginal, erotic soul requires willingness to experience a paradigm shift, not just to enjoy a new idea, but taking it seriously enough to allow the idea to change one's life. Each is a new worldview, with its own ways of being that require disciplined practice to be understood. Each is not simply about collecting information, but involves participation in a process of formation and transformation. One of the primary characteristics of a formative process is that one doesn't understand it until one has been experiencing it for a while. Formation is costly because understanding comes only after one has been changed by the process itself. Formation is not under one's control, neatly managed step by step; it is more a "suffering" than an acting.

Dying to the old ways of being is required in order to be born to the new life of the new way. And spiritual formation may involve major paradigm shifts, not just once but perhaps many times. If one refuses dying to the old ways, if one finds it impossible to accept or reconcile the past in its wholeness, it usually happens that one repeats the wounds and scars of the past, stuck in a vicious circle. Entering a creative and abundant future requires honesty about the past, both its beauties and its betrayals. And this is a pattern played out not only in individual life, but also in the larger life of the society as a whole.

Urban Holmes makes a distinction between open and closed stories, observing that the gospels are open stories. He observes that an open story "is a narrative that remains imaginative, developing, and capable of accompanying us into providing that essential ongoing nurture, the abyss....For the Christian with a closed story there is a lack of tension between his story and the Gospel story....Closed stories have no humor or terror. They are lifeless accounts."[3] Open, mythic stories celebrate a quality of tension between day-to-day existence and the gospel story, and are capable of dealing with both humor and terror. Lively myth is always fluid and full of surprises, as the Christian gospel tends to be.

Consider, for example, the "I am" statements of Jesus in the Gospel of John. Jesus speaks in metaphor as he tells his disciples that he is bread, shepherd, vine (chapters 6, 10, 15). He is, of course, not literally these things, but is inviting deeper consideration of what his relationship is with disciples. Lest a fixation develop on one meaning of one metaphor, Jesus piles images one on top of another, deepening the listener's confusion, which is to say, opening the heart to the new thing that he is and will become for his disciples then and now. In chapter 10 of John's Gospel, for example, Jesus says he is the shepherd, and also the door of the sheepfold. If that seems clear, Jesus adds that he is the door by which his sheep enter, and that he lays down his life and challenges the wolves. If the disciple is still following this, Jesus says he has other sheep not of this fold, and all of this invloves his death in some way. Today's Christian understands this language with far too much certainly and literalism if he or she does not expereince confusion, reflection, and eventually new openings in the heart toward fullness of life, the realm of Godde.

A certain foolish boldness characterizes this mythic re-visioning of theology. Each return to theological issues through the lenses of these mythic themes may bring uncertainty and new disorientation. The nature of the holy reality so encountered is ambiguous; but gradually as the soul deepens and the heart opens, an inner transformation can be experienced. Courage is required to persist in such a theological enterprise in a world largely committed at the moment to certainty, control, and singular truths. Yet I propose that only with a mythic theology does life deepen in meaningfulness, abundance, and relationship with the holy.

POSSIBLE "WORLDS"

If one looks at Christianity through the composite lens of this re-visioned theology, here is what might be found:

The Lens of Imagination and the Imaginal Realm

The imaginal lens offers the possibility that consciousness pertains not only to the realms of sensory perception and intellectual abstraction, but also to another realm—an intermediate and mediating realm of the imaginal. This realm, an aspect of reality no less authentic than the sensory world and the conceptual one, corresponds to a human faculty of imagination, of equal status with sensation and thought. The immediate issue is whether events and perceptions in the imaginal realm can bear truth in the same way that truth is understood in the sensory and conceptual realms. Can the imaginal realm be the source of personal truth claims, and perhaps more significantly, the source of communally valid experiences?

Recent explorations of imagination suggest that this faculty seems to be a uniquely productive aspect of consciousness, at work in most occasions of genuine synthesis, and is also an instrument of "semantic innovation."[4] In particular, metaphor and symbol involve imaginative leaps toward new and deeper understandings of the world. Imagination is fundamentally the ability to wonder "what if?" and to see things otherwise. This ability is crucial for envisioning a future worth living in, not remaining confined by the "as is." Einstein's aphorism is frequently quoted today, to the effect that problems cannot be solved with the same kind of thinking that created them. The shift to a different kind of thinking is the work of imagination. Imagination enables a vision of what "might be," or in Christian terms, exploring the nature of the kingdom/*kin-dom* of Godde as it might look today.[5] Godde's presence in the world is by its nature ambiguous, and imagination is needed to see beyond the surface into the depths of possibility.

In particular, a theological concept of imagination benefits from Sufi mysticism's concept of the imaginal realm as a place where the soul meets and is brought ever more fully into the divine

life itself. The practice of the prayer of imagination in Sufism functions in the context of both the general affirmations of Islamic
faith and the personal disciplined search for the beloved. This Sufi
concept has also been integrated into archetypal psychology as an
apt way to describe the soul's movement toward what Jung calls
"individuation" or full psychic maturity. James Hillman emphasizes that imagination is the way soul is honored in conversation
and life.

But, if imagination is regarded as having equal status with
sensation and thought, the question arises whether there is a truth
beyond multiple truths? Is every person caught in an imaginal web
of his or her own making, isolated from any common context? A
response begins with the reality that humans have access to something beyond individual fantasy through the inherited myths and
symbols of the past. While those myths and symbols are subject to
many interpretations, they retain a core of integrity that suggests a
connection to something deeper than any single interpretation can
reveal. In particular, the work of imagination in Sufi mysticism is
merely an effort to describe experiences that are beyond the reach
of words. Whether or not persons who have been caught up in an
"oceanic experience" believe in the reality of what has touched
them, enough humans have been touched in similar ways over time
to suggest something beyond. In a more technical mode, Ricoeur
describes a variety of ways of testing the validity of imaginative
experience beyond the logic of empirical verification. He suggests
in addition the logics of probability, of discovery, and of attesta-
tion/testimony as ways of strengthening and mediating between
the affirmations of sensation and of thinking.

Yet to affirm a truth beyond multiple truths is not to define
and contain the nature of that truth. The momentum of all the elements of this re-visioning is toward the affirmation of a core of
truth in theology, while learning to enjoy the ongoing ambiguity
and unfolding multiplicity of that truth. In the model of the rational
heroic ego, it is important to state problems and solve them, so
mysteries are considered to be like the puzzles in novels that
through careful sleuthing will be solved. But in the model of the
imaginal erotic soul, mysteries are to be enjoyed, and chaos is
understood as the place where life begins. The nature of Godde as

144

understood here is as mystery that will never be fully revealed, as pregnant spirit hovering over chaos. Yet this mystery and pregnant spirit penetrates daily life in many ways for those whose soul is attuned. Philosophy, religious experience, and psychology all attest to the fact that in disciplined imagination, persons encounter something beyond their own present knowing, something that seems oriented to their wholeness.

How might imagination's lens be helpful to Western Christianity? Imagination, especially in its forms of metaphor, symbol, and parable has long been a resource for Christianity, even if not always emphasized as such. In the New Testament, many of Jesus' teachings are presented in the form of a parable, such as "The kingdom of heaven is like a mustard seed that someone took and sowed in his field; it is the smallest of all the seeds, but when it has grown it is the greatest of shrubs and becomes a tree, so that the birds of the air come and make nests in its branches" (Matt 13:31–32). The full impact of this metaphor/parable tends to be lost on a contemporary Western reader, for in general there is little personal connection with mustard bushes. Apparently in Jesus' time, mustard shrubs often were considered a great nuisance, because they tended to spring up so quickly and unexpectedly that they could overwhelm the intended crop of the field. So with a bit of knowledge and imagination, the mustard seed becomes an image of something small that becomes very large, and also perhaps suggests a hint of subversive activity, where the thing that was excluded can in time become very important.

An extended example of how imagination could serve Christianity can be given in regard to the post-resurrection appearances of Jesus. Henry Corbin makes an interesting allusion when he says that the imaginal world is the world of "the resurrection body."[6] It is not clear what Corbin means by the term but it is certainly suggestive for Christians. After Jesus' tomb is found empty, the Gospels various report certain "sightings" of Jesus (e.g., Mark 16:9–14, Matt 28:9–10, Luke 24:13f., John 20:11–31, 21:1–25, and the first part of the Acts of the Apostles). Characteristic of these appearances is that the disciples do not at first recognize Jesus, evidently because something is different about his physical appearance, but they become convinced that Jesus is indeed the one in their presence. Jesus eats food but passes through locked doors. Sometimes he is not recognized at all; other times he is immediately worshipped. Also the stories themselves "are notoriously difficult to harmonize."[7] Yet the disciples become so convinced that Jesus is raised from the dead and appears to them that they subsequently act like different people—whereas before, they had been broken and in hiding, they now walk boldly forth and even preach in the temple (e.g., Acts 3:12f.). N. T. Wright observes that "the same *oddity* consistent across all the narratives...counts heavily in their favor as genuine recollection of deeply puzzling events."[8] Yet Wright goes on to insist that one must either skeptically rule out the resurrection because it can be challenged on empirical grounds, or affirm that Jesus was raised bodily from the dead.[9] Wright's conversation partner, Marcus Borg, suggests in contrast that these are metaphorical narratives with rich resonances of meaning. Borg stakes his claim on the fact that "the followers of Jesus, both then and now, continued to experience Jesus as a living reality after his death."[10] This claim comes closer to what an imaginal perspective might offer, but is still not quite as rich as it might be.

I suggest that the post-resurrection appearances of Jesus gain the most meaning if they are understood as occurring in the imaginal realm. The stories are all odd, but they have the *same* oddity. Jesus' disciples were those who had lived with him much of the time for many months prior to his death. They would have had time and space to build a common way of faith practice, a common set of understandings and expectations about how Godde is present in the world. Clearly, they didn't entirely "get it" before Jesus' death, because Jesus often calls the disciples hard of heart because of their lack of understanding (e.g., Mark 8:17). Yet some notions might have penetrated below conscious awareness. If it is credible to claim a realm of reality that is neither wholly sensate nor wholly intellectual, it seems obvious that Jesus appeared to the disciples after his death in the imaginal realm. It was a true appearing, validated by so many witnesses, yet the appearances were not in the fully sensate realm, so different people in different circumstances saw him differently. And people still do see Jesus in the imaginal realm. The imaginal is not a realm of private fantasy, but represents a common world where events occur that can be witnessed by more than one person. Such proof is not based on a logic of reason, but is based on logics of probability, discovery, and attestation.

One of the most cherished of the post-resurrection vignettes is the story of the travelers on the Emmaus road who are returning from Jerusalem greatly disheartened by Jesus' death (Luke 24:13–35). Jesus joins them on the road, and listens pastorally for a while. But then he calls them "slow of heart" (v. 25), and begins to interpret the scriptures to them "about himself" (v. 27). Ched Myers finds the key to this encounter in Jesus' question to these disciples: "Was it not necessary that the Messiah should suffer?" (v. 26). The importance of the question is not to support traditional atonement theories that Jesus death is "*necessary* given the character of God; it is, however, *inevitable*, given the character of the state."[11] Myers observes that there is a temptation in North America to want the good guys to win, to manage history from the top down—in short, what I would call the heroic fantasy. But the form of this story in the Gospel of Luke is like the form of epic: it demonstrates a reversal at the key point that brings the listeners up short and invites repentance. "With a jolt of recognition/revelation, the narrative reverses directions. The fugitive disciples now return to the capital city to face its dangers."[12] And when they arrive back in Jerusalem to tell the others their experience, Jesus appears to the whole group, and they are startled and terrified (Luke 24:37). The fear is natural, because they have come back to face the reality that their guide has been killed by the powers that be, and they too will face possible repercussions if they take up his way of discipleship. Generally speaking, the message of Christ does evoke an initial repressive reaction from those in power, because it is a call to "engage the way things *are* with a vision of what *could* be and *should* be."[13] But the disciples are also awestruck, amazed that the power of Rome had not defeated Jesus. "The Resurrection was overwhelming to the disciples because it signaled that Jesus's Way had been vindicated by God—especially that most difficult bit about dying for the cause rather than killing for the cause."[14]

Christians can benefit greatly from a sense of the imaginal realm that transcends time and is a place beyond whereness, enabling its participants to encounter and be strengthened by

Godde. This is not a realm that can be accessed solely by intellect, no more than solely by senses, though both are involved. The heart is the imagination's home, and the locus of its work.

The Lens of a Feminist Vision

Feminism, no less than imagination or hermeneutical philosophy, requires acceptance of a radical paradigm shift, with its attendant costs. Inevitably, questions emerge in the move toward that shift of paradigms: Is violence inherent in human nature, and the claim of feminism to bring greater peace merely an illusion? If theology ceases to function in terms of dualistic oppositions, what is to be done with evil? Are people fundamentally ignorant sheep, as Fyodor Dostoevsky's Grand Inquisitor claims, sheep incapable of dealing with true freedom who need forceful leaders to give the firm and directive shape of fixed rules and limits?[15] Does a serious spiritual life require an abandonment of the temptations of the world in an increasing withdrawal to a plane of wordless, imageless union with the One? Feminism challenges the assumptions underlying such questions, and calls for a radical rethinking of the way not only Godde is understood, but also the way a faith-filled life will be lived in the world.

Feminists generally are postmodernists, in the sense that they accept the claim that "no single theory of knowledge can ever adequately express, convey or provide an avenue to the whole truth."[16] This means that anything that can be said about Godde is necessarily partial and limited, for Godde will always be more than can be spoken. In particular, feminists tend to reject the notion of Godde identified with Aquinas as unchangeable, omnipotent, and omniscient. However, feminist Elizabeth Johnson takes Aquinas's reflections about Godde a step further. Aquinas says that Godde's very nature is "to be," suggesting that being is a more adequate term for Godde than any of the others, because it doesn't attempt to name any particular quality, rather referring to an indeterminate whole. Aquinas summarizes this perspective by saying that "He Who Is" is the most appropriate name for God. While Aquinas himself does fill his concept of being with transcendental modifiers like omnipotence, his actual language (*qui est*) can equally be translated "who is," "the one who is" or even "she who is."[17] For the feminist theologian, being is less a fixed quality of transcendental reality than a dynamic and flexible quality of "relational liveliness that energizes the world."[18]

Feminist theologians are exploring a number of metaphors for Godde to expand the ways in which the divine is understood to include more qualities associated with the feminine—Godde as mother, lover, friend, and even as the body of earth. Rosemary Reuther offers the image of Godde as "the primal Matrix, the great womb within which all things...are generated."[19] Overall, there is a sense that language about Godde matters, and a desire to shift the quality and nature of speech about Godde away from its fixation in heroic male imagery.

A primary feminist theological concern has been that Christian scriptures were written within a culture and context of male-centered power that tended to minimize stories and information about women and emphasize the primacy of men as Godde's representatives. Yet many continue to think that scripture remains a valuable resource because the Godde of scripture and of Jesus Christ is not only a past but a present resource for women and men in today's world.

In particular, feminists are exploring scripture as texts of wisdom. The wisdom tradition in scripture is found in the books of Psalms, Proverbs, Job, Ecclesiastes, Song of Solomon, and the apocryphal Ecclesiasticus and Wisdom of Solomon. Wisdom writing bears a quite different style and purpose from either the books of the law or those of the prophets. Wisdom scriptures are fundamentally this-world oriented, asking questions about how the fullness of life can be attained for human beings. The primary expression of Godde's wisdom in these books is the female figure *Hokmah* or *Sophia* (respectively, Hebrew and Greek for "wisdom"). The spoken words of Jesus in the New Testament bear a marked resemblance to the sayings of Sophia in the older testaments, and feminist theologians often speak of Jesus-Sophia, alluding to the possible identification of Jesus himself with the older figure of Wisdom.[20]

Like the figure of Wisdom, Jesus often finds himself challenging conventional values. One of the most marked characteristics of Jesus' life and ministry is thought by feminists to be that he ate with everyone! An anthropological term, *commensality*, specifically refers to meal behavior, and it suggests that one can tell much about a society by who eats with whom. Food exchanges are basic to life, and implicit in them are obligations of reciprocity and mutuality.[21] Typical of feminist concerns with daily life, an assessment is made of Jesus' core values by looking at what he does. And what he does is go to parties and tell stories about banquets, often with unexpected visitors at the table.

So, the phrase used to describe the heart of Jesus' ministry is "open commensality"—the sharing of meals—and it is increasingly used to describe the heart of Jesus' ministry. Jesus' teaching and practice was that of open commensality, a radically nonhierarchical or egalitarian way of living in the world. Not only were men of lesser social status invited to Jesus' table, but also women, even unmarried women—all treated with respect and affection. This is a practice profoundly strange to the customary practices of Jesus' time, a challenge to convention. How different an image is evoked by Jesus enjoying himself at table with friends, in contrast with that of Jesus as a Lord worshipped by his disciples. It might even be considered that the "Lord's Supper" or eucharistic mass, is less in memory of the violent death of Jesus than in memory of his inclusive way of being present with women and men in the midst of daily life.

Another similar example of Jesus' "strange" and challenging behavior occurs in John's Gospel, when a man who was blind from birth passes by, and Jesus' disciples ask him: "Rabbi, who sinned, this man or his parents, that he was born blind?" (John 9:2). The assumption behind the question reveals the purity codes of Jesus' time, suggesting that physical infirmity is directly linked with personal sin, and that physical deformity defiles sacred places.[22] But Jesus insists that neither of these things is true, that Godde is in the world working for healing and wholeness in all things. "I came into this world for judgment so that those who do not see may see, and those who do see may become blind." (John 9:39). This answer is all the more astonishing in light of a concern for re-visioning. Just as in the epic pattern there is a suggestion in Jesus' words that what has been seen is incomplete. And the invi-

150

tation of Godde is to become blind to the old vision, in order that one may come to see truly the invitation of the future. Consistently Jesus seems to challenge conventional thinking to the extent that one important question feminists are asking is, "Is such challenge central to the good news of Christianity?"

Although considerable thought has been given to ideas about Sophia/Wisdom in Western Christian thought, a feminist revisioning is enriched by the reflections of Eastern Christian sophiologists, notably the work of Sergei Bulgakov, who sees the figure of Sophia as twofold, with both divine and creaturely aspects. Whereas the earliest Christian councils decreed that God the Father and God the Son (Jesus) were of one substance (*ousia*), Bulgakov boldly proclaims that Sophia *is* the substance (the *ousia*) that unites them and the Holy Spirit.[23] Sophia is inherent in the nature of Godde, something like the connective glue of the three persons of Godde. She is not a fourth hypostasis or person, nor another Godde. If this sounds paradoxical, it is because the nature of Sophia (and of Godde, for that matter) is that of antimony, a form that enfolds the truth of two or more ideas that seem opposites but are in fact essential to each other.[24]

However, the way Sophia exists within the life of the Trinity is only the first of her antinomies. The second is that she exists also within creation; her "body" is the world. Sophia is a kind of eternal prototype of creation, an "eternal reality in God (that) also provides the foundation for the existence of the world of creatures."[25] Sophia is at the heart of the intersection of Godde and the world. Bulgakov is quite aware that his viewpoint affirms the sacredness of the created world, acknowledging that nature is penetrated with (but not identical to) divinity, and indeed points out that this reality calls forth a new attitude toward the world. Yet Sophia's presence in creation in no way precludes her presence in Godde's very being; she exists in both modes at once, thereby establishing the interdependence and interconnection of the eternal and the temporal.

This understanding of Sophia integrates several elements crucial to feminist theology. It shows how Sophia can be intimately part of Godde, without needing to develop a complex theological addition to the notion of Trinity or to assign femininity to one person of the Trinity and not to the other two. In addition, it suggests how Godde can be both immersed in creation and separate from it. Sophia does not fit into dualistic categories, being neither solely human nor solely divine, and it is exactly that unity in distinction that identifies who she is. Sophia also reveals a theological reality important to feminists: the goodness of creation. The flickering of her being between creaturely and divine forms is a vivid reminder of the way in which all of creation (and not just the spiritual part) yearns toward *theosis*, or God-becoming.

The Lens of Ricoeur's Open Philosophy

The project of re-visioning theology has enfolded the two lenses of the imagination and a feminist vision. The goal of this mythic re-visioning is to offer a contemporary theology centered in an open story, one that is always renewing itself. The final lens of soul, Paul Ricoeur's philosophy, adds scope and depth to the composite re-visioning instrument. What is the nature of this final lens? What is the special contribution of Ricoeur's phenomenological hermeneutics to the new vision? The imagination lens supplements the perspective of rationality so dominant in contemporary Western culture. The feminist lens supplements the perspective of the positivist heroic view, especially by emphasizing the life-force of the erotic rather than hierarchy and dualism. And Ricoeur's philosophy supplements the perspective of the individual ego, self as self-contained and autonomous subject, with an emphasis on the relational soul.

In his work on language and metaphor, Ricoeur demonstrates that meaning-effects, or new things, emerge in language as a surplus of meaning that can produce semantic innovation. Metaphoric truth shows the inadequacy of merely empirical verification, revealing a quality of reality that both is and is not, because it can only be encountered ambiguously through symbol. Poetic structure reveals the apparently random events of life to be necessary and probable, creating an "as if" world of past, present, and future in which tradition and innovation are combined. But it is not sufficient to abstract meaning from life events; the completion of narrative is to reintegrate some of the possibilities encountered in narrative, based on ethical commitment with others.

Ricoeur develops a philosophy that embraces postmodern concerns for the integrity of multiple perspectives, agreeing that rigid and absolute certainties are no longer tenable, and then goes the next step to show how truth claims can nevertheless be made and embodied in the lives of real persons. These truth claims continue to bear ambiguity and tension, and must be lived dynamically. In the language of epic, one continues to be invited to look afresh at the past and acknowledge its illusions and limitations, while one continues to explore future possibilities. There is no end to this process, and such a reality could be viewed with alarm and dismay. But this dynamic circling is not the empty repetition of existential phenomenology, because at each cycle, new meanings are appropriated and lived.

Ricoeur's self or soul is subject to a dynamic cycle, integrating sameness and newness. Not even self finds a point at which it stabilizes permanently, for it too is dynamic and continues to unfold through the rhythm of discordance and concordance, instability and continuity. Life must be lived as an ethical self, in relationships of solicitude and justice with others. The fact of relationship means that the self is constantly renewed in continuous encounter with other selves having conflicts of interpretation. Autonomy is valued equally with a principle of respect owed all others in a universal field of equality and justice. Others are essential to the self, because change and reappraisal are the conditions of the ongoing vitality of selfhood. Each genuine engagement with another enlarges interior capacity, and the longing for additional unfolding of meaning toward fullness of life is correspondingly expanded. Ricoeur's is a world of radical complexity and polyvalence in which all truth statements are provisional. Nevertheless, creative imagination, disciplined by the logics of probability, discovery, and attestation, can play an innovative role of mutual cocreation with the also-unfolding other.

Ricoeur himself does not make a point of comparing his philosophy with twentieth-century developments in quantum physics. But there are several key ways in which the two fields overlap. This overlap is important because at times of major shift in mythic perspectives, those hinge periods of history, physics and metaphysics begin to converge in an emergent worldview encompassing both. Ricoeur's return to a discussion of ontology, or foundational qualities of being, is a way of restoring metaphysics to the contemporary conversation. And by extension, philosophy and theology find parallels in physics. This is not the place for an extended discussion of modern physics, but Ricoeur's philosophy does have implications not only for Christianity's understanding of the physical world, but also for the way Godde is imagined or understood.[26]

1. *The interchangeability of matter and energy.* Experiments in the early twentieth century present the astonishing idea that light can sometimes take the form of waves or, at other times, the form of energy. No longer could there be a clear and permanent distinction between physical matter and dynamic process. This principle of physics appears in Ricoeur's reluctance to name either Godde or human self as a permanently fixed substance. Ricoeur alludes to Godde in the form of as yet unrealized possibilities, but does not endeavor to assigned fixed or certain qualities. The same is true of Ricoeur's treatment of self or soul: the person is dynamic, an "unquiet self" continually in process of becoming, a soul that is both material and spiritual. One can speak of ontology or essential being, but not by assigning fixed qualities of substance. Instead, being itself is ambiguous. The ambiguity does not negate the reality of either Godde or soul, but it means that all statements about either one are provisional and subject to later change. Christians can speak about Godde only in the knowledge that all language about Godde is inadequate. Even language about Jesus ought to astonish: both divine and human at once!

2. *Certainty and probability.* The scientific discovery of the multiple forms of light revealed that even the most careful empirical experiment in the subatomic world could not predict exact outcomes. Experiments could describe tendencies or probabilities but not certainties. In working with what was initially called the "human sciences," Ricoeur developed alternatives to the logic of empirical verification. His tests for truthfulness include the logic of probability and the logic of discovery, as alternatives to certainty. The essential instability of metaphor and myth caused Ricoeur to emphasize the illusion of certainty in favor of the ongoing possibility of multiple interpretations. This does not mean that all inter-

pretations are equal. There remain ways to verify truthfulness of any given interpretation, checking for congruence with other tests. A valid interpretation must be more probable, or at least as probable, as others.

The existence of God cannot be proved with certainty; there is risk involved in daring to commit oneself to a life of Christian discipleship. Christians can no longer assert with confidence that Jesus is the only way to Godde, for other religious and spiritual paths may be able to put forth equally probable ideas about Godde. To insist on certainty may be to explain away something essential. What if such insistence forecloses the possibility of a real experience beyond the reach of certainty? The lack of certainty does not mean that following the path of discipleship to Christ is foolish or misguided; it simply means this choice is an effective one for those who choose it, just as other choices may be effective. Christian theology must find ways to acknowledge the validity of other ways of faith while working alongside them for the common good of the world.

Myth, symbol, metaphor, and religious narrative are not subject to fixed and certain interpretations; there will always be conflicts of interpretation. The reality that both self and Godde live in ambiguity can be a cause of real tension. Yet it can also be a reminder of the way meaning never ceases to interpenetrate the physical world. The great mythic reality underlying all efforts to speak of it will always bear more meaning than any single interpretation can reveal. Life is precarious and baffling, but meaning and purpose can be encountered when one learns to be attuned to the surrounding mystery.

3. *Isolated entities or interrelated parts of a whole.* Classical physics could analyze discrete parts and their effects upon each other in a simple cause and effect model based on the behavior of machines. Quantum physics finds that model useless at the subatomic level and discovers instead a world of mutual interactivity. "As we penetrate into matter, nature does not show us any isolated 'building blocks,' but rather appears as a complicated web of relations between the various parts of the whole."[27] The world is seen more like an organism than a machine, in which each whole thing has autonomy and interiority, even as it also func-

tions as part of a larger whole. The notion of isolated entities in causal connection is expanded toward a concept of relational interaction. Ricoeur's dialectic method of comprehension rests on a conviction that any particular interpretation is strengthened when it engages with other interpretations toward a more complete understanding of an emergent whole. His notion of immersing oneself in an ongoing narrative through which new meaning is encountered is expressive of relational interaction.

In particular, the move away from a dualistic conception of the world toward an interrelational one suggests a notion of Godde that is not wholly separate from and different than the created world. There is no sharp distinction between Godde as an external, superhuman agent and creation as hopelessly flawed. The physical and spiritual worlds are an unbroken whole, including darkness, chaos, pain, and suffering, and Godde shares these experiences in an expanding horizon of divine belonging that includes all forms of life.[28] Godde is affected and possibly changed by interaction with human intentions and even nonhuman circumstances. Godde's engagement in human history is not as an external savior, but as an intimate, mutually involved participant in unfolding futures. And humans are cocreators with Godde in those unfolding futures, rather than passive recipients of Godde's will. The whole is more than the sum of its parts.

4. *Objectivity or participation?* One of the more astonishing aspects of quantum physics is the discovery that the observer changes the situation being observed. Subatomic particles respond differently, depending on the question posed by the experimenter. What was thought to be the neutral stance of a subject observing an object turns out to be a participatory engagement in which both parties are changed. In human affairs, this participatory engagement of the so-called objective observer has been understood for some time, but it is a shock to realize that participatory engagement describes the nature of the physical and spiritual worlds. This discovery in physics contributes an additional dimension to Ricoeur's insight that the fact of many diverse interpretations reveals that the cosmos itself inherently abounds in surplus meaning.

For Christians a participatory universe means that not only will humans have diverse ways of understanding reality, but that something in the nature of reality itself bears the capacity for infinite meaning. Further, the meaning evoked in any given situation depends on the intent with which it is sought. Statements such as "For you always have the poor with you," (Mark 14:7) must be seen, not as Jesus' prescription for the unfolding future, but rather as a description of a future *expected and thus co-created by his hearers.* What is perceived is at least partly relative to what one is willing to accept as sufficient. We participate in cocreating the reality we experience, and this is not a matter of private fantasy, but something that coheres in the nature of unfolding reality.

Objectivity functions best when used as an analytical tool, separating things into discrete units. Such an approach may be useful for a period of time, but when one is endeavoring to explore the nature of Godde, the layers of the self, or various subtle aspects of the world, eventually analysis alone is inadequate for the task. Analysis by its nature is divisive, and theology by its nature seeks to be integrative. Integration is a movement of synthesis or bringing things together rather than separating them. And integration requires releasing control, opening in receptivity to the other, and willingness to lose some independence in a dance of life that involves more than any single piece or person can bring. Wholeness of life is necessarily collaborative, participative, cocreative. These are ancient Christian principles, capable of rediscovery in relationship to ideas of quantum physics and Ricoeur's open philosophy.

The application of Ricoeur's philosophy to Western Christianity has a second dimension, and this concerns the implications of his philosophy for the Christian spiritual life. As noted, Ricoeur's is a world of radical complexity and polyvalence, in which all truth statements are provisional. One of the ingredients that helps sustain a vibrant life of faith in such a world is an explicit spiritual path.

The way Ricoeur engages postmodern philosophy offers a model for developing a spiritual practice that effectively engages contemporary life experience of diversity and complexity. My own spiritual path has been closely related to the monastic tradition of Benedictine spirituality, and I find many helpful analogies both to Ricoeur and for spiritual practice in a book by Raimundo

Panikkar that takes the monk as universal archetype. Panikkar has explored in depth significant changes that seem to be occurring in contemporary monastic practice, changes that parallel the shift toward more ambiguity and less certainty, the shift central to this re-visioning and to Ricoeur's philosophy. His reflections are included as a way of linking the theological and philosophical re-visioning with spiritual practice.

Panikkar observes first that the archetype of the monk can be found as a "*constitutive dimension of human life.*"[29] That is, the mythic archetype of monkhood is a foundational aspect of every human life, no matter whether or how it is activated. The monastic archetype aspires to something very like the pattern described throughout this book, an experience of a decisive break that turns one around "for the sake of that 'thing' which encompasses or transcends everything."[30] This aspiration is lived out in many ways toward the fullness of a meaningful, joyful life. Just as Ricoeur considers the work of consciousness or selfhood to be a task involving effort, so Panikkar understands the achievement of the monastic archetype within each person (and perhaps within each culture?) to be something that requires disciplined intention.

In *Blessed Simplicity*, Panikkar's intention is to contrast the shape of a spiritual life of blessed simplicity (a traditional monastic pattern) with a spiritual life of harmonious complexity (a more contemporary pattern). My own interpretation of a contemporary monasticism for oblates (lay affiliates of monasteries) corresponds more closely to harmonious complexity, which in turn corresponds well to the open philosophy Ricoeur has crafted.

The traditional monastic path seeks fullness of life through simplification while the contemporary way tends to seek it through integration.[31] The first risks reductionism, in the move toward simplification possibly rejecting too much of the world and doing violence to the real. The traditional spiritual path may be tempted to pessimism, finding the world too distracting or sinful. On the other hand, the contemporary monastic path risks gathering everything found without regard to its inherent value, in the move to find the goodness in complexity. The contemporary path is tempted to optimism, possibly ignoring or minimizing evil and suffering. In setting side by side these two spiritual paths, Panikkar (like Ricoeur) acknowledges a conflict of interpretations and seeks to honor both sides, while trying to move toward a vision beyond either.

Central to the distinction between traditional and contemporary paths is the move away from renunciation toward a hope for the transformation of all things. Emphasis is not so much on sin and suffering as rather on the harmonious embrace of everything. This is a bold shift, emphasizing inclusion rather than denial, in the endeavor to midwife the world into the fullness implicit in its potential as Godde's self-giving. Is this shift to be seen as a betrayal of the monastic calling, a new mutation in the same direction, or something new altogether "birthed within the womb of the old institutions"?[32]

The same questions might be asked of this theological re-visioning: is it faithful to Christianity's center, a mutation of its core, or something altogether new birthed within the old? These are fair questions, and only time will tell. But the intent in both cases is not betrayal but the essential work of love so that the institution remains vital and relevant in the contemporary world.

The very word *complexity* suggests the joining of many elements so that they may fit together in a whole. In particular, harmonious complexity assumes that there is no inherent incompatibility between and among the internal tendencies of the different constituents to be joined. Harmonious complexity assumes it is possible to reconcile all the elements in a situation, perhaps in the way that Ricoeur's hermeneutics assumes the possible reconciliation of conflicting interpretations. But since things are not already joined and fitted together, harmonious complexity is not automatic; it means that everything has to be transformed—as epic seeks transformation for a culture on the cusp of change—in order that all may fit together. Such transformation is only authentic if it expresses a movement by which things become what they really are, toward the natural fullness of their being.

If this effort is optimistic in its minimization of evil and its belief in the compatibility of all that is, it also reflects the kind of intentional and participatory presence that quantum physics suggests may be instrumental in effecting change. It is not the first naiveté of innocent hopefulness, but rather follows a journey of self-awareness, a clear assessment of diversity and who benefits

159

from existing ways, and a knowledge that change is likely to be challenged, with a readiness to stand firm in the face of such challenge. Suffering is inevitable, given the present character of the world, and engagement in the work of transformation is undertaken with full awareness of that inevitability and willingness to share it with joy. Finally, such engagement is also undertaken with confidence that Godde is working through human lives to bring about transformation even through what might appear to be failure or death. For the Christian, the contemporary spiritual path to transformed life is similar to the pattern epic reveals—requiring a break or rupture. Although it brings suffering, it also brings discovery and is the means by which a new future is claimed. Perhaps this perspective is what shapes Ricoeur's concept of a selfhood whose contours are intimately shaped both by "wounding" self-knowledge as well as by interactions with others where mutual respect and regard for humanity serve as a unifying ground and source of new meaning.

Finally, Panikkar turns to what he calls the sociological challenge, and what I might call the urgency of the need for re-visioning and corresponding action. Not only in the West, but in all societies engaged in the endeavor to modernize (which usually means to westernize),

> the system is breaking down...the social, political, economic, and religious order, seems to be collapsing.... For many the system seems merely imperfect and unsatisfying. But I daresay that it is unjust and even inhuman. It cannot just be reformed. It has to be redeemed. It represents the shift of the center from God, or Man, or Cosmos into one particular corner of reality with pretensions to universality. I suggest that the system is falling apart because it has tried to resolve the global human predicament by and with the means and insights of one particular culture and/or religion....The system is "de-centered," off-kilter, distorted; it has lost (or never found) its center.[33]

Many if not most of the institutions associated with Western culture, including Western Christianity, are collapsing. Mere reformation cannot solve this problem. Perhaps the main reason for the collapse is that the West and its socioeconomic version of Christianity have presumed that their mythic reality of the rational heroic ego is sufficient and suitable for all of humankind, and indeed for all of earth itself. This hubris, this presumption, though it may look strong, is without a center and cannot stand.

It is this presumption that is rightly contested by post-modernity, this claim to universality characteristic of the modern West and its Christian expression. But postmodernity without a theological or spiritual dimension does not have the resources to contest this claim all the way through, for postmodernity also has no center. Western Christianity is challenged today to see that in order to challenge effectively this political–economic–military claim of the West to universal relevance, Christianity will have to stop looking for Godde exclusively in a transcendent and abstract world. Postmodernity offers a gift in revealing that the old myth is shattered, with its center in the idea of a reasonable, heroic, iso-lated Godde disconnected from the world. Risky as the (monas-tic) strategy of harmonious complexity is, it may be an absolutely necessary risk in light of today's pressures.

In particular, harmonious complexity can be strengthened and stabilized by a rediscovery of "the place and function of *myth* in human life."[34] Mythos, especially a revised mythos of the imaginal, erotic soul, is the resource that grounds a spiritual path for this work of transformation. Myth is the bearer of possible worlds.[35]

Notes

INTRODUCTION:
PROBLEM AND POSSIBILITY:
LITERALISM AND A MYTHIC RESPONSE

1. C. G. Jung, *Psychology and Religion* (New Haven: Yale University Press, 1938), 21.

2. John Micklethwait, "In God's Name: A Special Report on Religion and Public Life," *The Economist* 385 (November 3–9, 2007): 1–22, Special Report.

3. The term *Western* society or culture as used here means the United States and Europe, as industrialized countries founded in the classic Greek cultural heritage and the underlying Hebrew mythology taken up in Christianity.

4. This pattern is described by Paul Ricoeur in John B. Thompson, ed., *Paul Ricoeur: Hermeneutics and the Human Sciences; Essays on Language, Action and Interpretation* (Cambridge: Cambridge University Press, 1981).

5. Wendy Doniger, *The Implied Spider: Politics and Theology in Myth* (New York: Columbia University Press, 1998), 79.

6. A good introduction to Jung's thought can be found in C. G. Jung, *The Essential Jung: Selected Writings*, trans. R. C. F. Hull and Richard and Clara Winston (Princeton: Princeton University Press, 1983).

7. James Hillman, *Re-Visioning Psychology* (New York: Harper & Row, 1975), 153.

8. Paul Ricoeur, *The Rule of Metaphor: Multi-Disciplinary Studies of the Creation of Meaning in Language*, trans. Robert

Czerny with Kathleen McLaughlin and John Costello, SJ (Toronto: University of Toronto Press, 1977), 6.

9. Norvene Vest, *No Moment Too Small: Rhythms of Silence, Prayer and Holy Reading* (Kalamazoo, MI: Cistercian Studies/Cowley Press, 1994), 68.

10. Thomas Cahill, *Hinges of History Series* (Random House/Anchor Books, including, e.g.): *Mysteries of the Middle Ages* (2006), *Desire of the Everlasting Hills* (2001), *How the Irish Saved Civilization* (1996); and Phyllis Tickle, *The Great Emergence: How Christianity Is Changing and Why* (Grand Rapids, MI: Baker Books, 2008).

11. Louise Cowan, "Introduction: The Epic as Cosmopoesis," in *The Epic Cosmos*, ed. Larry Allums (Dallas: Dallas Institute of Humanities and Culture), 3.

12. Ibid., 5.

13. Charles J. Billson, introduction to *Vergil's Aeneid* (Toronto: Dover Thrift Books, 1995).

14. Joseph Campbell, *The Hero with a Thousand Faces*, Bollingen Series XVII (Princeton: Princeton University Press, 1968), 30.

15. Joseph Campbell, *Flight of the Wild Gander: Essays in the Mythological Dimension* (Novato, CA: New World Library, 2002), 55, 130.

16. Francis Fergusson, ed., *Aristotle's Poetics*, trans. S. H. Butcher (New York: Hill and Wang, 1961).

17. C. G. Jung and Aniela Jaffé, *Memories, Dreams, Reflections*, trans. Richard and Clara Winston, rev. ed. (New York: Vintage, 1989), especially chapter VI, 170.

18. Joan D. Chittister, *Called to Question: A Spiritual Memoir* (Chicago: Sheed and Ward, 2004), 5.

19. St. John of the Cross, *Collected Works*, trans. Kieran Kavanaugh and Otilio Rodriguez (Washington, DC: Institute of Carmelite Studies, 1973).

20. Constance FitzGerald, "Impasse and Dark Night," in *Women's Spirituality: Resources for Christian Development*, ed. Joann Wolski Conn (New York/Mahwah, NJ: Paulist Press, 1996), 414.

21. Ibid., 422.

22. Thomas Kuhn, *The Structure of Scientific Revolutions* (Chicago: University of Chicago Press, 1970), 108, 153.

23. Lucy Tatman, *Knowledge That Matters: A Feminist Theological Paradigm and Epistemology* (Cleveland, OH: Pilgrim Press, 2001), 21.

24. Elisabeth Schüssler Fiorenza, *Wisdom's Ways: Introducing Feminist Biblical Interpretation* (Maryknoll, NY: Orbis, 2001), 12.

25. Khaled Hosseini, *The Kite Runner* (Canada: Anchor, 2003).

26. Toni Morrison, *Beloved* (New York: Penguin, 1987).

27. Paul Ricoeur, "Memory and Forgetting," in *Questioning Ethics: Contemporary Debates in Philosophy*, ed. Richard Kearney and Mark Dooley (New York: Routledge, 1999), 9.

28. FitzGerald, "Impasse and Dark Night," 423.

29. This observation is indebted to Campbell's *Hero with a Thousand Faces* and especially to Hillman's *Re-Visioning Psychology*.

30. Hillman, *Re-Visioning Psychology*, xv.

31. Ibid., xx.

32. Ibid., 48.

33. Ibid., 135.

34. Ibid., xvi.

35. Henry Corbin, *Alone with the Alone: Creative Imagination in the Sufism of Ibn 'Arabī*, Bollingen Series XCI (Princeton: Princeton University Press, 1969), 4.

36. R. W. J. Austin, introduction to *Ibn Al 'Arabī's Bezels of Wisdom*, Classics of Western Spirituality Series (New York/Mahwah, NJ: Paulist Press: 1980), 34.

37. Paul Ricoeur, *Rule of Metaphor*, 7 and *Oneself as Another*, trans. Kathleen Blamey (Chicago: University of Chicago Press), 22, 129.

38. This concept is well articulated in Audre Lorde, *Sister Outsider* (Freedom, CA: Crossing Press, 1984).

39. Paul Ricoeur, *The Conflict of Interpretations: Essays in Hermeneutics* (Evanston, IL: Northwestern University Press, 1974).

40. Paul Ricoeur, *Interpretation Theory: Discourse and the Surplus of Meaning* (Fort Worth: Texas Christian University Press, 1976), 75.

41. Paul Ricoeur, "Myth as the Bearer of Possible Worlds," in *States of Mind: Dialogues with Contemporary Thinkers*, ed. Richard Kearney (New York: New York University Press, 1995), 236–45.

42. Marcus Borg, *The Heart of Christianity: Recovering a Life of Faith* (San Francisco: Harper, 2003), 28.

CHAPTER 1:
WHAT IF...? IMAGINATION AND THE IMAGINAL REALM

1. Norvene Vest, "Is Reverie to Be Trusted? The Imaginal and the Work of Marija Gimbutas," *Feminist Theology* 13:2 (2005): 239–40.

2. Gilbert Durand, "Exploration of the Imaginal," trans. Ruth Horine, *Working With Images: The Theoretical Base of Archetypal Psychology* (Woodstock, CT: Spring Books, 2000), 53.

3. Gilbert Durand, "The Imaginal," in *The Encyclopedia of Religion*, vol. 7, ed. Mircea Eliade (New York: Macmillan, 1987), 109.

4. Durand, "Exploration," 55.

5. Richard Kearney, *Poetics of Imagining: Modern to Post-Modern*, Perspectives in Continental Philosophy, Series 6 (New York: Fordham University Press, 1998), 9.

6. Edward S. Casey, *Imagining: A Phenomenological Study*, Studies in Continental Thought Series, ed. John Sallis (Bloomington, IN: Indiana University Press, 2000), 3.

7. Richard Kearney, *The Wake of Imagination: Toward a Postmodern Culture* (London: Routledge,1988), 16.

8. Kearney, *Poetics of Imagining*, 4.

9. Kearney, *Poetics of Imagining*, 2.

10. Kearney, *Wake*, 39.

11. Ibid., 80.

12. Ibid., 87–88.

13. Edward S. Casey, Lecture notes from class in *Psyche and Nature* (Carpinteria, CA: Pacifica Graduate Institute, 2004).

14. Doniger, *Implied Spider*, 3.

15. Kearney, *Wake*, 106.
16. Ibid., 107.
17. Ibid., 106.
18. Aristotle, *Poetics*, 61.
19. Ibid.
20. Hillman, *Re-Visioning Psychology*, 1. To be fair to him, Hillman assigns responsibility for the contemporary fear of the imagination not only to Descartes, but also to the Christian emphasis on spirit to the exclusion of soul and on allegory to the detriment of authentic image and the related "idea of the person as the true focus of the divine and the only carrier of soul." Hillman is highly critical of Christianity in contrast to my own view, but he offers theology much of value, whether intentional or not. See "Peaks and Vales" in Sells, *Working With Images*, 113–16 and *Re-Visioning Psychology*, 1.

21. Susan Bordo, *The Flight to Objectivity: Essays on Cartesianism and Culture*, State University of New York Series in Philosophy, ed. Robert C. Neville (New York: State University of New York Press, 1987), 26.

22. Daniel Garber, "René Descartes," *Routledge Encyclopedia of Philosophy*, vol. 3, ed. Edward Craig (New York: Routledge, 1998), 8.

23. Edward Farley, "Fundamentalism: A Theory," *Cross Currents* 55:3 (2005): 385.

24. Colin Brown, *Philosophy and the Christian Faith: A Historical Sketch from the Middle Ages to the Present Day* (Downers Grove, IL: InterVarsity Press, 1968), 62.

25. Kearney, *Wake*, 155.
26. Ibid., 156–57.

27. F. H. Heinemann, *Existentialism and the Modern Predicament* (New York: Harper and Row, 1958), 66.

28. Lewis White Beck, trans., and introduction to *Immanuel Kant's Prolegomena to Any Future Metaphysics* (Indianapolis, IN: Bobbs-Merrill, 1950), xvi.

29. Kearney, *Wake*, 158.

30. Brown, *Philosophy and Christian Faith*, 91 (Note: This is Brown's translation and paraphrase of Kant's language in "Beantwortung der Frage: Was ist Aufklärung?" *Berlinisch*

Monatsschrift, December 1784 in *Gesammelte Schriften VIII,* (Berlin), 35.

31. Bordo, *Flight to Objectivity,* 17.

32. Ibid., 95.

33. Kearney, *Poetics of Imagining,* 14.

34. Casey, *Imagining,* 38; see also Robert Sokolowski, *Introduction to Phenomenology* (New York: Cambridge University Press, 2000), 59–60.

35. "Life-world" is the English translation of Husserl's term *Lebenswelt.*

36. Sokolowski, *Introduction to Phenomenology,* 49.

37. Kearney, *Poetics of Imagining,* 22.

38. Ibid., 19.

39. Ibid., 20.

40. Ibid., 6.

41. Gaston Bachelard, *Earth and Reveries of Will: An Essay on the Imagination of Matter,* trans. Kenneth Haltman, Bachelard Translation Series (Dallas: Dallas Institute Press, 2002), 1.

42. Gaston Bachelard, *Water and Dreams: An Essay on the Imagination of Matter,* trans. Edith R. Farrell, Bachelard Translation Series (Dallas: Dallas Institute of Humanities and Culture, 1983), 199, 50.

43. Casey, *Psyche and Nature.*

44. Kearney, *Poetics of Imagining,* 97.

45. Casey, *Psyche and Nature.*

46. Bachelard, *Water and Dreams,* 16.

47. Kearney, *Poetics of Imagining,* 106.

48. Jolande Jacobi, *Complex, Archetype, Symbol in the Psychology of C. G. Jung,* trans. Ralph Manheim, Bollingen Series LVII (Princeton: Princeton University Press, 1971), 52, 59.

49. Kearney, *Poetics of Imagining,* 102.

50. Ibid., 111.

51. Bachelard, *Earth and Reveries of Will,* 4–5.

52. Bachelard, *The Poetics of Reverie: Childhood, Language, and the Cosmos,* trans. Daniel Russell (Boston: Beacon Press, 1969), 11.

53. Ibid., 15.

54. Ibid., 13.

55. Seyyed Hossein Nasr, ed. *Islamic Spirituality: Foundations*, World Spirituality: An Encyclopedic History of the Religious Quest Series, gen. ed. Ewert Cousins, vol. 19 (New York: Crossroad, 1987), xxiii.

56. Seyyed Hossein Nasr, *Three Muslim Sages: Avicenna-Suhrawardi-Ibn ʿArabī* (New York: Caravan Books, 1964), 63.

57. Nasr, *Three Sages*, 52.

58. Zaman Stanizai, Lecture notes from class in *Islamic Traditions* (Carpinteria, CA: Pacifica Graduate Institute, 2005).

59. Nasr, *Three Sages*, 3.

60. Annemarie Schimmel, *Mystical Dimensions of Islam* (Chapel Hill, NC: University of North Carolina Press, 1975), 260.

61. Nasr, *Three Sages*, 64, 62.

62. Schimmel, *Mystical Dimensions*, 261.

63. Nasr, *Three Sages*, 73.

64. Ibid., 76.

65. Zaman Stanizai, *Islamic Traditions*.

66. Nasr, *Three Sages*, 92.

67. Ibid., 102.

68. Quoted in William C. Chittick, *The Sufi Path of Knowledge: Ibn al-ʿArabī's Metaphysics of Imagination* (Albany, NY: State University of New York Press, 1989), 4.

69. Schimmel, *Mystical Dimensions*, 267.

70. Chittick, *The Sufi Path of Knowledge*, 3.

71. Schimmel, *Mystical Dimensions*, 267.

72. Ibid.

73. Stanizai, *Islamic Traditions*.

74. Corbin, *Alone with the Alone*, 184.

75. Ibid., 14.

76. Austin, introduction to *Ibn Al ʿArabī*, 27.

77. Corbin, *Alone with the Alone*, 112.

78. Ibid., 189–90.

79. Schimmel, *Mystical Dimensions*, 270.

80. Austin, Introduction to *Ibn Al ʿArabī*, 34.

81. Nasr, *Three Sages*, 110.

82. Ibid.

83. Austin, introduction to *Ibn Al ʿArabī*, 34.

Notes

84. Quoted from *Ibn 'Arabī* I: verse 304.16 in Chittick, *The Sufi Path of Knowledge*, 117–18.

85. Chittick, *The Sufi Path of Knowledge*, 112.

86. Ibid., 117.

87. Henry Corbin, "Mundus Imaginalis: Or the Imaginary and the Imaginal," trans. Ruth Horine, *Working with Images: The Theoretical Base of Archetypal Psychology*, ed. Benjamin Sells (Woodstock, CT: Spring Books, 2000), 70–89.

88. Ibid., 77.

89. Corbin, *Alone with the Alone*, 4.

90. Corbin, "Mundus Imaginalis," 76.

91. Ibid.

92. Corbin, *Alone with the Alone*, 193.

93. Corbin, "Mundus Imaginalis," 88.

94. Schimmel, *Mystical Dimensions*. This point is elaborated on pages 98 to 130.

95. Ibid., 106.

96. Henri F. Ellenberger, *The Discovery of the Unconscious: The History and Evolution of Dynamic Psychiatry* (New York: Basic Books, 1970), 6–7, 11–12.

97. Richard Tarnas, *The Passion of the Western Mind: Understanding the Ideas That Have Shaped Our World View* (New York: Ballantine, 1991), 328. And a note to the reader: Please be aware that Freud is discussed at length in chapter 3 on Paul Ricoeur.

98. C. G. Jung's writings have been collected into a multivolume compendium, which is typically cited by volume and paragraph, as for example in this case as *CW*, 11.889. The full citation here is C. G. Jung, "Forward to *Suzuki's Introduction to Zen Buddhism*," *The Collected Works of C.G. Jung*, trans. R. F. C. Hull, Vol. XI, Bollingen Series XX (Princeton: Princeton University Press, 1967), 538–57.

99. Benjamin Sells, ed., introduction to *Working with Images: The Theoretical Base of Archetypal Psychology* (Woodstock, CT: Spring Books, 2000), 5.

100. Mary Watkins, *Invisible Guests: The Development of Imaginal Dialogues* (Woodstock, CT: Spring Books, 2000), 101.

101. Ibid., 66–67.

102. Glen Slater, Lecture notes from class in *Jungian Depth Psychology* (Carpinteria, CA: Pacifica Graduate Institute, 2005).

103. C. G. Jung Foreword in Jacobi, *Complex, Archetype, Symbol*, x.

104. Jacobi, *Complex, Archetype, Symbol*, 31.

105. *CW* 11. 222, or C. G. Jung, "A Psychological Approach to the Dogma of the Trinity," *The Collected Works of C. G. Jung*, Vol. XI, par. 222.

106. Jacobi, *Complex, Archetype, Symbol*, 6.

107. Ibid., 22–23.

108. C. G. Jung and Aniela Jaffé, *Memories, Dreams, Reflections*, 170.

109. Ibid., 173.

110. Ibid., 174.

111. Ibid., 176.

112. Ibid., 177.

113. Ibid.

114. Ibid., 183.

115. Quoted from Jung's reflections on Nietzsche's *Zarathustra*, in Watkins, *Invisible Guests*, 103.

116. Anthony Storr, introduction to C. G. Jung, *The Essential Jung: Selected Writings*, trans. R. F. C. Hull and Richard and Clara Winston (Princeton, Princeton University Press, 1983), 21.

117. Edward F. Edinger, *Ego and Archetype: Individuation and the Religious Function of the Psyche* (Boston: Shambhala, 1992), 110. The material in the following paragraphs is indebted to Edinger's *Ego and Archetype*, pages 78 and following, especially in reference to Jung's essay named "The Transcendent Function," found in Jung's *Collected Works*, vol. 8. Citations here and below are from that essay.

118. *CW* 8, 132.

119. *CW* 8,178.

120. Ibid.

121. Ibid.

122. *CW* 8,181.

123. Ibid.

124. Ibid.

125. Jung and Jaffé, *Memories, Dreams, Reflections*, 183.

126. Slater, *Jungian Depth Psychology*.

127. Edinger, *Ego and Archetype*, 110.

128. Jacobi, *Complex, Archetype, Symbol*, 28.
129. *CW* 8, 186.
130. Jacobi, *Complex, Archetype, Symbol*, 12.
131. *CW* 8, 189.
132. As noted above, Jung's essay "The Transcendent Function" is found in *The Collected Works*, vol. 8, and discussed in Edinger, *Ego and Archetype*, 78 and following.
133. *CW* 8, 145.
134. Watkins, *Invisible Guests*, 105–6.
135. Jung, *Psychology and Religion*, 2.
136. Tarnas, *The Passion of the Western Mind*, 387.
137. Hillman, "Why 'Archetypal' Psychology?" *Working with Images: The Theoretical Base of Archetypal Psychology*, ed. Benjamin Sells (Woodstock, CT: Spring Books, 2000); orig. pub. *Spring Journal*, 1970: 212–19.
138. Hillman, *Archetypal Psychology* (Woodstock, CT: Spring Books, 1983), 9.
139. Hillman, "Why 'Archetypal' Psychology?" 15–16.
140. Hillman, "An Inquiry into Image," *Spring Journal* (1977): 75.
141. Hillman, *The Soul's Code: In Search of Character and Calling* (New York: Random House, 1996), 92.
142. Hillman, *Re-Visioning Psychology*, xv.
143. Ibid., 115.
144. See for example his essay "The Seduction of Black," *Spring Journal* 61 (1997): 1–15; and his book, *The Dream and the Underworld* (New York: Harper & Row, 1979).
145. Hillman, *Re-Visioning Psychology*, 56.
146. Ibid., 173.
147. Ibid., 167.
148. See for example, Hillman, *Insearch: Psychology and Religion* (Woodstock, CT: Spring Books, 1967), 131.
149. Hillman, *Re-Visioning Psychology*, 168.
150. Hillman, *Insearch*, 43.
151. Ibid., 42.
152. See especially the essays in Part II "World" of *Blue Fire: Selected Writings*, ed. Thomas Moore (New York: Harper & Row, 1989).

153. Hillman, *Blue Fire*, 25.

154. Hillman, *Archetypal Psychology*, 62.

155. Ibid., 11.

156. Good examples of wordplay are offered in "Further Notes on Images," *Spring Journal* (1978): 163–7.

157. Hillman, *Blue Fire*, 25.

158. Hillman, "An Inquiry into Image," 68.

159. Ibid., 85.

160. Hillman, *Re-Visioning Psychology*, 17.

161. Ibid., 118.

162. Ibid., 123 (Hillman's repetition and italics).

163. Ibid., 151.

164. Kearney, *Wake*, 16.

165. Adriana Berger, "Cultural Hermeneutics: The Concept of Imagination in the Phenomenological Approaches of Henry Corbin and Mircea Eliade," *Journal of Religion* (1986): 141.

166. Ibid., 143.

167. Ibid., 156.

168. Durand, "Exploration of the Imaginal," 61.

CHAPTER 2:
THINKING OTHERWISE: A FEMINIST VISION

1. Sallie McFague, *Models of God: Theology for an Ecological Nuclear Age* (Philadelphia: Fortress, 1987), 35.

2. Elaine H. Pagels, "What Became of God the Mother? Conflicting Images of God in Early Christianity," *Womanspirit Rising: A Feminist Reader in Religion*, ed. Carol P. Christ and Judith Plaskow (San Francisco: Harper, 1979), 107.

3. Valerie Saiving, "The Human Situation: A Feminine View," *Womanspirit Rising: A Feminist Reader in Religion*, ed. Carol P. Christ and Judith Plaskow, 35–36 (San Francisco: Harper, 1979); orig. pub. *Journal of Religion* (1960).

4. See page 62 above for a more complete discussion, or see Jacobi, *Complex, Archetype, Symbol*, 22–23.

Notes

5. Elizabeth A. Johnson, *She Who Is: The Mystery of God in Feminist Theological Discourse* (New York: Crossroad, 1993). This exact phrase is repeated on pages 3, 5, 38.

6. Ibid., 4.

7. Carol Flinders, *At the Root of This Longing: Reconciling a Spiritual Hunger and a Feminist Thirst* (San Francisco: Harper, 1998), 45, 50.

8. Rita Gross, *Feminism and Religion: An Introduction* (Boston: Beacon Press, 1996), 16–17 (my italics).

9. Arvind Sharma and Katherine K. Young, ed., *Feminism and World Religions* (Albany, NY: State University of New York, 1999), 2.

10. Joan D. Chittister, *Heart of Flesh: A Feminist Spirituality for Women and Men* (Grand Rapids, MI: Eerdmans, 1998), 4.

11. Ibid., 5.

12. See for example Stephanie Y. Mitchem's article, "No Longer Nailed to the Floor," *Cross Currents* (53:1, 2003): 64–74.

13. Ann Belford Ulanov, *The Feminine in Jungian Psychology and in Christian Theology* (Evanston, IL: Northwestern University Press, 1971), 13.

14. Ann Belford Ulanov, *Receiving Woman: Studies in the Psychology and Theology of the Feminine* (Philadelphia: Westminster, 1981), 77.

15. The composite ideas set forth below are my own reflections, based on years of observation and reading feminist literature. The ideas are gathered from many sources, whom I shall cite when specifically relevant.

16. Luke Dysinger, OSB, Lectures given at St. Andrew's Abbey in summer retreats titled "Benedictine Spirituality for Laity" (Valyermo, CA: 1987–97).

17. Augustine of Hippo, *Confessions*, trans. Edward B. Pusey (New York: Modern Library, 1949). In response to John Chrysostom's observation that the "beauty of women is the greatest snare," St. Odo of Cluny cries: "How should we desire to embrace what is no more than a sack of dung!" as reported in Vern L. Bullough, *The Subordinate Sex* (Chicago: University of Illinois Press, 1973), 98, 187.

18. Susan Griffin, *Woman and Nature: The Roaring Inside Her* (San Francisco: Sierra Club Books, 1978).

19. One classic example is Erich Neumann, *The Great Mother: An Analysis of the Archetype*, trans. Ralph Manheim, rev. ed., Bollingen Series XLVII (Princeton: Princeton University Press, 1972).

20. Rita M. Gross, *Buddhism after Patriarchy: A Feminist History, Analysis, and Reconstruction of Buddhism* (New York: State University of New York Press, 1993), 292.

21. Rita M. Gross, *Feminism and Religion: An Introduction* (Boston: Beacon Press, 1996), 18, 22.

22. Ibid., 18–19.

23. Ibid., 20.

24. John Chrysostom as quoted in Merlin Stone, *When God Was a Woman* (New York: Harcourt Brace Jovanovich, 1976), 226.

25. Tertullian as quoted in Mary Daly, *Beyond God the Father: Toward a Philosophy of Women's Liberation*, 2d ed. (Boston: Beacon Press, 1973), 44.

26. Joseph Campbell, *Masks of God: Occidental Mythology* (New York: Penguin, 1970), 9.

27. Doniger, *The Implied Spider*, 82.

28. Carol P. Christ, *Rebirth of the Goddess: Finding Meaning in Feminist Spirituality* (New York: Routledge, 1997), 66.

29. Johnson, *She Who Is*, 11.

30. Rosemary Radford Reuther, *Sexism and God-Talk: Toward a Feminist Theology*, 2d ed., (Boston: Beacon Press, 1993), 18–19.

31. Fiorenza, *Jesus and the Politics of Interpretation* (New York: Continuum, 2001), 4–5 (my italics).

32. Mary Grey, *Introducing Feminist Images of God*, Introductions to Feminist Theology Series, ed. Mary Grey et al. (Cleveland, OH: Pilgrim Press, 2001), 11.

33. Joann Wolski Conn, "Dancing in the Dark: Women's Spirituality and Ministry," *Women's Spirituality: Resources for Christian Development*, ed. Joann Wolski Conn, rev. ed. (New York: Paulist Press, 1996), 13.

34. Ntozake Shange, *For Colored Girls Who Have Considered Suicide When the Rainbow is Enuf* (New York: Buddah Records, 1976).
35. Carol P. Christ, "Why Women Need the Goddess: Phenomenological, Psychological and Political Reflections," *Womanspirit Rising: A Feminist Reader in Religion*, ed. Carol P. Christ and Judith Plaskow, 2d ed., (San Francisco: Harper, 1992), 275.
36. Grey, *Introducing Feminist Images of God*, 9.
37. Ibid., 9–10.
38. William E. Paden, *Interpreting the Sacred: Ways of Viewing Religion*, 2d ed. (Boston: Beacon Press, 2003), 99.
39. Christ, *Rebirth of the Goddess*, 34–35.
40. Lorde, *Sister Outsider*, 53–56.
41. See for example David Bohm, *On Dialogue*, ed. Lee Nichol (New York: Routledge, 1996).
42. Carol P. Christ, *She Who Changes: Re-Imaging the Divine in the World* (New York: Palgrave/Macmillan, 2003), 93.
43. Michael Battle and Desmond Tutu, *Ubuntu: I in You and You in Me* (New York: Seabury Press, 2009).
44. See for example the active nonviolence work of *Pace e Bene*, a Franciscan nonprofit organization active for more than twenty years in nonviolence training and nuclear protests (contact 2501 Harrison Street, Oakland, CA 94612; *www.paceebene.org*; or 510-268-8765).
45. Gross, *Feminism and Religion*, 76 (her italics).
46. Ibid., 78–79.
47. Gross, *Buddhism after Patriarchy*, 298.
48. See for example Reuther, *Sexism and God-Talk*, 47, and Sandra M. Schneiders, "Feminist Spirituality: Christian Alternative or Alternative to Christianity?" in *Women's Spirituality: Resources for Christian Development*, ed. Joann Wolski Conn (New York: Paulist Press, 1996), 32.
49. Stone, *When God Was a Woman*, 1.
50. Gross, *Feminism and Religion*, 153.
51. Much of the scholarly work in this area has been done by archeomythologist Marija Gimbutas. Riane Eisler's "popular interpretation" of Gimbutas' erotic sacred narrative, *The Chalice and*

the Blade, has sold over 500,000 copies worldwide, evidence of widespread interest and response to this narrative.

52. The narrative below is based on a number of scholarly accounts, chief among which are Marija Gimbutas's, *Civilization of the Goddess: The World of Old Europe* (San Francisco: Harper, 1991); *The Language of the Goddess: Unearthing the Hidden Symbols of Western Civilization* (San Francisco: Harper, 1989); and "Women and Culture in Goddess Orientated Old Europe," in *The Politics of Women's Spirituality: Essays on the Rise of Spiritual Power within the Feminist Movement*, ed. Charlene Spretnak (New York: Anchor, 1982), esp. 23. Additional resources include J. P. Mallory, *In Search of the Indo-Europeans: Language, Archeology, and Myth* (London: Thames and Hudson, 1989); Nanno Marinatos, *Minoan Religion: Ritual, Image and Symbol* (Columbia, SC: University of South Carolina Press, 1993); Miriam Robbins Dexter, *Whence the Goddess: A Source Book* (New York: Teachers College Press, 1990), esp. 4–5; Melissa Raphael, *Introducing Thealogy: Discourse on the Goddess*, Introductions in Feminist Theology Series, ed. Lisa Isherwood et al. (Cleveland, OH: Pilgrim Press, 2000), esp. 78; Mary Condren, *The Serpent and the Goddess: Women, Religion, and Power in Celtic Ireland*, 2d ed. (Dublin: New Island, 2002), esp. 8; and Carol P. Christ, "Musings on the Goddess and Her Cultured Despisers, Provoked by Naomi Goldenburg," *Feminist Theology* 13:2 (2005): 143–49.

53. Winifred Milius Lubell, *The Metamorphosis of Baubo: Myths of Woman's Sexual Energy* (Nashville and London: Vanderbilt University Press, 1994); and Miriam Robbins Dexter and Victor H. Mair, "Apotropaia and Fecundity in Eurasian Myth and Iconography: Erotic Female Display Figures," in *Proceedings of the Sixteenth Annual UCLA Indo-European Conference, 2004*, ed. Karlene Jones-Bley, Angela della Volpe, Martin Huld, and Miriam Robbins Dexter (Washington, DC: 2005, Institute for the Study of Man Monograph), 97–121.

54. Condren, *Serpent and Goddess*, 8.

55. The concept of a time in human history, before the written period, in which the feminine principle was worshipped in the form of goddess(es), is not new with feminism. Indeed, that theory has been held in recent centuries by such historians and mytholo-

gists as J. J. Bachofen, Karl Marx, Friedrich Engels, Sigmund Freud, and James Frazer, as well as C. G. Jung's colleagues Karl Kerenyi and Erich Neumann, as pointed out by Raphael, *Introducing Thealogy*, 89. However, those male authors tend to see what they call the matriarchal period as negative. The mythology of the prepatriarchal "Rule of the Mothers" is consistently articulated in the male-authored theories of the eighteenth to twentieth centuries as a period of amorphous and all-absorbing psychic unconsciousness, dangerous to individual freedom.

56. For a scholarly resource on the interchange of Old European cultures and newer settlers, see Marija Gimbutas, *The Kurgan Culture and the Indo-Europeanization of Europe: Selected Articles from 1952–1993*, ed. Mariam Robbins Dexter and Karlene Jones-Bley, *Journal of Indo-European Studies Monograph*, no. 18 (Washington, DC: Institute for the Study of Man, 1997).

57. Calvert Watkins, ed., *The American Heritage Dictionary of Indo-European Roots* (Boston: Houghton Mifflin Company, 1985), 23.

58. Lucy Goodison and Christine Morris, eds. *Ancient Goddesses: The Myths and the Evidence*, 2d ed. (Madison, WI: University of Wisconsin Press, 1999), 12, 8.

59. For an elaboration of this point, see N. Vest, "Is Reverie to be Trusted?"

60. Mara Lynn Keller, "The Interface of Archaeology and Mythology: A Philosophical Evaluation of the Gimbutas' Paradigm," *From the Realm of the Ancestors: An Anthology in Honor of Marija Gimbutas*, ed. Joan Marler (Manchester, CT: Knowledge, Ideas and Trends, 1997), 384.

61. Ibid., 384–86.

62. Ibid., 386.

63. Ibid., 388.

64. Reuther, *Sexism and God-Talk*, 135.

65. Ibid., 48, 67.

66. Fiorenza, *Jesus and the Politics of Interpretation*, 1.

67. To explore my preference further, see Norvene Vest, "In the Image of Godde: Feminist Spiritual Direction," *Tending the Holy: Spiritual Direction across Traditions*, ed. Norvene Vest (Harrisburg, PA: Morehouse, 2003), 186.

68. Gross, *Feminism and Religion*, 85.
69. Tatman, *Knowledge That Matters*, 45.
70. Raphael, *Introducing Thealogy*, 58.
71. McFague, *Models of God*, xiii.
72. Shannon Schrein, OSF, *Quilting and Braiding: The Feminist Christologies of Sallie McFague and Elizabeth A. Johnson in Conversation* (Collegeville, MN: Liturgical Press, 1998), 6, 8; and Tatman, *Knowledge That Matters*, 220–21.
73. Sallie McFague, *Speaking in Parables: A Study in Metaphor and Theology* (Philadelphia: Fortress Press, 1975), 2.
74. Tatman, *Knowledge that Matters*, 232.
75. McFague, *Speaking in Parables*, 96.
76. McFague, *Models of God*, 33.
77. Schrein, 13.
78. Ibid., 10.
79. Sallie McFague, "God as Mother," *Weaving the Visions: New Patterns in Feminist Spirituality*, orig. publ. *Models of God*, 1987, ed. Carol P. Christ and Judith Plaskow (San Francisco: Harper, 1989), 139.
80. McFague, *Models of God*, 35.
81. McFague, *Metaphorical Theology: Models of God in Religious Language* (Philadelphia: Fortress Press, 1982), 54.
82. McFague, *Models of God*, 91.
83. McFague, "God as Mother," 142-46.
84. Ibid., 146.
85. Ibid., 143.
86. McFague, *Models of God*, 91.
87. Schrein, 41.
88. McFague, *Models of God*, 85.
89. This quotation is from Tatman, 218–19.
90. McFague, *The Body of God: An Ecological Theology* (Minneapolis: Fortress, 1993), 16.
91. Ibid., 111, 185.
92. Schrein, 86.
93. Johnson, *She Who Is*, 29.
94. Ibid., 11.
95. Schrein, 17.

96. Elizabeth A. Johnson, "The Symbolic Character of Theological Statements about Mary," *Journal of Ecumenical Studies* 22 (1985): 320.

97. Ibid., 322. This theme will be explored further in Chapter 3 in the work of Paul Ricoeur.

98. Johnson, *She Who Is*, 113.

99. Ibid., 114.

100. Ibid., 192.

101. Ibid., 193.

102. Ibid., 197 and 204.

103. Ibid., 225.

104. Ibid., 226. The experience of self not as encapsulated ego or as diffuse self denied is not only an emerging experience of women, but is also a model currently favored as a sign of psychological health.

105. Ibid., 236.

106. Daly, *Beyond God the Father*, 33–37.

107. John Macquarrie, *Principles of Christian Theology* (New York: Scribner, 1966), 179–185 as referred to and elaborated in Johnson, *She Who Is*, 239.

108. Johnson, *She Who Is*, 231.

109. Ibid., 225.

110. Ibid., 230.

111. Ibid., 247.

112. Ibid., 252.

113. Phyllis Trible, *God and the Rhetoric of Sexuality* (Philadelphia: Fortress Press, 1978), 33.

114. Johnson, *She Who Is*, 249.

115. Ibid., 254.

116. Ibid., 263.

117. Ibid., 269.

118. Ibid., 270.

119. Fiorenza, *Jesus and the Politics*, 3.

120. Ibid., 3, 6.

121. Ibid., 5.

122. Ibid., 15.

123. Ibid., 95.

124. Ibid.

125. For example, Colin Brown, Lecture notes from class in *Systematic Theology II* (Pasadena, CA: Fuller Theological Seminary, 1983).

126. Fiorenza, *Jesus and the Politics*, 165.

127. Ibid., 164.

128. Fiorenza, *In Memory of Her: A Feminist Theological Reconstruction of Christian Origins* (New York: Crossroad, 1985), 29.

129. Ibid.

130. Ibid., 45; and Fiorenza, *Jesus, Miriam's Child, Sophia's Prophet: Critical Issues in Feminist Christology* (New York: Continuum Books, 1994), 29.

131. Fiorenza, *In Memory of Her*, 41.

132. Fiorenza, *Wisdom's Ways*, 83.

133. Ibid., 43.

134. Ibid., see especially Chapter VI, 165–207.

135. Fiorenza, *Jesus, Miriam's Child, Sophia's Prophet*, 27–28.

136. Ibid., 131.

137. Fiorenza, *In Memory of Her*, 134.

138. For an extensive discussion and translations of the specific scripture passages pertaining to Sophia, see Susan Cady, Marian Ronan, and Hal Taussig, *Wisdom's Feast: Sophia in Study and Celebration* (San Francisco: Harper, 1989).

139. Fiorenza, *Jesus, Miriam's Child, Sophia's Prophet*, 135.

140. Ibid., 147, quoting from Sirach 24:3–7.

141. Ibid., 135.

142. Ibid., 157.

143. Ibid., 142.

144. Fiorenza, *Jesus and the Politics*, 7.

145. Ibid., 113.

146. Fiorenza, *In Memory of Her*, 118. *Praxis* can be understood as the action or practice flowing from a commitment.

147. Ibid., 119, 121.

148. See, for example, John Dominic Crossan, *Jesus: A Revolutionary Biography* (San Francisco: Harper, 1994), 66–70.

149. Fiorenza, *Wisdom's Ways*, 77.

150. Fiorenza, *Jesus, Miriam's Child, Sophia's Prophet*, 187.

151. Tatman, 45.

152. These four points were central to a lecture made by Catherine Keller at Syracuse University Conference II, *Postmodernism, Culture and Religion*, in April 2007.

153. Fiorenza, *Wisdom's Ways*, 42.

154. I have adapted this definition from Doniger, *The Implied Spider*, 2, as referenced earlier.

CHAPTER 3:
THE "OPEN" PHILOSOPHY
OF PAUL RICOEUR

1. Friedrich L. Schweitzer, *The Postmodern Life Cycle: Challenges for Church and Theology* (St. Louis: Chalice Press, 2004), 4.

2. Ibid., 22, quoting from Langdon Gilkey, *Religion and the Scientific Future* (New York: Harper, 1970).

3. Russell T. McCutcheon, ed., *The Insider/Outsider Problem in the Study of Religion: A Reader* (New York: Cassell, 1999), 9.

4. Doniger 10.

5. Kearney, *Strangers, Gods and Monsters: Interpreting Otherness* (London: Routledge, 2003), 9.

6. Paul Ricoeur, *Freud and Philosophy*, trans. Denis Savage (New Haven: Yale University Press, 1970), 32.

7. Bordo, *Flight to Objectivity*, 7.

8. Ricoeur, "Intellectual Autobiography of Paul Ricoeur," *The Philosophy of Paul Ricoeur*, ed. Lewis Edwin Hahn, Library of Living Philosophers, vol. XXII (Chicago: Open Court, 1995), 13.

9. Ricoeur, *Conflict of Interpretations*, 237.

10. Ricoeur, *Freud and Philosophy*.

11. Ibid., 6.

12. Ibid., 33.

13. Ibid., 34.

14. Ricoeur, *Conflict of Interpretations*, 165.

15. Ricoeur, *Freud and Philosophy*, 257.

16. Ibid., 117.

17. Ibid., 118.

18. Ibid., 120.
19. Ricoeur, *Conflict of Interpretations*, 100 (Ricoeur's italics).
20. Ibid., 121.
21. Ricoeur, *Freud and Philosophy*, 180.
22. Ricoeur, *Conflict of Interpretations*, 238.
23. Ricoeur, *Freud and Philosophy*, 250.
24. Ricoeur, *Conflict of Interpretations*, 145.
25. Ricoeur, *Freud and Philosophy*, 235.
26. Ricoeur, *Conflict of Interpretations*, 146.
27. Ricoeur, *Freud and Philosophy*, 15.
28. Ibid., 256.
29. Ibid.
30. Ibid., 262.
31. Ibid., 282.
32. Ibid., 292.
33. Ibid., 311.
34. Ibid., 269.
35. Ibid., 271.
36. Ibid., 213.
37. Ibid., 277.
38. Ibid., 279.
39. Ibid., 280.
40. Ibid., 421.
41. Ricoeur, *Conflict of Interpretations*, 241.
42. Ibid., 108.
43. Ricoeur, *Freud and Philosophy*, 439.
44. Ibid., 419.
45. Ibid., 449.
46. Ibid., 459.
47. Ricoeur, *Conflict of Interpretations*, 117.
48. Ibid., 120.
49. The term *second naivete* is one for which Ricoeur is well-known. In the *Symbolism of Evil* (Boston: Beacon Press, 1967), 351, Ricoeur observes that although the immediacy of belief is irremediably lost (by the critiques of a hermeneutics of suspicion), it is possible to aim at a second naivete by another step

of symbolic, communal interpretation that opens up new possibilities of being, a world in front of the text.

50. Ricoeur, *Freedom and Nature: The Voluntary and the Involuntary*, trans. Erazim V. Kohak, Northwestern University Studies in Phenomenology and Existential Philosophy Series, ed. John Wild (Evanston, IL: Northwestern University Press, 1966), 405.

51. Ibid.

52. Ibid., 472.

53. Ibid., 414.

54. Ibid., 424.

55. Ricoeur, *Interpretation Theory: Discourse and the Surplus of Meaning*, (Fort Worth: Texas Christian University Press, 1976), 37.

56. Ricoeur, "Intellectual Autobiography," 16.

57. Ricoeur, *Rule of Metaphor*, 74.

58. Ricoeur, *Conflict of Interpretations*,12.

59. Ibid., 13.

60. Ibid., 91.

61. Ibid., 17.

62. Ibid., 18.

63. Ricoeur, *Rule of Metaphor*, 6.

64. Ibid.

65. Ibid., 229–30.

66. Ibid., 221.

67. Ibid., 220.

68. Ibid., 227.

69. Ibid., 7.

70. Ibid., 249.

71. Ibid., 250.

72. Ibid., 251.

73. Ibid., 255.

74. Ibid., 307–8.

75. Ibid., 253.

76. Ricoeur, *Time and Narrative*, trans. Kathleen McLaughlin and David Pellauer, vol. I (Chicago: University of Chicago Press, 1984), 80.

77. Ricoeur, *Rule of Metaphor*, 254.

78. Ibid.

79. Ibid, 224.
80. Ricoeur, *Conflict of Interpretations*, 108.
81. Ricoeur, *Freedom and Nature*, 418.
82. Ricoeur, *Oneself as Another*, 3.
83. Battle and Tutu, *Ubuntu*, 3.
84. Ricoeur, *Oneself as Another*, 19.
85. Ibid., 17–18.
86. Ibid., 20.
87. Ibid., 115.
88. Ibid., 116.
89. Ibid., 128.
90. Ibid., 129.
91. Ibid., 22.
92. Fiorenza, *Wisdom Ways*, 14.
93. Ricoeur, *Oneself as Another*, 169.
94. Ibid., 169–70.
95. Ibid., 170.
96. Ibid., 171.
97. Ibid., 172.
98. Ibid., 180.
99. Ibid.
100. Ibid., 189.
101. Ibid.
102. Ibid., 190.
103. Ibid., 192.
104. Ibid., 194.
105. Ibid. Ricoeur borrows this idea from Hannah Arendt, *The Human Condition* (Chicago: University of Chicago Press, 1958), 143.
106. Ricoeur, *Oneself as Another*, 202.
107. Ibid., 221.
108. Ibid., 219.
109. Ibid., 240.
110. Ibid., 241.
111. Sophocles, *The Three Theban Plays*, trans. Robert Fagles (New York: Penguin Books, 1982).
112. Ricoeur, *Oneself as Another*, 248.
113. Ibid.

114. Ibid., 249.

115. Ibid., 254 and 256.

116. Ibid., 258.

117. Ibid., 260.

118. Ibid., 266.

119. Ibid., 267.

120. Ibid., 268.

121. Ibid.

122. Ibid., 273.

123. Ibid., 274.

124. Ricoeur, "Intellectual Autobiography," 50.

125. Ricoeur, *Oneself as Another*, 302.

126. Kearney, *Strangers, Gods, and Monsters*, 9.

127. Jürgen Habermas, "Discourse Ethics: Notes on a Program of Philosophical Justification," *Moral Consciousness and Communicative Action: Studies in Contemporary German Social Thought* (Cambridge, MA: Massachusetts Institute of Philosophy Press, 1983), 44.

128. Aristotle, "Poetics," 68.

129. Richard Kearney, *States of Mind: Dialogues with Contemporary Thinkers* (New York: New York University Press, 1995), 217.

130. Domenico Jervolino, "The Depth and Breadth of Paul Ricoeur's Philosophy," *The Philosophy of Paul Ricoeur*, ed. Lewis Edwin Hahn, The Library of Living Philosophers, vol. XXII (Chicago: Open Court Press, 1995), 533.

131. Thompson, introduction to *Paul Ricoeur: Hermeneutics and the Human Sciences*, 32.

132. Ricoeur, *Interpretation Theory*, 74.

133. Ricoeur, *Hermeneutics and the Human Sciences*, 111.

134. Ibid., especially chapter 4, "The Hermeneutical Function of Distanciation," 131–44.

135. Ibid., 142.

136. Ibid., especially chapter 7, "Appropriation," 182–93, esp. 185.

137. Ibid., 162.

138. Ricoeur, *Oneself as Another*, 288.

139. See especially Paul Ricoeur, *Critique and Conviction: Conversations with François Azouvi and Marc De Launay*, trans. Kathleen Blamey, European Perspectives: A Series in Social Thought and Cultural Criticism, gen. ed. Lawrence D. Kritzman (New York: Columbia University Press, 1998).

140. Ricoeur, *Critique and Conviction*, 139.

141. Jervolino, "Depth and Breadth," 536.

142. Ibid.

143. Ricoeur, *Conflict of Interpretations*, 153.

CONCLUSION:
A BOLD THEOLOGY

1. Gregory of Nyssa, *The Life of Moses*, trans. and introduction, Abraham J. Malherbe and Everett Ferguson, The Classics of Western Spirituality Series (New York: Paulist Press, 1978), 116, par. 219–39.

2. Ibid., 112.

3. Urban T. Holmes, *Ministry and Imagination* (New York: Seabury Press, 1981), 167–68.

4. Richard Kearney, *Poetics of Imagining*, 6.

5. Ada Maria Isasi-Diaz is one of the first theologians to use the term, *kin-dom*. See *Mujerista Theology: A Theology for the Twenty-First Century* (Maryknoll, NY: Orbis Books, 1996), 65 and 125 endnote.

6. Corbin, "Mundus Imaginalis," 83.

7. Marcus Borg and N.T. Wright, *The Meaning of Jesus: Two Visions* (San Francisco: Harper, 1999), 121.

8. Ibid., 123.

9. Ibid., 125.

10. Ibid., 134–35.

11. Ched Myers, "Easter Faith and Empire: Recovering the Prophetic Tradition on the Emmaus Road," *Getting the Message: Challenging the Christian Right from the Heart of the Gospel*, ed. Peter Laarman (Boston: Beacon Press, 2006), 60.

12. Ibid., 63.

13. Ibid., 62.

14. Ibid., 64.

15. Fyodor Dostoevsky, *The Grand Inquisitor* (Seven Treasures Publications, 2009), 39.

16. Tatman, *Knowledge That Matters*, 98.

17. Johnson, *She Who Is*, 242.

18. Ibid., 243.

19. Reuther, *Sexism and God-Talk*, 67.

20. This is common practice in the books of Fiorenza, Johnson, and Borg.

21. Crossan, *Jesus*, 69.

22. Borg, *Meeting Jesus Again for the First Time* (San Francisco: Harper, 1999), 50.

23. Sergei Bulgakov, *Sophia, The Wisdom of God: An Outline of Sophiology*, trans. Patrick Thompson, O. Fielding Clarke and Xenia Braikevitc (Hudson, NY: Lindisfarne Press, 1993), 33.

24. Ibid., 77.

25. Ibid., 71.

26. The reflections below are gathered in part from a paper by my (physicist and priest) husband, Doug Vest, "Some Correspondences Between Atomic Physics and Formative Spirituality: A Term Paper" (unpublished) (Pittsburgh: Duquesne University, 1981); and also from Diarmuid O'Murchu, MSC, *Quantum Theology* (New York: Crossroad, 1998); and Fritjof Capra, *The Tao of Physics* (New York: Bantum, 1975).

27. Capra, *The Tao of Physics*, 56.

28. O'Murchu, *Quantum Theology*, 198.

29. Raimundo Panikkar, *Blessed Simplicity: The Monk as Universal Archetype* (New York: Seabury, 1982), 11.

30. Ibid.

31. Ibid., 33.

32. Ibid., 35.

33. Ibid., 106.

34. Ibid., 110.

35. Ricoeur, "Myth as the Bearer of Possible Worlds," 243.

Bibliography

Arendt, Hannah. *The Human Condition*. Chicago: University of Chicago Press, 1958.

Aristotle. *Poetics*. Translated by S. H. Butcher. Edited by Francis Fergusson. New York: Hill and Wang, 1961.

Augustine of Hippo. *Confessions*. Translated by Edward B. Pusey. New York: Modern Library, 1949.

Austin, R. W. J. Introduction. *Ibn al-'Arabī: The Bezels of Wisdom*. Translated by R. W. J. Austin. Classics of Western Spirituality Series. New York: Paulist Press, 1980.

Bachelard, Gaston. *Earth and Reveries of Will: An Essay on the Imagination of Matter*. Translated by Kenneth Haltman. The Bachelard Translation Series. Edited by Joanne H. Stroud and Robert S. Dupree. Dallas: Dallas Institute Press, 2002.

———. *The Poetics of Reverie: Childhood, Language, and the Cosmos*. Translated by Daniel Russell. Boston: Beacon Press, 1969.

———. *Water and Dreams: An Essay on the Imagination of Matter*. Translated by Edith R. Farrell. The Bachelard Translation Series. Edited by Joanne H. Stroud. Dallas: Dallas Institute of Humanities and Culture, 1983.

Battle, Michael, and Desmond Tutu. *Ubuntu: I in You and You in Me*. New York: Seabury Press, 2009.

Beck, Lewis White, Introduction. *Immanuel Kant: Prolegomena to Any Future Metaphysics*. Translated by Lewis White Beck. Indianapolis, IN: Bobbs-Merrill, 1950.

Berger, Adriana. "Cultural Hermeneutics: The Concept of Imagination in the Phenomenological Approaches of Henry Corbin and Mircea Eliade." *Journal of Religion* (1986): 141–57.

Bibliography

Billson, Charles J. *Vergil's Aeneid*. Translated by Charles J. Billson. Toronto: Dover Press, 1995.

Bohm, David. *On Dialogue*. Edited by Lee Nichol. New York: Routledge, 1996.

Bordo, Susan. *The Flight to Objectivity: Essays on Cartesianism and Culture*. State University of New York Series in Philosophy. Edited by. Robert C. Neville. New York: State University of New York Press, 1987.

Borg, Marcus. *The Heart of Christianity: Recovering a Life of Faith*. San Francisco: Harper, 2003.

———. *Meeting Jesus Again for the First Time*. San Francisco: Harper, 1994.

Borg, Marcus, and N. T. Wright. *The Meaning of Jesus: Two Visions*. San Francisco: Harper, 1999.

Brown, Colin. *Philosophy and the Christian Faith: A Historical Sketch from the Middle Ages to the Present Day*. Downers Grove, IL: InterVarsity Press, 1968.

———. Lecture Notes from class in *Systematic Theology II*. Pasadena, CA: Fuller Theological Seminary, 1983.

Bulgakov, Sergei. *Sophia, the Wisdom of God: An Outline of Sophiology*. Translated by Patrick Thompson, O. Fielding Clarke, and Xenia Braikevitc. Originally published in 1937. Hudson, NY: Lindisfarne Books, 1993.

Cady, Susan, Marian Ronan, and Hal Taussig. *Wisdom's Feast: Sophia in Study and Celebration*. San Francisco: Harper, 1989.

Cahill, Thomas. *Hinges of History Series*. New York: Random House/Anchor Books. Including for example: *Mysteries of the Middle Ages* (2006), *Desire of the Everlasting Hills* (2001), and *How the Irish Saved Civilization* (1996).

Campbell, Joseph. *The Flight of the Wild Gander: Essays in the Mythological Dimension*. Novato, CA: New World Library, 2002.

———. *The Hero with a Thousand Faces*. Originally published in 1949. Bollingen Series XVII. 2d ed. Princeton: Princeton University Press, 1968.

———. *The Masks of God: Occidental Mythology*. New York: Penguin, 1970.

Capra, Fritjof. *The Tao of Physics*. New York: Bantum Books, 1975.

Casey, Edward S. *Imagining: A Phenomenological Study.* Studies in Continental Thought. Edited by John Sallis. 2d ed. Bloomington, IN: Indiana University Press, 2000.

———. Lecture Notes from class in *Psyche and Nature.* Carpinteria, CA: Pacifica Graduate Institute, Spring 2004.

Chittick, William C. *The Sufi Path of Knowledge: Ibn al-'Arabī's Metaphysics of Imagination.* Albany, NY: State University of New York Press, 1989.

Chittister, Joan D. *Called to Question: A Spiritual Memoir.* Chicago: Sheed & Ward, 2004.

———. *Heart of Flesh: A Feminist Spirituality for Women and Men.* Grand Rapids, MI: Eerdmans, 1998.

Christ, Carol P. "Musings on the Goddess and Her Cultured Despisers, Provoked by Naomi Goldenberg." *Feminist Theology* 13.2 (2005): 143–9.

———. *Rebirth of the Goddess: Finding Meaning in Feminist Spirituality.* New York: Routledge, 1997.

———. *She Who Changes: Re-Imagining the Divine in the World.* New York: Palgrave/Macmillan, 2003.

———. "Why Women Need the Goddess: Phenomenological, Psychological and Political Reflections." In *Womanspirit Rising: A Feminist Reader in Religion.* Edited by Carol P. Christ and Judith Plaskow, 273–87. Originally published in 1979. 2d ed. San Francisco: Harper, 1992.

Condren, Mary. *The Serpent and the Goddess: Women, Religion, and Power in Celtic Ireland.* Originally published in 1989. 2d ed. Dublin: New Island, 2002.

Conn, Joann Wolski. "Dancing in the Dark: Women's Spirituality and Ministry." In *Women's Spirituality: Resources for Christian Development,* edited by. Joann Wolski Conn, 9–29. Originally published in 1986. New York: Paulist Press, 1996.

Corbin, Henry. *Alone with the Alone: Creative Imagination in the Sufism of Ibn 'Arabī.* Translated by Ralph Manheim. Bollingen Series XCI. Princeton: Princeton University Press, 1969.

———. "Mundus Imaginalis: Or the Imaginary and the Imaginal." Translated by Ruth Horine. In *Working with Images: The Theoretical Base of Archetypal Psychology,* edited by Benjamin Sells, 70–89. Originally published in 1972 in *Spring Journal.* Woodstock, CT: Spring Books, 2000.

Cowan, Louise. "Introduction: The Epic as Cosmopoesis." In *The Epic Cosmos*, edited by Larry Allums, 1–26. Dallas: Dallas Institute of Humanities and Culture, 1992.

Crossan, John Dominic. *Jesus: A Revolutionary Biography*. San Francisco: Harper, 1994.

Daly, Mary. *Beyond God the Father: Toward a Philosophy of Women's Liberation*. Originally published in 1973. 2d ed. Boston: Beacon Press, 1985.

Dexter, Miriam Robbins. *Whence the Goddess: A Source Book*. New York: Teachers College Press, 1990.

Dexter, Miriam Robbins, and Victor H. Mair. "Apotropaia and Fecundity in Eurasian Myth and Iconography: Erotic Female Display Figures." In *Proceedings of the Sixteenth Annual UCLA Indo-European Conference, 2004*, edited by Karlene Jones-Bley, Angela della Volpe, Martin Huld, and Miriam Robbins Dexter, 97–121. Washington, DC: Institute for the Study of Man Monograph: 2005.

Doniger, Wendy. *The Implied Spider: Politics & Theology in Myth*. New York: Columbia University Press, 1998.

Dostoevsky, Fyodor. *The Grand Inquisitor*. Originally published in 1880. Seven Treasures Publications, 2009.

Durand, Gilbert. "Exploration of the Imaginal." Translated by Ruth Horine. In *Working with Images: The Theoretical Base of Archetypal Psychology*, edited by Benjamin Sells, 52–68. Woodstock, CT: Spring Books, 2000.

———. "The Imaginal." Translated by Sally Gran. In *The Encyclopedia of Religion*, edited by Mircea Eliade. Vol. 7, 109–114. New York: Macmillan, 1987.

Dysinger, Luke, OSB. Lecture Notes from workshop on *Benedictine Spirituality for Laity*. Valyermo, CA: St. Andrew's Abbey, Summer, 1995.

Edinger, Edward F. *Ego and Archetype: Individuation and the Religious Function of the Psyche*. Boston: Shambhala, 1992.

Eisler, Riane. *The Chalice and the Blade: Our History, Our Future*. San Francisco: Harper, 1987.

Ellenberger, Henri F. *The Discovery of the Unconscious: The History and Evolution of Dynamic Psychiatry*. New York: Basic Books, 1970.

Farley, Edward. "Fundamentalism: A Theory." *Cross Currents* 55.3 (2005): 378–403.

Fergusson, Francis, ed. and introduction to *Aristotle's Poetics*. Translated by S. H. Butcher. New York: Hill and Wang, 1961.

Fiorenza, Elisabeth Schüssler. *In Memory of Her: A Feminist Theological Reconstruction of Christian Origins*. New York: Crossroad, 1985.

———. *Jesus and the Politics of Interpretation*. New York: Continuum, 2001.

———. *Jesus: Miriam's Child, Sophia's Prophet: Critical Issues in Feminist Christology*. New York: Continuum, 1994.

———. *Wisdom Ways: Introducing Feminist Biblical Interpretation*. Maryknoll, NY: Orbis, 2001.

FitzGerald, Constance. "Impasse and Dark Night." In *Women's Spirituality: Resources for Christian Development*, edited by Joann Wolski Conn, 410–35. Originally published in 1986. New York: Paulist Press, 1996.

Flinders, Carol. *At the Root of This Longing: Reconciling a Spiritual Hunger and a Feminist Thirst*. San Francisco: Harper, 1998.

Garber, Daniel. "René Descartes." *Routledge Encyclopedia of Philosophy*. Edited by Edward Craig. Vol. 3:1–19. New York: Routledge, 1998.

Gilkey, Langdon. *Religion and the Scientific Future*. New York: Harper, 1970.

Gimbutas, Marija. *The Civilization of the Goddess: The World of Old Europe*. San Francisco: Harper, 1991.

———. *The Kurgan Culture and the Indo-Europeanization of Europe: Selected Articles from 1952–1993*. Edited by Mariam Robbins Dexter and Karlene Jones-Bley, Journal of Indo-European Studies Monograph No. 18 (Washington DC: Institute for the Study of Man, 1997).

———. *The Language of the Goddess: Unearthing the Hidden Symbols of Western Civilization*. Originally published in 1989. 2d ed. San Francisco: Harper, 1991.

———. "Women and Culture in Goddess Orientated Old Europe." *The Politics of Women's Spirituality: Essays on the Rise of Spiritual Power within the Feminist Movement*. Edited by Charlene Spretnak. 22–31. New York: Anchor, 1982.

Goodison, Lucy, and Christine Morris, ed. *Ancient Goddesses: The Myths and the Evidence.* Originally published in 1998 in Great Britain. 2d ed. Madison, WI: University of Wisconsin Press, 1999.

Gregory of Nyssa. *The Life of Moses.* Translated and Introduction by Abraham J. Malherbe and Everett Ferguson. The Classics of Western Spirituality Series (New York: Paulist Press, 1978).

Grey, Mary. *Introducing Feminist Images of God.* Introductions in Feminist Theology. Edited by Lisa Isherwood, Mary Grey, Catherine Norris, and Janet Wootton. Cleveland, OH: Pilgrim Press, 2001.

Griffin, Susan. *Woman and Nature: the Roaring Inside Her.* San Francisco: Sierra Club Books, 1978.

Gross, Rita M. *Buddhism after Patriarchy: A Feminist History, Analysis, and Reconstruction of Buddhism.* New York: State University of New York Press, 1993.

———. *Feminism and Religion: An Introduction.* Boston: Beacon, 1996.

Habermas, Jürgen. "Discourse Ethics: Notes on a Program of Philosophical Justification." *Moral Consciousness and Communicative Action: Studies in Contemporary German Social Thought,* 43–115. Originally published in 1983 in German. Cambridge MA: Massachusetts Institute of Technology Press.

Heinemann, F. H. *Existentialism and the Modern Predicament.* New York: Harper & Row, 1958.

Hillman, James. *Archetypal Psychology.* Woodstock, CT: Spring, 1983.

———. *A Blue Fire: Selected Writings.* Edited by Thomas Moore. New York: Harper & Row, 1989.

———. *The Dream and the Underworld.* New York: Harper & Row, 1979.

———. "Further Notes on Images." *Spring Journal* (1978): 152–82.

———. "An Inquiry into Image." *Spring Journal* (1977): 62–88.

———. *Insearch: Psychology and Religion.* Woodstock, CT: Spring Books, 1967.

———. "Peaks and Vales." *In Working with Images: The Theoretical Base of Archetypal Psychology.* Edited by Benjamin Sells, 112–35. Woodstock, CT: Spring Books, 2000.

———. *Re-Visioning Psychology.* New York: Harper & Row, 1975.

———. "The Seduction of Black." *Spring Journal* 61 (1997): 1–15.

———. *The Soul's Code: In Search of Character and Calling.* New York: Random House, 1996.

———. "Why 'Archetypal' Psychology?" *Working with Images: The Theoretical Base of Archetypal Psychology.* Edited by Benjamin Sells, 10–18. Originally published in Spring Journal 1970: 212–9. Woodstock, CT: *Spring Books* 2000.

Holmes, Urban. *Ministry and Imagination.* New York: Seabury Press, 1981.

Hosseini, Khaled. *The Kite Runner.* Canada: Anchor, 2003.

Isasi-Díaz, Ada Maria. *Mujerista Theology: A Theology for the Twenty-First Century.* Maryknoll, NY: Orbis, 1996.

Jacobi, Jolande. *Complex, Archetype, Symbol in the Psychology of C. G. Jung.* Originally published in 1959. Translated by Ralph Manheim. Bollingen Series LVII. Princeton: Princeton University Press, 1971.

Jervolino, Domenico. "The Depth and Breadth of Paul Ricoeur's Philosophy." In *The Philosophy of Paul Ricoeur.* Edited by Lewis Edwin Hahn. The Library of Living Philosophers. Vol. XXII, 533–48. Chicago: Open Court, 1995.

Johnson, Elizabeth A. *She Who Is: The Mystery of God in Feminist Theological Discourse.* New York: Crossroad, 1993.

———. "The Symbolic Character of Theological Statements About Mary." *Journal of Ecumenical Studies* 22 (1985): 312–35.

Jung, C. G. *The Essential Jung: Selected Writings.* Translated by R. F. C. Hull and Richard and Clara Winston. Introduction and edited by Anthony Storr. Princeton: Princeton University Press, 1983.

———. "Forward to *Suzuki's Introduction to Zen Buddhism.*" In *The Collected Works of C. G. Jung.* Translated by R. F. C. Hull Vol. XI. Bollingen Series XX. Princeton: Princeton University Press, 1967.

———. "A Psychological Approach to the Dogma of the Trinity." *The Collected Works of C. G. Jung.* Translated by R. F. C. Hull. Vol. XI. Bollingen Series XX, 148–63. Princeton: Princeton University Press, 1967.

———. *Psychology and Religion.* New Haven: Yale University Press, 1938.

———. "The Transcendent Function." In *The Collected Works of C. G. Jung.* Translated by R. F. C. Hull. Vol. VIII. Bollingen XX, 67–91. Princeton: Princeton University Press, 1967.

Jung, C. G., and Aniela Jaffé. *Memories, Dreams, Reflections.* Translated by Richard and Clara Winston. Revised ed. New York: Vintage, 1989.

Kearney, Richard. *Poetics of Imagining: Modern to Post-Modern.* Perspectives in Continental Philosophy. Vol. 6. New York: Fordham University Press, 1998.

———. *Strangers, Gods and Monsters: Interpreting Otherness.* London: Routledge, 2003.

———. *States of Mind: Dialogues with Contemporary Thinkers.* New York: New York University Press, 1995.

———. *The Wake of Imagination: Toward a Postmodern Culture.* London: Routledge, 1988.

Keller, Catherine. Lecture at *Postmodernism, Culture and Religion* conference. Syracuse: Syracuse University, April, 2007.

Keller, Mara Lynn. "The Interface of Archeology and Mythology: A Philosophical Evaluation of the Gimbutas' Paradigm." In *From the Realm of the Ancestors: An Anthology in Honor of Marija Gimbutas.* Edited by Joan Marler, 381-98. Manchester, CT: Knowledge, Ideas and Trends, 1997.

Kuhn, Thomas. *The Structure of Scientific Revolutions.* 2d ed. Chicago: University of Chicago Press, 1970.

Lorde, Audre. *Sister Outsider.* Freedom, CA: Crossing Books, 1984.

Lubell, Winifred Milius. *The Metamorphosis of Baubo: Myths of Women's Sexual Energy.* Nashville and London: Vanderbilt University Press, 1994.

Macquarrie, John. *Principles of Christian Theology.* New York: Scribner, 1966.

Mallory, J. P. *In Search of the Indo-Europeans: Language, Archaeology and Myth.* London: Thames & Hudson, 1989.

Marinatos, Nanno. *Minoan Religion: Ritual, Image and Symbol.* Columbia SC: University of South Carolina Press, 1993.

McCutcheon, Russell T, ed. and introduction to *The Insider/Outsider Problem in the Study of Religion: A Reader.* New York: Cassell, 1999.

McFague, Sallie. *The Body of God: An Ecological Theology.* Minneapolis, MN: Fortress, 1993.

———. "God as Mother." *Weaving the Visions: New Patterns in Feminist Spirituality.* Edited by Carol P. Christ and Judith Plaskow, 139–50. Originally published 1987 in *Models of God.* San Francisco: Harper, 1989.

———. *Metaphorical Theology: Models of God in Religious Language.* Philadelphia: Fortress, 1982.

———. *Models of God: Theology for an Ecological Nuclear Age.* Philadelphia: Fortress, 1987.

———. *Speaking in Parables: A Study in Metaphor and Theology.* Philadelphia: Fortress, 1975.

Mickelthwait, John. "In God's Name: A Special Report on Religion and Public Life." *The Economist* 385 (November 3–9, 2007): 1-22. Special Report.

Mitchem, Stephanie Y. "No Longer Nailed to the Floor." *Cross Currents* 53.1 (2003): 64–74.

Morrison, Toni. *Beloved.* New York: Penguin, 1987.

Myers, Ched. "Easter Faith and Empire: Recovering the Prophetic Tradition on the Emmaus Road." *Getting on Message: Challenging the Christian Right from the Heart of the Gospel.* Edited by Peter Laarman, 51-67. Boston: Beacon, 2006.

Nasr, Seyyed Hossein, ed. *Islamic Spirituality: Foundations.* World Spirituality: An Encyclopedic History of the Religious Quest Series. Vol. 19. Gen. ed. Ewert Cousins. New York: Crossroad, 1987.

———. *Three Muslim Sages: Avicenna-Suhrawardi–Ibn ʿArabī.* New York: Caravan Books, 1964.

Neumann, Erich. *The Great Mother: An Analysis of the Archetype.* Translated by Ralph Manheim. Originally published in 1955. Bollingen Series XLVII. Princeton: Princeton University Press, 1972.

O'Murchu, Diarmuid, MSC. *Quantum Theology.* New York: Crossroad, 1998.

Pace e Bene Franciscan non-violence organization, www.paceebene.org.

Paden, William E. *Interpreting the Sacred: Ways of Viewing Religion.* 2d ed. Boston: Beacon Press, 2003.

Pagels, Elaine H. "What Became of God the Mother? Conflicting Images of God in Early Christianity." *Womanspirit Rising: A Feminist Reader in Religion*. Edited by Carol P. Christ and Judith Plaskow, 107–19. San Francisco: Harper, 1979.

Panikkar, Raimundo. *Blessed Simplicity: The Monk as Universal Archetype*. New York: Seabury, 1982.

Raphael, Melissa. *Introducing Thealogy: Discourse on the Goddess*. Introductions in Feminist Theology Series. Edited by Lisa Isherwood, Mary Grey, Catherine Norris, and Janet Wootton. Cleveland, OH: Pilgrim, 2000.

Reuther, Rosemary. *Sexism and God-Talk: Toward a Feminist Theology*. Originally published in 1983. 2d ed. Boston: Beacon Press, 1993.

Ricoeur, Paul. *The Conflict of Interpretations: Essays in Hermeneutics*. Portions translated by Kathleen McLaughlin, Robert Sweeney, Willis Domingo, Peter McCormick, Denis Savage, and Charles Freilick. Evanston, IL: Northwestern University Press, 1974.

———. *Critique and Conviction: Conversations with François Azouvi and Marc De Launay*. Translated by Kathleen Blamey. European Perspectives: A Series in Social Thought and Cultural Criticism. Edited by Lawrence D. Kritzman. New York: Columbia University Press, 1998.

———. *Freedom and Nature: The Voluntary and the Involuntary*. Translated by Erazim V. Kohak. Northwestern University Studies in Phenomenology and Existential Philosophy Series. Edited by John Wild. Evanston, IL: Northwestern University Press, 1966.

———. *Freud and Philosophy*. Translated by Denis Savage. New Haven: Yale University Press, 1970.

———. *Hermeneutics and the Human Sciences: Essays on Language, Action and Interpretation*. Translated, edited, and introduction by John B. Thompson. Cambridge: Cambridge University Press, 1981.

———. "Intellectual Autobiography of Paul Ricoeur." *The Philosophy of Paul Ricoeur*. Edited by Lewis Edwin Hahn. The Library of Living Philosophers. Vol. XXII, 3–53. Chicago: Open Court, 1995.

———. *Interpretation Theory: Discourse and the Surplus of Meaning*. Translated by David Pellauer (chap. 3). Fort Worth: Texas Christian University Press, 1976.

———. "Memory and Forgetting." *Questioning Ethics: Contemporary Debates in Philosophy*. Edited by Richard Kearney and Mark Dooley, 5–11. New York: Routledge, 1999.

———. "Myth as the Bearer of Possible Worlds." *States of Mind: Dialogues with Contemporary Thinkers*. Edited by Richard Kearney, 236–45. New York: New York University Press, 1995.

———. *Oneself as Another*. Translated by Kathleen Blamey. Chicago: University of Chicago Press, 1992.

———. *The Rule of Metaphor: Multi-Disciplinary Studies of the Creation of Meaning in Language*. Translated by Robert Czerny with Kathleen McLaughlin and John Costello, SJ. Toronto: University of Toronto Press, 1977.

———. *Symbolism of Evil*. Boston: Beacon Press, 1967.

———. *Time and Narrative*. Translated by Kathleen McLaughlin and David Pellauer. Volume I of three volumes. Chicago: University of Chicago Press, 1984.

Saiving, Valerie. "The Human Situation: A Feminine View." *Womanspirit Rising: A Feminist Reader in Religion*. Edited by Carol P. Christ and Judith Plaskow, 25–42. Originally published 1960 in the *Journal of Religion*. San Francisco: Harper, 1979.

Schimmel, Annemarie. *Mystical Dimensions of Islam*. Chapel Hill, NC: University of North Carolina Press, 1975.

Schneiders, Sandra M. "Feminist Spirituality: Christian Alternative or Alternative to Christianity?" *Women's Spirituality: Resources for Christian Development*. Edited by Joann Wolski Conn, 30–67. Originally published in 1986. New York: Paulist Press, 1996.

Schrein, Shannon, OSF. *Quilting and Braiding: The Feminist Christologies of Sallie McFague and Elizabeth A. Johnson in Conversation*. Collegeville, MN: Liturgical Press, 1998.

Schweitzer, Friedrich L. *The Postmodern Life Cycle: Challenges for Church and Theology*. St. Louis, MO: Chalice, 2004.

Sells, Benjamin, editor and introduction to *Working with Images: The Theoretical Base of Archetypal Psychology*. Woodstock, CT: Spring Books, 2000.

Shange, Ntozake. "For Colored Girls Who Have Considered Suicide When the Rainbow Is Enuf." New York: Buddah Records, 1976.

Sharma, Arvind, and Katherine K. Young, ed. *Feminism and World Religions.* Albany, NY: State University of New York Press, 1999.

Slater, Glen. Lecture notes from class in *Jungian Depth Psychology.* Carpinteria, CA: Pacifica Graduate Institute, Spring 2003.

Sokolowski, Robert. *Introduction to Phenomenology.* New York: Cambridge University Press, 2000.

Sophocles. *The Three Theban Plays.* Translated by Robert Fagles. New York: Penguin Books, 1982.

Stanizai, Zaman. Lecture notes from class in *Islamic Traditions.* Carpinteria, CA: Pacifica Graduate Institute, Spring 2005.

St. John of the Cross. *Collected Works.* Translated by Kiernan Kavanaugh and Otilio Rodriguez. Washington DC: Institute of Carmelite Studies, 1973.

Stone, Merlin. *When God Was a Woman.* New York: Harcourt, Brace Jovanovich, 1976.

Storr, Anthony. Introduction to *C. G. Jung, The Essential Jung: Selected Writings.* Translated by R. F. C. Hull and Richard and Clara Winston. Princeton, Princeton University Press, 1983.

Tarnas, Richard. *The Passion of the Western Mind: Understanding the Ideas That Have Shaped Our World View.* New York: Ballantine, 1991.

Tatman, Lucy. *Knowledge That Matters: A Feminist Theological Paradigm and Epistemology.* Cleveland, OH: Pilgrim Press, 2001.

Thompson, John B., ed. *Paul Ricoeur: Hermeneutics and the Human Sciences: Essays on Language, Action and Interpretation.* Cambridge: Cambridge University Press, 1981.

Tickle, Phyllis. *The Great Emergence.* Grand Rapids, MI: Baker Books, 2008.

Trible, Phyllis. *God and the Rhetoric of Sexuality.* Philadelphia: Fortress, 1978.

Ulanov, Ann Belford. *The Feminine in Jungian Psychology and in Christian Theology.* Evanston: Northwestern University Press, 1971.

———. *Receiving Woman: Studies in the Psychology and Theology of the Feminine.* Philadelphia: Westminster, 1981.

Vergil. *Aeneid*. Translated by Charles J. Billson. Edited by Stanley Appelbaum. Previously published in English in 1906. Toronto: Dover Thrift Editions, 1995.

Vest, Douglas C. *Churchianity Lite: An Insider's Loving Look*. Longwood, FL: Xulon Press, 2007.

———. *Entering the Mystery: Lectio on Life*. Longwood, FL: Xulon Press, 2006.

———. *Homes for the Heart: Scripture and Poems on the Essence of Home*. Longwood, FL: Xulon Press, 2005.

———. "Some Correspondences between Atomic Physics and Formative Spirituality, A Term Paper" (unpublished). Duquesne University: Pittsburgh, PA, 1981.

Vest, Norvene. "In the Image of Godde: Feminist Spiritual Direction." *Tending the Holy: Spiritual Direction across Traditions*, 186–203. Edited by Norvene Vest. Harrisburg, PA: Morehouse, 2003.

———. "Is Reverie to Be Trusted? The Imaginal and the Work of Marija Gimbutas." *Feminist Theology* 13.2 (2005): 239–48.

———. *No Moment Too Small: Rhythms of Silence, Prayer and Holy Reading*. Kalamazoo, MI: Cistercian Studies/Cowley Publications, 1994.

Watkins, Calvert, ed. *The American Heritage Dictionary of Indo-European Roots*. Boston: Houghton Mifflin Company, 1985.

Watkins, Mary. *Invisible Guests: The Development of Imaginal Dialogues*. Woodstock, CT: Spring Books, 2000.

Index

Index

Self-constancy, 131, 132
Self-esteem, 127, 128, 131, 132
Self-respect, 127, 132
Shange, Ntozake, 77
She Who Is: The Mystery of God in Feminist Theological Discourse (Johnson), 93–94
Slater, Glen, 48, 52
Solicitude, 127–28, 131
Sophia (Wisdom), 99–100, 131, 149, 151–52
Sophocles, 129
Soul, 46–47, 106, 134, 153; archetypal psychology and, 55–56, 144; *see also* Self
Stone, Merlin, 82
Suffering, 95, 160
Sufism, 16, 31, 37–46, 61, 143–44
Suspicion, 109, 111–12, 117, 119, 120, 128
Suhrawardi, 38, 39–40

Tatman, Lucy, 89–90
Tertullian, 75
Theology, 2, 6–7, 138–39; psychology and, 56; *see also* specific headings, e.g.: Feminist theology
Thomas Aquinas. *See* Aquinas, Thomas
Tickle, Phyllis, 7
Trinity, 94

Ulanov, Ann, 67
Unconscious, 11, 47, 49–50, 51–52, 53–54, 112; collective unconscious, 53–54

Virgil, 8

Weber, Max, 14
Wisdom, 99, 149, 151–52
Woman and Nature (Griffin), 69
Wright, N. T., 146

www.ingramcontent.com/pod-product-compliance
Lightning Source LLC
Chambersburg PA
CBHW031250090426
42742CB00007B/391